Four Brothers From Lowell

Jim Turcotte

Pocol Press
Punxsutawney, PA

POCOL PRESS
Published in the United States of America
by Pocol Press
320 Sutton Street
Punxsutawney, PA 15767
www.pocolpress.com

Publisher's Cataloguing-in-Publication

Names: Turcotte, Jim, author.
Title: Four brothers from Lowell / Jim Turcotte.
Description: Punxsutawney, PA: Pocol Press, 2021.
Identifiers: LCCN: 2021947932 | ISBN: 978-1-929763-96-2
Subjects: LCSH Turcotte family. | Turcotte, Lionel--Biography. |
Turcotte, Robert--Biography. | Turcotte, Jim--Biography. | Turcotte,
Walter--Biography. | Lowell (Mass.)--Biography. | United States.
Navy--Biography. | World War, 1939-1945--Biography. | Soldiers--
Massachusetts--Biography. | BISAC BIOGRAPHY &
AUTOBIOGRAPHY / Military | HISTORY / United States / 20th
Century | HISTORY / Military / World War II
Classification: LCC D773 .T87 T87 2021 | DDC 940.54/5973.092--
dc23

Library of Congress Control Number: 2021947932

Front Cover: The four brothers; clockwise starting from top left:
Robert Turcotte, Lionel Turcotte, Walter Turcotte, James Turcotte.

Acknowledgements

I would like to first acknowledge and thank my father for taking the time to share with me, from a very young age, his time and tales. A lot of WWII fathers didn't discuss their experiences with their kids. My dad was the exception. He told me stories about his time growing up, about his mom and dad, and his adventures with his brothers and sisters. But most of all I enjoyed hearing about his experiences during the war. When he was in his eighties, I asked him to put his memories on tape. These tapes didn't include all the stories I heard throughout my lifetime, but it contained many of them. Because the tapes did not contain all the stories, some of his tales have survived only in my memory.

I would like to acknowledge my three uncles; Lionel, Robert (Bob) and Walter (Bud) for their service to our country. These four brothers truly define the phrase "the greatest generation".

I would like to lovingly acknowledge my aunt, Mary O'Connell, the last surviving sibling of seven Turcotte children. She freely shared photos and stories of her childhood, tales of growing up with her brothers and some of the details of what it was like in their home during the war. Although it must have been painful to revisit some of these memories, she was able to talk to me about her parents and the loss of Robert and Lionel. Both she and her daughter Helen have been extremely supportive of this project.

I would like to thank my uncle Walter's daughter, Patricia Cossette. She shared photos, letters, and stories of her father. These materials greatly enriched the book, and I am forever grateful for her generosity and support.

I would like to thank my childhood friend Johnny Mayo for his time, patience, and skill in reviewing and editing this manuscript. He spent countless hours making a lawyer sound like a writer. Not an easy task. I would like to acknowledge John Lion, Frank "Buddy" Leonard, Matt Thomsen, Gary "Squez" Vasquez, Ron DeBarge, Tim

Reardon, Mary Zambrello, Torie DeBarge, Andrew Lawrence, Louis Blandon, and Helen O'Connell. Thank you for your suggestions and constructive criticism. To the boys from 188. "Jeckyl." Remember, The Hoseman always rings twice.

I would like to acknowledge my sisters for their unwavering love and support during the project. To my brother Tom. I will always love you. To my brother Bud, I will always miss you.

To my grandparents, Helen and Herman: Until this book, I never fully appreciated the depth of your sacrifice to the cause of freedom.

I would like to thank and acknowledge all of the employees of the National Archives. You serve a great function for the people of the United States.

To the United States Navy Archives: you have an amazing library of photographs from WWII. The visual impact of these photos is immeasurable.

Finally, I would like to acknowledge and thank my wife and children. Thank you. Jean, I love you more than you will ever know. Kids, I am proud of each one of you and the fine adults you have become. Kilroy was here.

While this book pertains to historical events, is not intended to be a "history book." I am absolutely certain that there are things in this book that are not historically accurate. This book merely reflects the personal stories as described by the people who wrote the letters and newspaper articles, took the photographs, narrated the tapes and told me the tales. As often as I could, I used materials from official government reports, articles written by the United States military, newspaper articles, materials from The National Archives, or published memoirs to corroborate the story. On other occasions, I used less "academic" sources. Generally, these secondary sources were used to describe only a small fact or detail. It is my hope that they, in no way, took away from the overall purpose or quality of the book or telling of the story.

This book is dedicated to the Four Brothers From Lowell-Lionel, Bob, Jim and Bud.

Table of Contents

Prologue

"The Navy Department deeply regrets to inform you that your son..."

During World War II, Helen Gertrude Turcotte had four sons in the U.S. Navy – Lionel, Robert, Jim, and Walter. During wartime, no mother wants to receive a telegram from the Navy Department. Helen received two.

Helen Turcotte, center, at Gold Star Mothers dinner, November 12, 1957.

The name "Gold Star Mothers" comes from the custom of families of servicemen hanging a banner, called a service flag, in the windows or on the flag poles of their homes. Each service flag had a star for each family member in the armed forces. Living servicemen were represented by a blue star, and those who had lost their lives in combat were represented by a gold star.

Membership in the organization was open to any woman who had lost a son in active service in the U.S. military, regardless of the place or time of their service or if they were missing in action. It is not an organization any mother hopes to join. The cost of admission is much too high. Helen Turcotte paid double the price of admission into the Gold Star Mothers with the loss of her two oldest sons, Lionel and Robert.

Helen was a very active member of the Lowell, Massachusetts, Chapter of the American Gold Stars Mothers, pouring her heart and soul into the organization. She enjoyed being with other women who could understand her loss and pain, as she understood theirs. Over time, Helen held several positions in the organization, including social chair and vice president. On November 12, 1957, she was inducted as the chapter's president.

At the ceremony that evening, she would be recognized for her sacrifice and dedication in helping other mothers whose sons also paid the ultimate price to defend our freedom. Even on a day of great honor, you can see the sadness in her smile. She appears lost in thought, perhaps the thought of her sons.[1]

You are cordially invited to attend the

INSTALLATION OF OFFICERS

of the

American Gold Star Mothers Inc.
Lowell Chapter

Tuesday, November 12, 1957, at 8 P.M.

Liberty Hall, Memorial Auditorium

East Merrimack St., Lowell, Mass.

Helen Turcotte, Pres. Elect.

At a Gold Star function in 1958, Senator Jack Kennedy's wife, Jackie, was a special guest and graced those assembled with her presence. All of the ladies attending had lost a son in service. The

---

[1] Between the first and second photos, Helen had turned 60. It would be fair to say that losing two boys aged her.

Kennedy family knew the Gold Star Mothers all too well. With the loss of Joe Kennedy Jr., Jack Kennedy's mother, Rose, was a Gold Star Mother herself. John F. Kennedy, Jr. first spoke to the Gold Star Mothers in 1946 when he was running for U.S. Congress. It may have been the first time that the young, politically awkward but driven future president first connected with an audience. It could certainly be argued that the Gold Star Mothers helped launch Jack's political career. He never forgot these special groups of ladies and attended many Gold Star functions in his Congressional district. Jack's wife, Jackie, was also a faithful attendee.

Helen G. Turcotte, front row, center left;
Jackie Kennedy, front row, center right, 1958.

By June of 1944, at the Turcotte home at 113 Varnum Avenue in Lowell, Massachusetts, there were four stars in the window – two blue, two gold. They represented Helen's four sons that served their country and went to war. They were "Four Brothers from Lowell." This is their story.

Family History

Lowell was a New England mill town. By 1850, its population was 33,000, making it the second largest city in Massachusetts and, at the time, America's largest industrial center. One of the keys to its success was an intricate canal system that produced 10,000 horsepower and provided energy to forty mills. Some 10,000 workers used an equal number of looms fed by 320,000 spindles to produce 50,000 miles of cloth annually. Over time, other industries developed in Lowell as well, including service industry businesses that were critical in feeding and supporting a growing population of a growing city.

As a huge influx of immigrants arrived to work in the mills, by 1880, Lowell's population was almost 60,000 (39 percent foreign born). Many of these immigrants were French Canadians. With this influx came resentment and, at times, open hostility toward this new population from the north. In response, French Canadians started the St. Jean Baptiste procession to help counteract anti-French Canadian propaganda. The procession was part of a popular annual celebration by Roman Catholics in French Canada on June 24 (the feast day of St. John the Baptist). St. Jean Baptiste was recognized as the Patron Saint of Canada in that community. The tradition of the procession in Canada goes back to 1636. It began as a religious feast but soon became much more a social and political event. The celebration included the lighting of bonfires and, later, parades were organized. By the mid-1880s, the French-Canadian community in Lowell established the St. Jean Baptiste Roman Catholic Church, where they opened a night school to teach English. More than 400 people enrolled. In addition, J.H. Guillet founded L'Abielle, the first Franco-American daily newspaper to survive in the United States, and L'Etoile, the first French-Canadian newspaper was put in operation. Before long, French Canadians had set their foothold in the city.

There certainly was plenty of work for all comers in the mills, as well as in the surrounding businesses needed to support the growing community, businesses like bakeries, laundries and markets.

It was this supporting service industry that brought the Turcotte family to Lowell in 1885.

Nazaire Turcotte was born in 1847 in the little town of L'Assomption, just outside of Montreal, Quebec, Canada. He was a baker by trade. His son, Oswald, also was born in L'Assomption, in 1877. In 1885, Nazaire moved his family to Lowell for more opportunity and a better life, working as a baker at various locations throughout Lowell. He passed away in 1905 at the age of 57.

Like his father, Oswald became a baker, finding work at G.J. & D. Bradts, a manufacturer of breads, cakes and crackers of all kinds that was located in the French District of Lowell, an area later known as The Acre. On July 12, 1898, the then 22-year-old Oswald married Emilina "Minnie" Gaudet. The pair didn't waste any time starting a family. Their first child was Herman Oswald Turcotte, born May 10, 1899. By 1906, Oswald was a naturalized citizen. Over the course of the next 21 years, Minnie had twelve more children, a very fitting "baker's dozen," given her husband's profession. Sadly, not all survived into adulthood. In the 1930s, Oswald bought Bradt's Cracker Bakery and put his 10 boys – Herman, Paul, Arthur, Charles, Ernest, Eugene, David, Frederick, Richard and Robert – to work there. It was a family business and, as such, the boys filled a multitude of roles, as bakers, salesmen or drivers. You name it, they did it. The Turcotte family was well known and respected in The Acre. They were good neighbors. They lived in The Acre where their children attended school and they worshiped at the Catholic church.

The ovens at Bradt's had to be kept hot all the time, seven days a week. It was too costly to shut them down for the weekend and then reheat them come Monday morning. So, someone had to be at the bakery over the weekend to keep the ovens fired and watch the premises.

At that time, homemade baked beans with Saturday dinner was a tradition in many households in Lowell. Everyone had their own family recipe, usually with one or more "secret ingredients" that made their beans special. On Saturday morning, many families in The

Acre would bring their bean crock to the loading dock at Bradt's. One of the Turcotte boys would put the beans in the oven and let them bake, low and slow, all day. At around dinner time, one of the boys would bring the hot beans out to the loading dock where the neighbors would come back and pick up their crock of hot baked beans. Everyone knew their crock and no one would touch anyone else's (and that's no crock).

The commercial bakery business was hard, built upon long hours in a hot environment. Not all the boys saw this as their chosen profession. Eugene became a lawyer. Richard found a career in the military. Herman initially went to the University of Ottawa to earn a degree, but eventually returned to the family business as a baker. But even though it was steady work, baking wasn't in Herman's future.

Herman liked working with his hands. He liked fixing and building things. So, he left the comfort of the family business and tried something else. He took a job as a fixer at the United States Cartridge Company in Dracut, Massachusetts. One of the first things he worked to build was a family. On May 9, 1918, Herman married Helen Gertrude Willett. Helen's father was a blacksmith who had come from Chazy, New York, in the early 1880s for the same reason Nazaire Turcotte did – a promise of steady work. Herman and Helen were young and had no money, so they lived with her parents on Mammoth Road in Dracut.

They had their first child, Lionel Oswald Turcotte, on June 6, 1919. He was a handsome lad and very outgoing from the start. He always seemed to have a mischievous smile, as if he knew something you didn't. Herman and Helen could not have been happier.

Herman and Helen on their wedding day, May 9, 1918.

Lionel at approximately age 2.

In 1920, along came their second child, Robert Thomas Turcotte. Herman and Helen still lived with her parents, Thomas and Henrietta Willett, for almost a year more until they found their own place to live. Returning to Lowell, Herman was indeed building a family, and quick. On February 27, 1922, Jim was born, and then sister Maude in 1923. They called her "Sis", because she was their first sister. Mary was born in 1925 and the youngest of the four brothers, Walter (also known as Bud), was born in 1926. Ernest died at birth in 1930, and Dorothy was born in 1932. Helen gave birth to eight children in all.

From left, Mary, Maude, Jim, Bob and Lionel Turcotte.

It was the time of the Great Depression, a time when scores of men were getting laid off. With a growing family and a lot of mouths to feed, the 33-year-old Herman decided to open his own business in Lowell, Turcotte's Shell Station. It was a risky venture during the depression, but Herman was hardworking. He fixed cars and sold gasoline. Being the oldest son from a large Lowell family, it seemed that everyone knew Herman or someone from the Turcotte family. This brought him a lot of customers.

Like his father, Herman was a well-respected fixture in the community. He believed that if you took care of your customers, they would take care of you. He understood the concept of goodwill. During the hard times of the Great Depression, people didn't have a lot of disposable income. So, Herman would fix cars on credit or barter.

Herman Turcotte at Turcotte's Shell Station in Lowell, Massachusetts.

Things were tight in the Turcotte household and Herman's boys were expected to help out any way they could. The three boys all started caddying golf around the age of nine at the Vesper Country Club in Tyngsboro. They earned 25 cents a bag for carrying 18 holes. It was routine for each of the boys to carry two bags each round they caddied. They brought the money home and put it in the "meat jar." If the family saved up enough, they could buy some beef or pork. Otherwise, vegetables and dumplings served to stretch meals. They knew the meaning of hard work and sacrifice, traits their mother and father instilled in the children at a young age. As a side benefit, occasionally the club allowed the caddies to play a round of golf at the club for free, as long as they were behaved, and they didn't dig up the course with divots.

The family was in regular attendance at Sunday mass in St. Rita's Catholic Church, and the church played a significant role in each member's development. It was there that they received the sacraments of the church – Baptism, First Confession, First Holy Communion, and Confirmation. The children were members of the St. Rita's Cadets. This was the youth group at the church. There they sang in the choir, acted in plays and shows, and played in the St. Rita's Marching Band. It was at St. Rita's that young Jim developed his love of music and singing. Herman loved his family and his family loved him. He was strict in his rearing of the boys and they knew to toe the line. Herman had mechanic's hands – big, strong and hard – and he wasn't afraid to use them to instruct his boys on proper behavior. The threat itself was usually enough to straighten them out. The three oldest boys – Lionel, Robert and Jim – slept in the same room and in the same bed. When the boys raised a little too much hell at bedtime, Herman would walk into the darkened room without saying a word, his cigar glowing in the darkness. The shenanigans usually stopped immediately.

But Herman wasn't just a disciplinarian. He was also a teacher, instructor and mentor. He took the time to teach his children about the importance of family, God, nature, mechanics and hard work. By all accounts, he was a very good father. The oldest boys were known as "The Three Turks." They were inseparable. They also were very competitive and loved all sports, and played them all, including football, baseball, hockey, and golf. There were not many organized sports teams in Lowell at the time until you got to high school. Games were mostly of the sandlot variety, which the boys played in an open lot by the firehouse known as "The Cow Field." If they got thirsty, they ran over to the firehouse and got a drink of water from the outside hose. Right next to the firehouse was Stoddard's Bakery. If the boys could scrape together a nickel, they could buy a bag of "edges," the scraps cut from all the various fruit squares baked that day – fig squares, lemon squares, cherry squares, blueberry squares and other flavors all mixed together in a bag. If you were lucky, the edges would have a little bit of fruit still on them. Stoddard's also made whoopie pies, chocolate cake with a cream filling that came two in a pack. They also were called Black Moons or Stoddard Twins.

The Three Turks loved to play practical jokes on each other. On one occasion, the entire neighborhood was in Herman's backyard listening to a heavyweight title boxing match. He had a radio with a loudspeaker attached to a lower roof broadcasting the fight. It was in the evening and there must have been 30 to 40 people in the yard. The boys wanted to stay up and listen to the fight with the adults, but Herman said no. Still, the boys were so excited, with all those people in the backyard and the sound of the fight being broadcast. Bob and Lionel grabbed Jim, the youngest of the three, stripped him naked and threw him out onto the roof for all the neighbors to see. Jim was simultaneously trying to cover up and get back into the window. All the neighbors laughed and applauded. Jim, embarrassed and blushing, scrambled headlong back in the window. Lionel and Bobby were laughing so hard they were nearly crying. Herman quickly made his way upstairs and quieted things down. He didn't admit to the boys that he got a big kick out of the prank.

In the summer, Herman would rent a cabin on Althea Lake, which the family affectionately referred to as "Mud Pond." The lake was in Tyngsboro, Massachusetts, near the Lowell-Dracut-Tyngsboro State Forest, and just a short drive from their home. The family would spend the whole summer living out at the camp. While Herman was at work, the kids spent their days swimming, fishing, and boating. As a result, the boys became rather strong swimmers. It was a skill that would come in handy later in life.

Left to right: Lionel, Bob, Jim, Sis and Mary at Mud Pond.

The Turcotte family summering at Lake Althea
(affectionately called "Mud Pond").

Herman, Lionel, and Helen (inside the car) at Lake Althea.

Herman constantly was looking to improve himself and his family's situation. After a long day of working in the garage, he went to school at night to learn more about auto mechanics, diesel engines, carburation, electronics, and related matters. The boys would help run the garage while their dad was at school. They did whatever they could, pumping gas, feeding the furnace in the winter months and helping around the garage. From a very young age, they were exposed to engines, transmissions, ignitions, and carburetors. Herman taught them the basics and even some more advanced skills of auto repair – all skills that would come in handy later in life.

The boys would jockey cars around the gas station, moving them in and out of the bay and around the parking lot. When Lionel was about 13 years old, he, Bobby and Jim took a customer's car for a joy ride while Herman was at night school. Lionel, the oldest, was driving. With Bobby and Jim as his wingmen. Lionel, despite having driven cars around the parking lot had not yet honed his driving skills on the streets of Lowell and when he took a corner a little sharply, he hit a parked car. The customer's car had a large dent in the front quarter panel. The boys knew they had to tell their dad. They knew he would be angry, but they also knew it would be worse if they didn't tell him. They couldn't hide the damage on the car, and they knew their dad would know right away who did it.

To say the least, Herman was not at all pleased. He had the boys bring him to the other car, which also had a significant dent in the rear quarter panel. He brought the boys to the respective owners and made them confess. Herman promised the cars would be fixed without charge. True to his word, the cars were fixed better than new, and the boys were with their father every minute he worked on the two cars and were made to help repair the damage they had caused. They learned many valuable lessons on many different levels from this incident, not the least of which was the love of their father. Herman not only wanted to improve himself, but his children as well. He never missed an opportunity to teach a valuable lesson to his kids.

Besides cars, Herman also had a fascination with aviation. He loved airplanes and all aspects of aircraft. He worked on them, studied them and, eventually, learned how to fly them. It began by doing a favor for one of his automobile customers. He worked on a customer's plane engine. In exchange, the customer gave him some flight lessons. In a very short time, Herman became very proficient at flying and got his pilot license. He started studying the physics and mechanics of airplanes. Before he knew it, he knew airplanes inside and out. In fact, Herman began to literally build planes from the ground up in the garage at his home. He would salvage parts from an old wreck and rebuild it. He would build the frame of the fuselage out of wood inside the garage. He would cover the frame in canvas, or later, sheet metal, Then, once the frame was complete, he would move the body outside, put the wings on it, install an engine and fly it. As the oldest boy, Lionel spent the most time with his father building airplanes.

Since the Turcotte family home was just a stone's throw from the Merrimack River, Herman used the river as his own private runway. During the summer, he outfitted the plane with pontoons. In the winter, the plane would have skis. Herman used the planes to make extra income for the family. He delivered newspapers in the airplane up and down the Merrimack River Valley. He would take his boys with him to help load copies of the *Lowell Sun* on and off the plane. When they returned from a trip, Herman and the boys would land, tie the plane off to a tree and walk home. Over his lifetime, Herman had numerous planes and exposed the boys to this passion.

Just as with the workings of an automobile, Herman taught the boys the basic principles of flight and airplanes including propulsion, engine maintenance, and carburation. These were lessons they would not soon forget and, not surprisingly, all three boys took an interest in flight and mechanics.

Building a plane at the garage at Herman's house. Notice the air frame leaning against garage door on far right. Also note the tail rudder in rear center of photo.

Herman building a plane at this home (wings not yet attached).

Herman on the frozen Merrimack River with one of his numerous planes.

At Lowell High School, as with many schools of the time, each of the boys was required to have two years of compulsory military training. They wore khaki WWI calvary-style uniforms with breeches and leggings. The students drilled regularly. Instruction was provided by military officers who taught them discipline and how to carry out orders. They earned a great deal of respect for the military services.

1938 Lionel Turcotte's Enlistment

All of the Turcotte children learned the value of serving their community and their country through their parents and grandparents. As a result, one by one, all four of the Turcotte boys joined the U.S.

Navy. They served in the United States, guarding the homeland, as well as in both the Atlantic and Pacific theatres. Lionel was the first to join.

The Commonwealth of Massachusetts

The Adjutant General's Office

State House, Boston, July 19, 193 8

.. The name of ..

LIONEL O. TURCOTTE

of Lowell, Massachusetts , is borne upon the records of this office as follows:

Enlisted on the twenty-ninth day of April 1 937 , and mustered-in to the service of the State on the twenty-ninth day of April 1 937 for three years, as a Private in Hq.Btry and Combat Train, 1st Battalion 102d REGIMENT FIELD ARTILLERY

National Guard, Massachusetts.

HONORABLY Discharged by reason of S.O. No. 132,par.1, AGO Mass. "TO ENLIST IN U.S. NAVY"

on the nineteenth day of July 1 938

PORTER B. CHASE
The Adjutant General.

Form No. 31. A. G. O.
5m-1-'37. No. 9443.

Lionel Oswald Turcotte was 18 years old, had just graduated from Lowell High School and, according to the July 22, 1938, edition of the *Lowell Sun*, had already been a member of the Massachusetts Army National Guard for more than a year as a private in the 1st Battalion, 102 Regiment Field Artillery. On July 20th that year, Lionel went into Boston to the Navy Recruiting Station and enlisted in the

U.S. Navy (having previously been granted permission to discharge from the Army National Guard).

According to his Physical Examination Report, Lionel had a "good general appearance with a ruddy complexion." He was approximately five-feet, seven-inches tall, weighed 134 pounds, had light brown hair and hazel eyes, and his blood pressure was 130/70. This marked the first of many "poking and prodding" events the Navy would give him. He had his whole life ahead of him and, with the help of the U.S. Navy, he was going to see the world.

Everything on his exam was "normal." His vision was 20/20, which was important as he wanted to be a Navy pilot. A *Lowell Sun* article didn't mention it but, before he left the recruiting station, Lionel had signed up for a four-year enlistment.

As an apprentice seaman, Lionel was sent to Naval Station Newport, Rhode Island, for basic training. The facility continues today to be one of many U.S. Navy "boot camps" located throughout the country. He spent 12 weeks there learning all the basics. He easily qualified in swimming and was able to swim 160 yards in 4 minutes and 30 seconds, broken down to a 40-yard breaststroke, 20-yard right-side stroke, 20-yard left-side stroke, 40-yard back stroke, and 40-yard crawl. He performed life-saving to a drowning person and was able to swim 20 yards to safety with a potential victim and apply the taught method of resuscitation.

Lionel was required to take an aptitude test to determine how well he did in various designated areas. This information would help the Navy in determining what position he was most qualified to serve. Due to his exposure to his father's garage and passion for planes, he was hoping for something in aviation. He didn't want to do it just for fun. Now he wanted to do it as a career and for his country.

Lionel, front row, second from left, at U.S. Navy "boot camp."

Lionel completed basic training in mid-November and on November 15, 1938, while still in boot camp, was given orders to the Naval Air Station in Pensacola, Florida (hereafter, NAS Pensacola). Lionel must have thought he died and went to heaven as NAS Pensacola was known as the "Cradle of Naval Aviation." It was best known as the initial primary training base and advanced training operations for all U.S. Navy, Marine Corps, and Coast Guard officers pursuing designation as naval aviators and flight officers. NAS Pensacola also became home to the Naval Air Technical Training Center (NATTC) Pensacola. NATTC Pensacola provided technical training schools for all enlisted aircraft maintenance and enlisted aircrew specialties in the U.S. Navy, U.S. Marines, and U.S. Coast Guard.

Only two days after reporting for duty in Pensacola on November 18, 1938, Lionel was promoted to seaman second class and assigned to Squadron Four. Life fell into a routine of assigned duties, various training, and physical-fitness requirements.

The Navy judged Lionel's proficiency on a quarterly basis. If he didn't have a bad conduct rating, he would be promoted to seaman first class in nine months., Lionel advanced to seaman first class on August 16, 1939. The routine continued, and so did Lionel's training. He was training as an aviation mechanic, but he wanted to fly.

On January 16, 1940, Lionel was physically examined in order to qualify as a pilot. Unfortunately, he failed the examination. Records show that despite reading 20/20, he had vision issues. While he was not physically disqualified for duty involving aviation training, Lionel was just not going to be a Navy pilot. No matter what, hard work and studying was not going to fix Lionel's eyes. To say the least, he was disappointed.

⚓ ⚓ ⚓

1939 Robert Turcotte's Enlistment

Robert Turcotte in Newport, R.I.

Robert Thomas Turcotte was born December 1, 1920. At 19 years old, he became the second son to join the Navy (for a while he had jokingly been referred to as #2 son). He enlisted in the U.S. Navy on December 11, 1939, at the Navy Recruiting Station in Boston, about 18 months after Lionel had, "Rob," "Robbie," but mostly known as "Bob," signed up for a six-year hitch as he wanted to make the Navy his career. He was immediately ordered to Newport for training.

Because Bob was so thin, at his weight of 128 pounds, he looked taller than his five-feet, nine-inches. He had dark brown hair, brown eyes and, just like his brother Lionel, a ruddy complexion.

It was reported in the *Lowell Sun* on January 11, 1940, that Bob was one of four Lowell recruits that joined the Navy in December 1939. All four enlisted as apprentice seamen and all were under training at the Newport Training Station. At the end of February 1940, the *Lowell Sun* reported that Bob was home on leave visiting his family. He had completed boot camp and was given leave from February 10-19. When he returned from leave, he received orders to report to San Diego, California, for assignment and reported on February 27, coincidentally, his brother Jim's birthday. He was to report to Capt. Byron McCandless, a fascinating man from a fascinating family. McCandless was a long-time U.S. Navy officer who was awarded the Navy Cross during World War I. He developed an interest in flags, a field later termed vexillology, and in 1917 was described by *National Geographic* Magazine as the "foremost flag expert of the United States Government and probably the leading authority in the world on flag usages among maritime nations." On March 2, 1940, Bob was assigned as an apprentice seaman aboard the USS *Cincinnati* in San Francisco. The *Cincinnati* (CL-6), was the third Omaha-Class light cruiser in the Navy fleet, was 555 feet long, weighed more than 7,600 tons and was designed to travel 35 knots per hour.

She was built for a peace-time crew of 29 officers and 429 enlisted men. For armament, the ship carried numerous torpedoes and mines, as well as various guns and cannons. That weaponry was to be used for both offensive and defensive purposes against enemy ships, planes, and submarines. In addition, the *Cincinnati* was equipped with two aircraft – floatplanes which could be launched from amid ship catapults and retrieved by cranes. Although the planes were armed, they were generally used for scouting missions rather than for offensive purposes as attack fighters or bombers. These were two-seater biplanes (two-winged) that carried a pilot and a passenger. Their wings folded back when stored aboard ship.

While stationed in San Diego, Bob completed instruction in the Elementary Machine Gun School at San Clemente Island, with a final grade of 3.51. Records indicate that he was qualified as a gunner with average ability. He was also instructed on the use of a gas mask, measured for a proper fit and found to take a "size 1 gas mask." In the Navy, this was like having a children's sized mask. Jim and Lionel had always kidded Bob about how small his head was. Like all good, loving brothers, if they ever found out that the Navy confirmed it, they would have teased him relentlessly and mercilessly. On April 11, 1940, Bob's rating was changed from an apprentice seaman to a seaman second class (Sea2c).

USS *Cincinnati* floatplanes, circa 1937

Lionel had hoped he and his brother Bob would be assigned duty together at Pensacola and was disappointed that it had not yet happened. Lionel was hoping that if he was promoted next quarter, he would put in for a transfer to be with Bob, provided that Bob got duty on a carrier, cruiser or battleship. If not, Lionel would wait until Bob could arrange a transfer.

At that time, the Navy allowed brothers to serve together. A sibling could apply for a "brother transfer" in order to get assigned along with their sibling. That policy ended on November 13, 1942, when the five Sullivan brothers all went down on the USS *Juneau* at Guadalcanal. Even earlier, just after Pearl Harbor, the Navy distributed informational bulletins discouraging the practice.

The Bureau considers that it is to the individual family interest that brothers not be put on the same ship in war time, as the loss of such a ship may result in the loss of two or more members of the family, which might be avoided if brothers are separated. An instance of this was the loss of three brothers on the USS Arizona at Pearl Harbor, T. H. (Territory of Hawaii), on December 7, 1941. In view of the above, Commanding Officers will not forward requests for brothers to serve in the same ship or station.

Issued July 1942, the article forbade commanding officers from forwarding requests from brothers to serve in same ship/station, although it doesn't appear it was universally enforced in practice.

At the end of February 1940, Lionel sent a letter to his dad from Pensacola:

February 27, 1940

Dear Dad,

I had to wait a couple of days before I could answer you as we've been kept hopping for the last week. We have been sending planes up to A&R (alternation & repair) for overhaul. We also are trying to fix up that big XPBS (it's that big four engine Sikorsky) and we have been having quite a time to obtain parts. There are only eight engines like them in the world. Four are on the plane and the others are on their way to Honolulu. So it has been holding us up for a while.

I was disappointed myself that Rob couldn't get to do duty here. But if I get third class next quarter and I have good chances of doing it I am going to put in for a transfer to get with Rob providing he gets a carrier, cruiser or a battleship. If not we will just have to wait until Rob can arrange a transfer.

You and I are in the same fix I guess, Dad. Nothing much goes on here that is much worth writing about with the exception of the airshow we had last week. It was pretty good. One fellow was supposed to show how not to fly and he certainly did. He had only a little cub but he certainly put that little ship through more than its share of the paces. I was surprised at the power, maneuverability and general safety features it has. It sure was a darn swell little ship. Kind of makes me wish I had one.

Next week (Mar.6) I am being sent to Key West for a week on a working party to fix up one of our planes that came down with a busted stub wing. Coming back I will have to drive one of the fellows cars as he is going to mech the plane back to the station.

It looks kind of black concerning my leave this year, Dad. They just don't seem to want to let anyone go. So, keep your fingers crossed and hope I can make it. I am going to try like hang anyway even if it is only to say hello and goodbye.

I have the rest of the day today off and all of tomorrow as I have to work all night tonight in order to get planes back in commission. No kidding, Dad, this place is a mad house now. You hardly know which way to turn once you set foot in the squadron area.

Well I'll see ya, Dad, as I've got to shave and take a shower before I go back to work.

Your #1 Son,

Lionel

P.S No paper since January 1ˢᵗ

P.S. Tell the gang I was asking for them.

Whenever Lionel wrote his parents, he almost always signed off with some reference to the fact that he was the #1 son. It was either, "your #1 son, Lionel" or "Lionel, #1." It was part of a running joke between he and his brother Robert (the #2 son).

Inside the letter he sent a copy of a soldier's prayer. It is supposed to be said at taps and reveille;

O GOD of power and love behold me before thee this night (morning) to add my faltering prayers to those which a little child daily brings to thee in my behalf. Make me a soldier (sailor, marine, aviator) worthy of the great cause for which we fight. Give me the strength when the going is hard. Give me courage when danger is near. In thee I place my trust. Lead me through the perils of this war to the peace of that [illegible] world to which I have dedicated myself, but if the service of thee and my country calls for the sacrifice of my life I only ask dear GOD that thee be with me at that moment, confident that peace awaits me in eternity. Amen.

Lionel was a natural airplane mechanic, having worked alongside his father for many years. Because of his vision issues, he worked to become an aviation machinist mate. He was looking forward to a short trip to Key West the following week on a working party to fix a plane that had a broken wing. Once they fixed it, one of the crew was going to fly the plane back to Pensacola.

Lionel, front row, second from left, with his fellow squad members.

Lionel was to be rated again only a month later on March 31, 1940. The next rate was petty officer. He would have to put in for promotion. Petty officer third class is the first of the Navy's petty officer grades (the Navy's variation of non-commissioned officers). A petty officer third class serves both as a leader and as a technical expert. To receive a promotion from seaman to this level, sailors must complete a specialty test for their rating and apply for advancement. The exact title with which a petty officer is addressed depends on their specialty. Only a certain number of petty officer third class billets are available to be filled every year, and competition for promotion can be extremely fierce among qualified seamen. A petty officer third class serving as a machinist's mate, for example, would have the full title of machinist's mate third class.

According to the U.S. Navy, aviation machinist's mates were aircraft engine mechanics who inspect, adjust, test, repair, and overhaul aircraft engines and propellers. In addition, they perform routine maintenance, prepare aircraft for flight, and assist in handling aircraft on the ground. These technicians may also volunteer to fly as aircrew. Aircrew perform numerous in-flight duties and operate various aircraft systems. Aircrew can earn additional pay for flight hours. Lionel got what he hoped for – his brother Bob was assigned to a cruiser (the *Cincinnati*) and Lionel was advanced to aviation machinist's mate third class (AMM3c) on May 16, 1940. Now, the question remained. Could they transfer to be together?

Bob (L) Lionel (R).

While Lionel was in Pensacola, Rob and the *Cincinnati* were transferred to Pearl Harbor, Hawaii, in April 1940. Pearl Harbor is a lagoon harbor located just to the west of Honolulu on the island of Oahu. In order to enter Pearl Harbor, a ship must pass through a relatively narrow channel on the south side of the island from Mamala Bay in the Pacific Ocean. This lagoon provides a great deal of natural protection to ships from storms. The big drawback, however, of this configuration is that there is only one way in and one way out through the narrow channel. During an attack, this could lead to a bottleneck and disaster.

Famous Waikiki Beach was only a short distance away from Pearl Harbor. From there, you could see out to Diamond Head. In 1940, the beach area had some hotels, but it was certainly not as developed as it is today. This must have seemed like paradise to Bob, though. He was 19 and had never been outside New England and here he was in Honolulu, Hawaii. Bob had no way of knowing at the time, but his younger brother Jim would be in the same exact spot in less than a year.

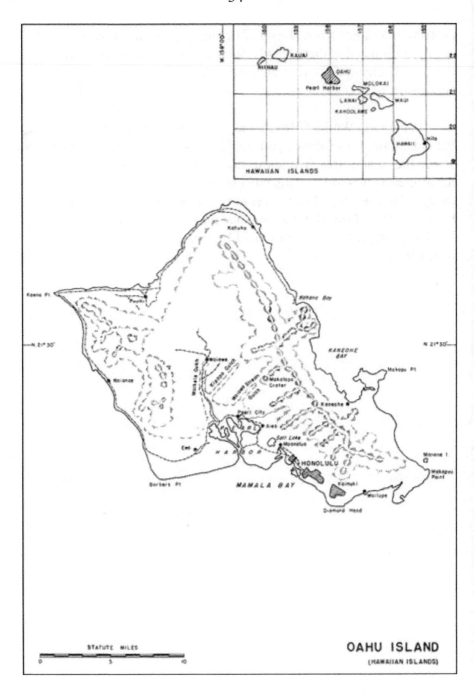

HAWAIIAN ISLANDS

OAHU ISLAND
(HAWAIIAN ISLANDS)

STATUTE MILES
0   5   10

On October 14, 1940, Bob was temporarily based on shore with the Cruiser Scouting Squadron aboard the *Cincinnati*. The scouting squadron was referred to as VCS-3. Their insignia was a green winged seahorse. This land assignment was training for the VCS program.

VCS-3 was a U.S. Navy Aviation designation or abbreviation used from 1920 to the 1950s for the Cruiser Scouting Squadrons. As seen from the photo of the floatplane aboard the *Cincinnati*, the insignia is affixed to the side of the plane and designates it as part of the *Cincinnati* scouting squadron. The plane, a two-man aircraft, would be sent out on scouting missions looking for enemy contacts from land, sea, or air.

On November 20th, Bob returned on board with the VCS Squadron 3. Though not a pilot, he had been given new orders involving flying for enlisted men and was authorized to participate, as a crew member, in regular and frequent aerial flights. With this order, Bob could get as many flight hours as possible in the scout plane.

A warship rarely stays in one place for very long, and the *Cincinnati* was no different. The *Cincinnati* was almost always on the move. After a year in the Pacific, it was ordered to return to the Atlantic to join her sister ships in the expanding neutrality patrols in the Western Atlantic.

On the way back to the East Coast, the *Cincinnati* crossed the 180th Meridian, making Bob a Golden Dragon. The U.S. Navy has many maritime traditions. When a naval vessel crosses the 180th Meridian, there is a ceremony that takes place and each sailor crossing for the first time gets a certificate marking the occasion.

The certificate reads as follows:

Kingdom of the Golden Dragon

Ruler of the 180th Meridian

Greetings:

Know ye that on this Twelfth day of Dec. 1940 in latitude 20 degrees 25 feet and longitude 180 degrees, there appeared within my Royal Kingdom the USS Cincinnati bound from Honolulu, Hawaii.

Harken ye

The said Vessel Officers and Crew have been inspected and passed on by my Royal Body and Staff. And know ye: Ye that are chit signers, squaw men, opium smokers, Ice men and all land lubbers that

R.T. Turcotte

Having been found sane and worthy to be numbered a dweller of the Far East have been gathered in my fold and duly initiated into the

Silent Mysteries of the Far East

Be it further understood:

That by virtue of the power in me invested, I do hereby command all money lenders, wine sellers, cabaret owners, taxi drivers, carromata drivers and all my other subjects to show due honor and respect to all his wishes whenever he may enter my realm. Disobey this command under penalty of my Royal Displeasure

Golden Dragon

By the end of the year, the *Cincinnati* was sailing on its way to Guam and the Philippines. Bob sent his mother and father a postcard, postmarked Guam:

Dear folks, Well here I am half way around the world headed for manila. Never-the-less I still wish I was in Lowell.

Bob

Shortly, thereafter, he sent a Christmas card with a Hawaiian sunset and palm trees on the front. Inside, the sentiment reads,

Across the miles between us this message wings its way to wish you Aloha on this Christmas Day.

Bob.

There was a short personal note,

A little early but I either go the Mech school or Manila tomorrow.

                              Love,
                              Bob

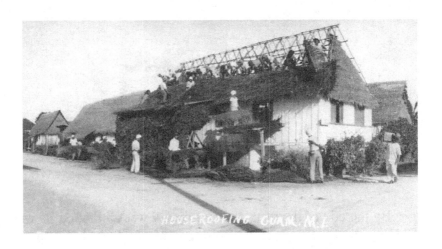

⚓ ⚓ ⚓

1940 Jim Turcotte's Enlistment

James Harold Turcotte was the #3 son, the youngest of "The Three Turks." The three boys were the oldest children in the Turcotte Clan, and it was rare if they weren't all together when they were kids. They were thick as thieves and competitive in all things, especially sports. All the Turcotte boys were good athletes and in excellent physical shape. While they were small-framed and wiry, they could all fend for themselves. Each could throw a punch, but more importantly, each could take a punch. Often times, it was two against one and Jim was often the "one." As a result, he had to learn to stand up for himself. The Turcotte boys would fight between themselves on a regular basis. However, as the saying goes, "Blood is thicker than water." If someone got into a scrap with one of the Turks, the other two had his back. Due to the way they were brought up, they didn't take kindly to bullies and believed it was a sign of weak character. If a bully was picking on a smaller or weaker kid, any one of The Three Turks had no problem stepping in.

For example, growing up Jim worked carrying golf bags at the Vesper Country Club in Tyngsborough, to pick up extra money for the family. At the club, there was an older caddy named Gino who liked picking on the younger, smaller caddies. Gino would push the kids around, knock them down or belittle them. One day, Jim saw Gino picking on a young kid and he stepped in and told Gino to "knock it off." Gino thought he would bully Jim as well. "What are you going to do about it?" asked Gino, moving into Jim's face. "Knock it off Gino," Jim said. Gino started to push Jim but, before Gino knew what hit him, Jim had hit Gino numerous times in the head and body, dazing him. Using both hands, Jim grabbed Gino by the front collar of his shirt and threw him into a nearby pond. The other caddies cheered. Jim dragged Gino out of the pond and told him outright, in no uncertain terms, not to bully any more kids or he would get more of the same. That was the end of Gino's bullying at The Vesper Country Club.

As with most kids their age, The Three Turks spent most of their time outside playing or on a ball field. They learned their love of sports from their father. Herman played sports in his younger days and coached in his older years, including baseball, basketball, hockey, and football. The boys also loved to swim, spending time down by the bridge on the Merrimack River or up at Mud Pond. Jim was a particularly strong swimmer. While he wasn't fast, he didn't tire easily.

Jim graduated from Lowell High School in 1939. He had enough credits to have graduated the year previous, but instead took a post-graduate year.[2] The Great Depression had lasted nearly 10 years, and while the economy began growing again in 1938, unemployment remained above 10 percent until 1941. At that moment, he thought the best place for him was in school. By the time Jim finished high school, his two older brothers were in the Navy, and Jim felt that it was a good idea for him to enlist also.

Jim enlisted on September 16, 1940 as an apprentice seaman. He was just 18 years old. His father brought him to the recruiting station in Boston. On the way in, Jim tripped over the curb – "ass over tea kettle" – and he wondered if it was a sign to stop him from joining up. He quickly decided it wasn't and went in and signed up for a six-year hitch. On his application, he stated the reason why he wanted to enlist was to learn a trade. Right after signing up, Jim, as his brothers before him, was sent to boot camp at Newport.

While there, somebody was always pulling a prank or dirty trick on another recruit. In their assigned quarters, the new recruits slung hammocks and slept in them throughout bootcamp. Every once in a while, some "wise guy" would re-sling another guy's hammock with a slip knot on the end. When he jumped into his hammock he'd immediately crash to the floor. While a few times Jim ended up on the deck, he luckily completed boot camp at the end of November 1940 without any major injuries and then stayed in Newport until early December of 1940.

---

[2] A postgraduate year usually refers to an academically minded gap year spent post-high school graduation, in order to strengthen candidacy for admission and potential in college. It was more common in private schools. Lowell High School offered such an option.

Jim, second row, right, upon graduation from boot camp in Newport, R.I.,1940.

Jim's boot camp unit in Newport, R.I., 1940. Jim, second row, dead center

Upon graduation, for Jim's first duty station, he had the privilege of serving aboard one of the oldest commissioned sailing vessels in the U.S. Navy, the USS *Constellation*. She was a sloop-of-war built in 1854 and the last sail-only warship in the U.S. Navy. Jim was serving aboard an 85-year-old square rigger ship, sleeping in a hammock. If you were six feet tall, you couldn't stand upright while below decks. It was cold, damp, cramped, and crowded. After all, it was Newport in the winter. The Navy Department ordered that the *Constellation* be decommissioned for preservation on June 16, 1933. Later, when World War II broke out in Europe, the *Constellation* was recommissioned just before Jim came aboard on August 24, 1940, without any new work being done on her to bring her up to modern standards. This was Jim's introduction to the Navy. For his service on a square rigger, Jim earned his first unofficial naval recognition. He became a member of the Order of the Square Rigger. Membership is only available to a sailor that serves on a ship with square rigs. At that time, this was a rare event. In December 1940, there were only two U.S. ships that qualified. The USS *Constitution* and the USS *Constellation*.

The *Constellation* (starboard side) at wharf in Philadelphia
Navy Yard June 11, 1926.

For his first assignment, Jim was assigned to "pheasant watch" where he received a sidearm and had to patrol a fenced-in area surrounding some land that officers would use to hunt pheasant. It was cold and lonely duty. Fortunately for Jim, that duty didn't last long. Within a few weeks, he was put aboard a civilian ship out of Cape May, New Jersey, to be transferred to Norfolk, Virginia. He had only a few bucks in his pocket and was given a room aboard ship. Not that his lack of funds mattered. While there was gambling and drinking aboard ship, Jim was too young to participate in either activity.

In Virginia, Jim had his first payday, receiving eight dollars. Unbeknownst to Jim, it would be his last payday for a long time. Like his brother Lionel, Jim had put in for a "brother transfer" so that he could serve with his brother Bob. His request was granted and shortly thereafter, Jim was issued a "brother transfer" to the *Cincinnati* so they could serve together, thus beginning Jim's odyssey.

Jim got word that the *Cincinnati* was in the Pacific but, due to security reasons, no one could officially tell him where the ship was. In an effort to locate his brother, Jim went ship to ship in Norfolk Harbor and talked to other sailors aboard whether they had any scuttlebutt on where the *Cincinnati* was. Finding the *Cincinnati* was going to be like finding a needle in a haystack. This was really frustrating for Jim. He had the transfer, he just had to get there. The only problem was he didn't know where "there" was.

At that point, Jim decided he was going to board the USS *King* (DD-242), an old, four-stack destroyer that previously had been decommissioned in 1938. However, soon after the Nazi aggression began the Second World War in Europe, the *King* was recommissioned and, at that time, ordered to join the Caribbean Neutrality Patrol. The *King* operated along the East Coast out of Boston and Key West, ranging into the Caribbean.

Now, the *King* had new orders as part of a group of four ships to head for the Panama Canal and then sail on for the West Coast. A World War II-era destroyer was often referred to as a "tin can" or "can," and its sailors were referred to as "tin can sailors." Historians are not exactly sure of the exact origin of the phrase, but the popular expression appeared to come from one of two of the sailors' perceptions – that the thin armor of a destroyer was no thicker than that of a "tin can" (unlike destroyers, battleships, aircraft carriers and cruisers that had belts of "armor" around them, giving them much greater protection), or that the very successful U.S. metal drives being held had resulted in the recycling of millions of "tin cans" used to build the ships. It is true that the U.S. assembly line production model put thousands of ships of different classes and types into service in just a few years and much of the steel came from recycling.

The USS *King.*

If you haven't spent much time around ships, you might not know that the manner in which a ship moves as it plows through the water is an important thing for a sailor to know. It affects everything the sailor does, including simple things such as walking and keeping balanced. It's often referred to as "getting your sea legs," which is the ability to walk steadily on the deck of a boat or ship. Different types of ships move differently. Some pitch, some roll and still others pitch and roll. Pitching is when the bow of the ship moves up and down. Rolling is when the ship tips side-to-side. How the ship moves affects how you move, the pace of your walk, your gait, and your stability.

Battleships and carriers pitch forward. Light and heavy cruisers usually roll. But as a destroyer plows through the ocean, it both pitches and rolls. This type of movement requires the most getting used to since, as you walk, you are being thrust side-to-side as well as backward and forward. It requires the body to adjust to all these forces acting on it at one time. After a while, operating in this environment becomes instinctual but, initially, you walk like a "drunken sailor." It's said that you could always pick out a sailor on leave from a destroyer by the strange way he walked. After being on a ship for weeks or months at a time and then going back on land, it can feel like everything is still rising and falling, as if you're still on the boat.

Jim had been around water his whole life, having grown up on the Merrimack River and Lake Althea. However, he had never been to sea. This was supposed to be an easy sail into the Caribbean, but Jim was seasick – sick as a dog – the first four days aboard. During the day, he still had duties to perform, spending his time either painting below deck in a small forward hatch or scraping rust from the deck. If he was below deck and had to get sick, he would run like mad to make it to the deck rail. Not that it was any better working on the deck, where it was extremely hot and there was no shade. He often worked wearing just a pair of dungarees or, sometimes, just a pair of trunks. Although over time he sported a bronzed tan, spending most of the day in the Caribbean sun without any sunscreen resulted in quite a sunburn. At night, he couldn't sleep below deck for fear of getting sick. Since it was still hot, he slept up on deck inside a torpedo tube. He'd peel back the metal shield on the end of the tube, put his thin mattress inside and try to grab a few hours of shut eye. If he needed to get sick, he could run to the ship's rail. These were tough days.

He didn't eat much, didn't sleep well, and was nauseous the whole time. While he tried his best to stay hydrated, by the end of the fourth day he was so drained that you could have rolled him off the side of the ship and he wouldn't have cared. Still, there were some early pleasures, though. He saw beautiful sunrises and sunsets. He watched dolphins breach the ocean's surface and race the ship. And he loved being out in the fresh air at two or three in the morning because it was the coolest time of the day.

On the fifth day, the boatswain's mate called Jim and, with a bit of a sadistic grin, told him he had the watch (or look-out duty). Inside, Jim questioned whether he had the strength or stamina to be able do it. On old "tin can" destroyers like the *King* there's a forward mast with a crow's nest just above the yardarm (the two tapering outer ends of a ship's yard). As seen in the photo of the *King*, the crow's nest on the *King* was nothing more than a large open bucket strapped to the forward mast. In order to get in, the lookout needed to climb the mast and get himself in without falling off. Easier said than done, particularly for someone in Jim's condition. On a ship that pitches and rolls, the fixed mast acts like the pinnacle of an inverted cone. The base of the mast stays in a fixed position, while the top of the mast moves in a circular rotation, generally in a clockwise position. As the lookout climbs the ladder, the relative position keeps changing as the crow's nest moves in the circular rotation. It's easier to climb as the position leans you forward and much more difficult when the position leans you backward. So, the lookout needed to time his movements, alternating climbing forward and holding on for dear life.

Imagine Jim – seasick, sunburned, dehydrated and exhausted – climbing the mast to the bucket. Once there, he needed to hang on to the mast and push open a trap door in the bottom of the bucket. Then he needed to climb in, put his feet on a miniscule rim inside the bucket and close the trap door, which would then become the floor of the crow's nest. For the next four hours he would be on an amusement park ride, moving round and round and up and down. And, God forbid if he got sick. To say the least, the sailors down below would not be happy. Jim gritted his teeth, literally, and rode it out. He wasn't sure if it was mind over matter or if he just didn't have anything left inside him but, either way, he made it through his shift and didn't throw up. Grit.

On day six, Jim still not feeling much better, was assigned to help a second-class boatswain's mate take apart a steel drum. Jim was to hold the drum while the boatswain's mate struck the metal band that held it together with a hammer. The hammer had a flat end on one side and a sharp, pointed punch on the other. The boatswain's mate swung back with the hammer and struck Jim right between the eyes with the punch end. He went down and out like a light and lay there, unconscious and bleeding. There was no doctor aboard. The boatswain's mate called for the closest thing to a medical provider, a pharmacist mate third class, who brought Jim around, quickly examined him, wiped off the blood and put a tiny bandage on the large lump that had formed on his forehead. Jim was put right back to work. Welcome to the Navy, Jim!

Jim and the USS *King* were on their way to Cristobal, Panama, and the Canal Zone. Cristobal is at the Atlantic Ocean entrance to the Panama Canal. As soon as the lookout saw land, he began yelling, "Land Ho!" The ship stopped off in Gatun Lake for a day to allow the barnacles to drop off in the fresh water. Jim's section had duty the night they pulled in so he was unable to go into Cristobal. The next day, December 11, they refueled and started through the canal around 3:30 in the afternoon. It takes a day to pass through the series of locks in the canal. Jim was taken by the raw beauty of Panama – the lush green trees, the sound of the exotic birds, the beautiful color of the hills on both sides, and the slowly sinking sun. One section of the canal is called the Caillard Cut, a spot cut through solid rock. It had a bronze plaque with the picture of a man with a shovel on it, showing the cut was created by man. By the next day, the *King* had cleared the canal.

On the other side is Balboa, a district of Panama City at the Pacific Ocean entrance to the canal. It was approximately 8:00 p.m. when they reached the other side of the canal and anchored in the bay. Jim finally slept well that night. When he awoke, he was excited because he was going to get liberty and go into Balboa. He finished shining his brightwork and swabbing the decks and then grabbed some chow. After quickly showering and dressing, he grabbed the 1:00 p.m. liberty boat into Balboa. From there, he headed into Panama City. He was in desperate need of a haircut and went looking for a barbershop. In a letter to his parents, he described what happened:

I needed a haircut so bad that I was about ready to buy a violin. I asked an American how much it would cost me for a haircut. 25 cents was the price that he told me. So into the barbershop I walked. He was a young barber with one of those "Caesar Romero haircuts." "Seet down senior" he says to me. "O.K. Chum" say I. "Geef to me a haircut", say I. "O.K. Chum", says he. Now we know each other. It took him exactly one hour and seventeen minutes to give me a haircut. You couldn't put the amount of hair in your eye that he took off in that time. Just then a Marine officer walks in and sat in the next chair. "How much is it?" I asked. Just because a damn old marine was sitting in the next chair I had to pay that Romeo 70 cents for the haircut. 50 cents for the haircut and 20 cents for 4 drops of hair tonic.

When Jim asked how much for the haircut, the barber looked over at the Marine, who was in dress uniform and looked like he could afford to pay a lot more, and then gave Jim the inflated price. Jim had a great head of hair as a young man and he took his haircuts seriously. Needless to say, he wasn't happy about this one. However, he made the best of it and continued his liberty.

Jim had gone into town with a guy named Ingalls. Between them, they ate three dozen bananas since they were cheap and filled them up. As they toured around the city, Jim would ask other U.S. sailors he saw if they had any information on where the *Cincinnati* was located. No luck. At the last minute, they bought a couple of post cards and stamps and made their way back to the liberty boat in a taxi (the ride cost them a nickel). Jim was a little concerned, inasmuch as they drove on the left-hand side of the road in Panama as they do in England. He kept getting the feeling they were going to crash head-on into someone. White knuckled and heart pumping, Jim made it back safely to the dock. When they were waiting for the liberty boat, one of the sailors from the *King* brought back a huge stalk of bananas, which must have weighed 60 pounds. He was bent over and had them slung over his shoulder, resting on his back. Jim watched as this sailor tried to get the bananas aboard without falling into the water as his timing needed to be perfect. He struggled, but made his way from the rocking liberty boat, up the gangplank and onto the *King*. Once onboard, the sailor fixed the bananas to a line and hoisted them up on the yardarm of the mast to ripen. It was quite a sight.

On December 13, the *King* left Panama first thing in the morning and was back on its way to San Diego. When Jim and the crew left Panama and headed out to sea, he became a member of the Order of the Ditch. This would be the second of many such maritime milestone recognitions for Jim. The Order of the Ditch is one of the many traditions for sailors that pass a maritime position – in this case, the Panama Canal. It's recognized due to the significance the canal made in maritime travel, saving about 8,000 nautical miles in a trip between the Atlantic and Pacific oceans.

Jim was back scraping and painting the *King* as it badly needed a good patching up. He was now assigned to paint the deck on the port side. Jim was starting to feel a little bit better. The time spent in Panama helped settle his stomach a little. However, back under way, he still had some nausea. He worked under a variety of the chief boatswain's mates over the next few days. They seemed to like Jim as he was hardworking and friendly, despite his current physical condition. On a couple of mornings, they brought him out some cake and ice-cold water while he was working. On topside, the water for the crew was always warm, so cold water was a huge treat and the cake helped settled his stomach. He continued to scrape and paint his way around the Pacific. It was slow going from Balboa to San Diego because the captain was concerned that they would run out of fuel. They crept along at 8 to 10 knots. During the evening and nighttime hours Jim could not help but be mesmerized. He told his parents that he never saw such beautiful sunsets and so many stars in all his life. It was so peaceful and quiet in the moonlight, except for the sounds of the ship's engines and music coming from the crew's radio. Jim particularly loved when he was on night watch with an officer named Ensign Barr. Barr hooked up a horn to the speaking tube leading to the radio room. He would tell the radioman to "put a nickel in it." In response, the radioman would serenade them with music from the radio room. Jim loved the music. It kept them awake and broke up the monotony of looking for ship's lights. Jim finished painting the entire deck on the port side just before they reached their next port.

On December 23, 1940, the *King* pulled into San Diego. As soon as they pulled into port, two unfortunate things happened. First, an oiler came alongside to refuel the *King*. The oiler's hose spilled out and fuel got all over the deck, which had to be cleaned and hosed off. But when they did that, half of the new paint had washed away as well. Jim thought, "All that hard work for nothing!" In addition, he got word that his brother Bob's ship had sailed to the Hawaiian Islands. His heart sank as that meant that sometime soon, he would be transferred to another ship going to the islands and he'd still be a transient passenger and not a member of the crew, resulting in more missed paydays. Jim had not been paid since he left Virginia. The only silver lining to this whole mess was that some other "snook" would have to repaint the *King*.

1941 Build-up to December 7, 1941

On December 18, 1940, Lionel received orders that he had been transferred to the Naval Air Station (NAS) in Jacksonville, Florida, and was to report for duty on January 3, 1941. This was a brand-new Naval facility and had only become an official air station in mid-October of 1940. Much of the site was still under construction, including the airstrips. On Christmas Eve, just over a week before Lionel's arrival, the station's first set of training aircraft arrived. The planes were 10 Boeing N2S Stearman, which flew in directly from the factory in St. Louis. The N2S Stearman was an open cockpit biplane, built to be a primary training aircraft for pilots in the Army Air Force and Navy.[3] On January 2, 1941, the first primary training squadron in Jacksonville, designated VN-11, was commissioned.

Essentially, Lionel Turcotte was there at the base's inception, arriving the day after the commissioning. NAS Jacksonville took off fast. By March 5, seaplane squadrons had been established, using nine P2Y and P2Y-3 aircraft. On June 24, 1941, NAS Jacksonville began its first class of aviation cadets and, within six months, they had received their wings. While there, Lionel was trained and certified on instrument and radio-beam flying.

On February 21, 1941, Lionel voluntarily agreed to extend his enlistment for two full years, resulting in another transfer back to NAS Pensacola for Link Trainer School. The term Link Trainer, also known as the "Blue Box" and "Pilot Trainer," is commonly used to refer to a series of flight simulators produced in the early 1930s by Link Aviation Devices, Inc., founded in 1929 in Binghamton, New York. During World War II, it was used as a key pilot training aid by almost every combatant nation. The original Link Trainer was created out of the need for a safe way to teach new pilots how to fly by instruments. The company's founder, Ed Link, used his knowledge of pumps, valves, and bellows gained at his father's Link Piano and Organ Company to create a flight simulator that responded to the

---

[3] The Stearman was flown by future President George H.W. Bush during his flight training.

pilot's controls and gave an accurate reading on the included instruments.

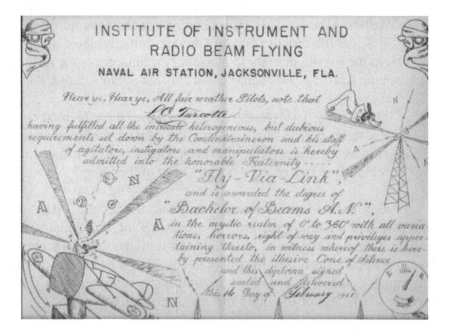

The trainer could simulate various flight conditions, including wind drift, turbulence and radio static, and could put the aircraft in various flight orientations. Air nozzles even produced the sound effect of the slipstream. Better still, the cost to operate the device was incredibly low. Each instrument flight in a training aircraft cost the military $10 per hour, while the Link Trainer only cost four cents per hour. Further, and most importantly, no cadet could lose his life if he committed an error in the simulator. The Link Flight Trainer was so important to military aviation that it was later designated as a Historic Mechanical Engineering Landmark by the American Society of Mechanical Engineers (one is on display at the National Museum of Naval Aviation in Pensacola).

Even though Lionel could not be a Navy pilot, the Link Training allowed him to work toward being an aviation chief machinist mate and crew chief aboard naval aircraft. Lionel knew there was more than one way to skin a cat. If he couldn't pilot an aircraft, he would be a chief aboard one. Grit.

The *Cincinnati* split her pre-World War II career between the Atlantic and Pacific fleets, continuing to go back and forth between oceans until March 1941, when she was assigned to Neutrality Patrol in the Western Atlantic. This area encompassed the Atlantic from 20° W to 20° S, off the coast of South America. Initially, the *Cincinnati* went from the Pacific directly to Norfolk, Virginia, for some refitting and then, on April 5, 1941, departed on her first South Atlantic Patrol.

On May 18, 1941, Robert Turcotte joined the esteemed ranks of many a sailor before him, crossing the equator for the first-time aboard ship on the *Cincinnati*, after which he was duly initiated into the "Solemn Mysteries of the Ancient Order of the Deep."

Bob became a "Shellback," or "Son of Neptune," part of a time-honored tradition marking the crossing of the equator and initiation through a series of tests and trials until the sailor is accepted by King Neptune as one of his trusty Shellbacks. When a ship crosses the equator, there is usually a line-crossing ceremony for Navy members crossing for the first time and a certificate for each.

A "Pollywog" is someone who has yet to cross the equator. And a "landlubber" is someone altogether unfamiliar with the sea or seamanship. Rooted in history, these line-crossing ceremonies are practiced in several countries. They were first thoroughly documented in the early 1800s and likely boosted morale, serving as proof of endurance. Over time, it appears that the intention of these ceremonies changed slightly. In the 1940s, there was an element of hazing involved. The ceremony commences as King Neptune comes aboard to exercise authority over his domain and to judge charges brought against Pollywogs that they are only posing as sailors and haven't paid proper homage to the god of the sea. High-ranking members of the crew and those who have been Shellbacks the longest dress up in elaborate costumes and each play a part in King Neptune's court. For instance, the ship's captain might play the part of King Neptune himself. What proceeds is a day of festivities, which builds camaraderie among the seafaring crew.

After crossing the line, Pollywogs receive subpoenas to appear before King Neptune and his court (usually including his first assistant, Davy Jones; Her Highness Amphitrite; and often various other dignitaries, who are all represented by the highest-ranking seamen). The king and his court officiate at the ceremony, which is often preceded by a beauty contest of men dressing up as women, with each department of the ship being required to introduce one contestant in swimsuit drag. Afterwards, some "Wogs" may be "interrogated" by King Neptune and his entourage with the use of "truth serum" (hot sauce + after shave) and whole uncooked eggs put in the mouth. During the ceremony, the Pollywogs undergo a number of increasingly embarrassing ordeals, like wearing clothing inside out and backwards; crawling on hands and knees on nonskid-coated decks; being swatted with short lengths of firehose; being locked in stocks and pillories and pelted with mushy fruit; being locked in a water coffin of salt-water and bright green sea dye; crawling through chutes or large tubs of rotting garbage; kissing the "Royal Baby's" belly, coated with axle grease; and having their hair chopped, all largely for the entertainment of the initiates.

The ceremony is still practiced today and is usually orchestrated in a controlled manner. It's a significant event for a sailor and something they remember for life, including where they crossed and much of the ceremony. The certificate refers to a maritime ceremony called "Crossing the Line." The certificates are unofficial, so the U.S. Navy usually keeps no official records of them. Occasionally, there is an entry in the sailor's file. Officially recognized or not, as with many other milestone events, they are treasured and taken as a sign of honor by the sailor. Each certificate is slightly different, depending on the circumstances under which the ship was sailing. For instance, if the ship crossed the line during wartime, the certificate would likely mention that. In addition, due to wartime censorship, the exact location of the crossing would not be included. Seeing as Bob's crossing occurred prior to the war, we know the exact location where he became a Shellback – Latitude 0-00, Longitude 32-minutes 57-seconds West.

The certificate reads:

To All Sailors Wherever Ye May Be: and to all Mermaids, Whales, Sea Serpents, Porpoises, Sharks, Dolphins, Eels, Skates, Suckers, Crabs, Lobsters and all other Living Things of the Sea

Greeting: Know ye: That on this 18th day of May 1941 in Latitude 00000 and Longitude 32 Minutes 57 Seconds there appeared within Our Royal Domain the USS Cincinnati bound South for the Equator in the Southwest Pacific

Be it Remembered that the said Vessel and Officers and Crew thereof have been inspected and passed on by Ourself and Our Royal Staff

And Be It Known: By all ye Sailors, Marines, Land Lubbers and others who may be honored by his presence that Robert T. Turcotte U.S. Navy having been found worthy to be numbered as one of our Trusty Shellbacks he has been duly initiated into the Solemn Mysteries Of The Ancient Order Of The Deep

Be It Further Understood: That by virtue of the power invested in me I do hereby command all my subjects to show due honor and respect to him wherever he may be

Disobey this order under penalty of Our Royal Displeasure.

Given under our hand and seal this 18th day of May 1941

Davey Jones His Majesty's Scribe

Neptunus Rex Ruler of the Raging Main By His Servant

E.N. Senn, Captain

Many sailors, once ashore, would acknowledge this event by way of a nautical tattoo, often of a shellback turtle and, sometimes, with King Neptune. The two symbols are interchangeable for this initiation into King Neptune's Court.

The U.S. Navy is a giant bureaucracy. Administration can be an overwhelming challenge. At any given time, people are being enlisted, transferred, discharged and, unfortunately, sometimes there are deaths. The Navy is tasked with keeping track of each sailor through a series of files. When a sailor moves from one assignment to the next, his records are supposed to follow him. These files are critical to the smooth administration of naval functions. During World War II, all records were paper records. They were a physical object and, like any object, they could get lost, mislaid, or accidently destroyed. One of those paper files were pay records. Without pay records, a sailor does not get paid. Period.

Unfortunately for him, it seems that somewhere between Newport and San Diego, Jim's pay records were either lost, misplaced, or sent to Bob's ship, the *Cincinnati*. Or they could have been on any one of 100 different ships in any of 100 different ports anywhere in the world. No matter what, until Jim got to the *Cincinnati* or his pay records were found, he wasn't getting paid. At first, he didn't mind. "So much for that," he wrote his parents. But then it started to sink in. He didn't have a lot of money to begin with and now he had even less. He still had no idea when he would get paid again.

Christmas Eve and Christmas Day 1940 were spent at the dock in San Diego. On Christmas, Jim's section got liberty. Instead of going, Jim took over the mess cook's job in the chief's quarters. The $8.00 he was paid in Norfolk hadn't gone very far. With that money he had to buy his dungarees to work in and soap to wash his uniforms to stand his daily watch in. After going to Panama, getting a haircut, buying some post cards and the bananas, Jim didn't have much left. Since it appeared that he wouldn't see a payday for a while, he spent Christmas working. He was paid three bucks to pick up the Christmas shift.

Nonetheless, he was thankful. Christmas on board was fairly quiet. Every ship had a Christmas tree and Jim had a swell dinner. He mess-cooked for and ate with the chiefs who remained on board. As Christmas gifts, they gave Jim three packs of cigarettes and three, ten-cent Robert Burns cigars. So far, despite no pay records, Jim thought he was a pretty lucky sailor. After cleaning up, Jim washed himself down with a bucket of water, put on his dress blues, and headed into San Diego. The first thing he did was send his parents and grandmother a Christmas telegram. Given his financial circumstances, that was all he could afford. He then went to a cheap movie with another mess cook. It was a comedy which he thought was really good, adding he "almost busted a gut from laughing."

Even though it was an old rust bucket, Jim had liked the *King*. He had gotten to know most of the guys pretty well. According to him, there wasn't a guy on the ship that didn't treat him fine. All in all, it wasn't a bad Christmas. Jim always looked on the bright side. Things could be worse which, unfortunately, he would soon find out.

While in San Diego, the *King* had picked up 40 more passengers. On December 26, Jim woke up to the call of "All hands on deck!" It was anchors aweigh with a destination of San Pedro, California, part of the Port of Los Angeles. The trip featured rough seas and all 40 of the new passengers got seasick. Jim knew their pain and suffering. Luckily, it only took about seven hours to reach San Pedro.

Upon arrival, Jim, along with the 40 other passengers, went from the *King* to the Battleship *Colorado* (BB-45), which was headed for the Hawaiian Islands. He was still hoping to meet up with the *Cincinnati* there. Jim was bothered by a couple of things. First, that the *Colorado* was not scheduled to go to Hawaii until January 20. Even if they immediately rendezvoused, it wouldn't be until after January 30 that he would get paid next. He was starting to get a little concerned about his lack of funds. He knew sooner or later he would come into some money, but he was pretty close to broke now. Second, on the *King*, they slept in bunks. On the *Colorado*, they slept in hammocks, which were definitely not as comfortable. His mind harkened back to boot camp and the *Constellation*. He hoped some joker wouldn't pull that slip knot trick on him again.

He recalled years later an incident when he was aboard the *Colorado* and still in San Pedro waiting to head out to Hawaii. A Japanese freighter came into the harbor. There were rumors and inklings of possible hostilities between the United States and Japan. All the American warships trained their guns on the freighter and tracked her as she cruised into the harbor. No one was taking any chances.

Off the *Colorado* went to Hawaii. Once it arrived, Jim was aboard for only a short time. He went through a quick series of transfers, looking for the *Cincinnati*. Jim was quite literally a transient. He went to the light cruiser *Trenton* (CL- 11); the *Henderson* (AP-1), a transport vessel; and the *Concord* (CL-10), another light cruiser. With each transfer, the lack of pay became more and more difficult to resolve. January turned to February and February to March. He went from ship to ship, port to port, looking to join up with his brother, Bob. He traveled from San Diego to Pearl Harbor, from Pearl Harbor to the Philippines, back to Pearl Harbor, and then to San Francisco. Despite being promoted to seaman second class on March 13, 1941, he still had no money for even the simplest of things. The heels on his shoes were broken and needed to be fixed. He hadn't had a haircut in months, not since Panama, and that wasn't much of a haircut. He started to look shabby. He tried to borrow money from fellow sailors but given his transient status, most figured they would never see their dough returned to them. He tried borrowing a few bucks from the ship's chaplain but was politely declined for the same reason.

In April, while in the San Francisco Bay area, Jim was with the *Concord* at Repair Station, Mare Island. Mare Island is located inside San Pablo Bay after you pass through San Francisco Bay near Vallejo, California. While there, he befriended a signalman who went into the radio shack and was able to find out that Bob's ship was part of the Southern Atlantic Neutrality Patrol. This was frustrating for Jim. The government had known where his brother was and had refused to share it with him. He had been running in circles around much of the globe. At this point, Jim had had enough of being a vagabond. He was upset by this turn of events and really wanted to serve with his brother, but it was not working out. At this point in time, Jim was a seaman second class, but he had no permanent duty station or job assignment. He hadn't stayed long enough on any one ship to be given a regular job assignment. The use of the word "rank" for Navy enlisted personnel is incorrect. The correct terms are "rate," which refers to the pay grade and "rating," which refers to the occupational specialty or job assignment. Because Jim had no permanent duty station, he couldn't get a rating or job assignment. Without a rating, Jim couldn't really advance in rate beyond a certain point, and he was getting close to that point. To top it off, it had been nearly six months without getting paid. He felt like a prisoner.

Jim, left, San Francisco 1941.

Jim wrote his brother Bob a short but heartfelt letter telling him that he couldn't continue in this way and he had decided that he was going to give up the "brother transfer" and try to get a sea assignment with the next ship. He hoped his brother would understand. Jim notified the Navy and requested duty on the next available ship. It didn't take long for them to grant Jim's request. On April 30, 1941, Jim transferred to the USS *Northampton* (CA-26) in San Francisco.

The *Northampton* was a heavy cruiser, 600-feet-long and could cruise at 32 knots. She had a complement of 90 officers and more than 600 enlisted men. The *Northampton* had nine, eight-inch guns; four, five-inch anti-aircraft guns; and six torpedo tubes. Jim finally had a ship to call his own.

When Jim reported aboard the *Northampton*, he didn't have a dime to his name. All he had was a small ditty bag with personal hygiene gear, a towel and his sea bag with his clothes, and his hammock. He hung up the ditty bag on a jack stand on the well deck and reported to the officer of the deck. He was with him for approximately ten minutes when he went back and discovered that someone had stolen his bag with his shaving gear, toothbrush, and towel. Things aboard the *Northampton* weren't starting out so well. He literally had to beg to replace his toothbrush and shaving gear. Every new sailor that came aboard was assigned a battle station. Jim's battle station was in a five-inch ammo magazine supplying ammunition for the five-inch guns. This magazine was located three decks down. The *Northampton* had three hollow mast legs that held up the bridge. If anything were to happen while he was in the magazine, all the sailors were to climb through a tiny hole and climb up the three decks to the ship's bridge on a ladder on the inside of one of the hollow mast legs. The only hatch from which he could escape was out on the bridge, way up top.[4] No matter how small you were it was not easy to climb up a ladder inside such a dark confined space. Even if you weren't claustrophobic, it was claustrophobic.

In addition, Jim was finally given his rating. Jim was assigned to the S Division, or the Supply Division, and he was given the rating of storekeeper apprentice (SK). Storekeepers are tasked with maintaining ship military supply stores. Their responsibilities generally include purchasing and procurement, shipping and receiving, and the issuing of equipment, tools, consumable items or anything else obtained through the Naval Supply System. Storekeepers are referred to, as with all other Navy rates, by rate and rank combined. If a sailor is a petty officer third class holding the rate of storekeeper, he or she would be referred to as storekeeper third class or, more commonly, SK3. Jim was at the bottom of the food chain as an entry-level SK. He worked for the storekeeper in charge, Charlie Fortier. In addition to being a storekeeper first class, Jim thought Charlie was a "first-class storekeeper." Charlie wasn't a micro-manager. He showed Jim what had to be done and let Jim do it. He allowed him to do a lot of different work without a lot of supervision, thus building up Jim's self-confidence. The position fit Jim's personality as he was a very organized person and he and Charlie worked well together. As time went on, if things were quiet, Charlie allowed Jim to find a place out of the way and out of sight to study. Jim would borrow math and history books out of the ship's library to read. He knew it was a long shot, but he wanted to go to officer's school and Charlie encouraged him.

Jim still wasn't getting paid, but he was getting three square meals a day and a bunk of his own. Despite having his gear stolen on his first day, he felt like this was a ship on which he could put down

---

[4] See photo NH94596. The bridge is the highest point of the ship, supported by the three hollow mast legs, each containing a ladder.

some roots. He was a jovial fellow and made friends easily. He felt like his luck was about to change.

Lionel continued to work hard and study while at his new assignment in Jacksonville. On May 1, 1941, his rating was changed from aviation machinist mate third class to aviation machinist mate second class. Six days later, Lionel was again examined to determine whether he could be an aviator. Again, his eyes were the disqualifier. These preliminary flight exams would go on periodically throughout his service. Each and every time, his eyesight prevented him from becoming a pilot. He knew deep down he wasn't going to be a pilot but, each time he was examined, he secretly hoped his luck would change and a miracle would happen.

Despite how busy he was, on June 15, 1941, Lionel remembered his father for Father's Day. He sent a telegram. "When we picked a dad, we picked the very best they had. Lionel." Being so far away from home for so long – Father's Day, Mother's Day, and birthdays – seemed to take on greater importance. After all Herman had done for Lionel, he wanted to make sure his father knew he was thinking of him.

FATHER'S *Greetings* DAY

by POSTAL TELEGRAPH

B6 748 FDG=JACKSONVILLE FLO
MR HERMAN O TURCOTTE=
113 VARNUM AVE LOWELL MASS=

WHEN WE PICKED A DAD, WE PICKED THE VERY BEST THEY HAD=
=LIONEL.

By September 1940, U.S. military aircraft began flying neutrality patrols over the western Atlantic. They were employed to observe and report the movement of foreign warships, including German U-boats. The reporting areas were soon expanded to the east coast of Canada and down to the West Indies. Although the United States was not yet in the war, U.S. surface ships and aircraft on neutrality patrol were of significant assistance to Great Britain. The objective of the British Fourth Fleet was to dominate the strategically important Atlantic Narrows between Natal, Brazil, and the Freetown-Accra portion of Africa by finding and destroying Axis Power submarines and blockade runners that were funneling essential war materials from the Japanese Empire through the South Atlantic Narrows between Brazil and Africa into Europe.

An additional purpose was to halt the sinking of Brazilian and other Allied merchant ships by the Axis Power's naval units. Because the Mediterranean Sea was hazardous for Allied shipping, control of the South Atlantic Narrows was strategically critical.

Effective January 10, 1941, Bob transferred to VCS Squadron 2 on the USS *Cincinnati*. Same ship, same job, different plane. Shortly thereafter, he was again promoted. On February 16, 1941, his rating changed from seaman second class [Sea.2c] to aviation machinist mate third class [AMM.3c]. Just like his brother Lionel, Bob performed routine maintenance, prepared aircraft for flight and assisted in handling aircraft on the ground. In addition, during the quarter ending June 30, 1941, he had logged four flights with 5.2 hours of flight time as a member of the VCS Squadron. While he wasn't a pilot, he was the crew member that served with the pilot aboard the floatplane. As an aircrewman, Bob earned additional pay for flight hours.

Before it became part of the neutrality patrols, the *Cincinnati* was scheduled for an overhaul during the month of July 1941. One of the things the Navy scheduled was enhancement of the armaments aboard the ship. As a result of the scheduled overhaul, effective July 17, Bob was temporarily transferred to shore with the *Cincinnati* VCS-2 Squadron Unit to Naval Air Station Norfolk.

The USS *Cincinnati*, July 8, 1942.

Once the overhaul was completed, the *Cincinnati* began patrols along the eastern seaboard of the United States and down to South America. At the end of 1941 through 1942, the *Cincinnati* was working out of Recife, Brazil, on neutrality patrols, along with her sister ships, to prevent supplies getting to German submarines and to Japan.

On December 1, 1941, just days before the attack on Pearl Harbor and America's entry into World War II, Bob was again promoted. His rating was changed from an aviation machinist mate third class [AMM.3c] to aviation machinist mate second class [AMM2c]. In addition, he was ordered to continue duty involving flying, participating in regular and frequent aerial flights.

By mid-1941, Jim and the *Northampton* had set sail for Pearl Harbor. At this point, his pay records had finally caught up to him

(Hallelujah!). He had gone more than six months without pay. Jim was paid $21 per month. Now, at 20 years old and in Hawaii, he was sitting on six months of back pay – a whopping $126. The first thing he did with his new-found wealth was get a new pair of shoes and a real haircut.

Jim, right, in white bathing suit on Waikiki Beach in 1940.

Jim loved Pearl Harbor and thought it was a great assignment. What wasn't to love? The weather was spectacular, the beaches were nice, and he loved to swim in the beautiful, blue Pacific Ocean. He loved to hang out with his buddies near the Royal Hawaiian Hotel, which catered to the rich and famous. At the time, the Royal Hawaiian was advertised as an ultra-luxury hotel in a tropical paradise. For many wealthy people, the Royal Hawaiian was *the* destination.

At night, Jim and his buddies would occasionally go to the movies at a theater in downtown Honolulu. Jim loved a good picture and thought this theater was a real beauty. As the picture was playing, the windows were usually kept open. Often there would be a slight breeze coming through the window which kept the theater comfortably cool and carried with it the sweet fragrance of flowers from a nearby garden. For Jim, this really was paradise. Even if they didn't do anything else after the movie, he thought just walking around downtown at night was a treat. All the sailors would be out in their uniforms, and all the girls would be dressed up, looking their best. Music from the clubs would come wafting out into the streets. It was a wonderful atmosphere. Jim stayed away from the clubs and bars. He was still only 19 years old and was too young to legally drink.

Because he was still so young and so far from home, Jim enjoyed getting mail from Lowell. He loved to hear about how his parents were doing, if they had heard from his brothers, Lionel and Bob, and about how the rest of the family was doing. He had his three sisters, Maude, Mary and Dorothy, still at home. In addition, his youngest brother, Walter (Bud), had just turned 15 years old. They all had plenty going on and Jim wanted to hear about everything. The mail wasn't as regular as Jim liked, but his family was very good about writing to all three boys. When Jim was lax in responding, he got a gentle nudge in the letters that followed from family members.

In late June 1941, the *Northampton* was given its first real assignment since Jim came aboard. The *Northampton*, the *Salt Lake City* and two destroyers were tasked with a secret mission. In early 1941, President Franklin Roosevelt had signed a secret executive order authorizing retired Air Force Major Claire Chennault to recruit volunteer pilots and ground crews from Army, Navy, and Marine squadrons. They would be formally called "The American Volunteer Group" (AVG). Informally, they were known as the "Flying Tigers."

Interestingly, during this time, the AVG was technically part of the Chinese Military. The squadrons were put together by President Roosevelt's order as well as an executive order by Generalissimo Chiang-Kai-shek to aid the Nationalist Government of China against the Japanese Empire and to protect the Burma Road. By outward appearances, the Tigers were employed by a military contractor, but they were bought and paid for by the U.S. government. At various times throughout the summer and fall of 1941, some 300 men of the AVG, carrying civilian passports, boarded ships ultimately destined for Burma, where they would be stationed.

The *Enterprise* was only one of three aircraft carriers commissioned just prior to World War II. It was stationed at Pearl Harbor at the same time as the *Northampton* and assigned a group of destroyer and cruiser escorts to protect it when out at sea. In the summer of 1941, the *Northampton*, a heavy cruiser, was assigned as one of those escorts. The group of ships was to meet up with a foreign-flagged ship and escort it to Java, part of Indonesia, located just north of Australia. Jim identified the ship as the Dutch vessel, the *Argus Fontaine*. The ship was carrying nurses, pilots and Flying Tigers aboard. The orders for the U.S. Navy vessels were to protect the *Argus Fontaine* at all costs. The "cover story" for the cruise was that it was heading to Australia. The ships headed out as ordered to rendezvous with the *Argus Fontaine*.

To defeat boredom aboard ship, sailors will do most anything – make wagers on when the first land bird will be spotted, when it will rain next or what night they'd have meatloaf for dinner. On this trip there was a challenge put out to all the lookouts and sailors alike aboard the *Northampton*. Whoever was the first lookout to spot the ship they had to rendezvous with would win a carton of cigarettes. Winning a carton of cigarettes was like winning the lottery. For days, every man aboard scanned the horizon for a glimpse of anything that could possibly be the *Argus Fontaine*. Finally, the shout went up, "Ship on the horizon!" It was the *Argus Fontaine*. A young seaman claimed his prize to the shouts and cheers of his fellow sailors.

The *Northampton* would remain about 1,000 yards off the side of the *Argus Fontaine* but, every morning, every available sailor would grab a pair of binoculars and peer over at the Dutch vessel. Nurses on board often gathered on deck to the delight of the U.S. sailors. One particular nurse, all dressed in black, would take an early morning walk around the deck. The Americans thought she was beautiful, and the sailors would raise a commotion and yell and she would wave back to everybody. With that one wave, she raised the blood pressure of thousands of guys in the fleet. Once at Java, they were met by another foreign ship that would take over the escort of the Tigers into Burma. Being escorted into Burma by American warships would have drawn too much attention. As the U.S. ships departed, all the sailors lingered at the railing and waved goodbye, whistled and yelled to their beautiful "companions." Each was both thrilled and heartbroken when they got a final wave goodbye from the nurse in black. The mission was successful as the Flying Tigers got to Burma and were well-established before the end of the year. It was a good thing they went when they did. The Tigers saw action against the Japanese by December 12, 1941, a week after the bombing of Pearl Harbor.

True to their cover story, the U.S. Navy vessels headed to Brisbane, Australia. As part of their trip, on July 21, 1941, Jim crossed the equator at 165 degrees 50' west, heading south for Brisbane, becoming a Shellback like his brother.

The *Northampton* arrived in Brisbane by August 5. Australia had been at war since September 1939, entering the conflict alongside Britain and sending troops to Europe and the Middle East. The Australian people were thrilled to have American warships visit Brisbane.

The *Northampton* stayed in Australia for several months. With so many Australian men absent due to military service, the remaining Australian population loved the Americans and treated them well, throwing numerous parties and celebrations for the sailors. The sailors loved it, but still had to mind their behavior. They were representatives of the United States and had to make a good impression on the Australian people. Australian women greeted the Americans with great excitement. According to Jim, the Aussie women loved the Americans so much and treated them so well that nearly 50 sailors from the *Northampton* crew alone jumped ship and got married, honeymooning with their new wives and enjoying the good life.

On October 1, 1941, after successfully testing to be a petty officer in his rating, Jim was promoted to storekeeper third class. In October, when the *Northampton* shipped out for return to Pearl Harbor, nearly 50 men were missing, as most of the newlyweds had stayed behind. Officially the sailors were AWOL (Away Without Leave). However, the Navy took a lenient approach. Each of the sailors was required to report to the police station in Brisbane and sign in each day. They had to keep the Navy informed of where they were and what they were up to. At that time, no other punitive action was taken against the sailors. After December 7, 1941, each of the "AWOL" sailors raced back to Pearl Harbor to rejoin the *Northampton*. Their only punishment was a $50 fine and being stationed back aboard the *Northampton*. Most of the sailors never saw their young Australian wives again until the war was over in 1945. Some never did.

On their return voyage back to Pearl Harbor, Jim crossed the equator at the 180th Meridian. When a sailor crosses the equator for the first time, he becomes "a shellback".

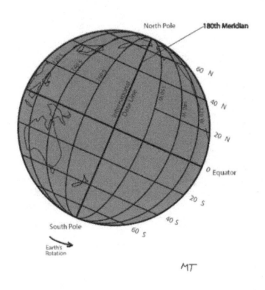

Map of world showing the equator and 180th Meridian and International Date Line.

When a sailor crosses the 180th Meridian, or International Date Line, for the first time he becomes a "Golden Dragon". But when a "pollywog" sailor crosses both the equator and the 180th Meridian at the same time, he becomes a Golden Shellback. For a sailor crossing the equator for the first time at the 180th Meridian, it's an extremely significant and rare event. The sailor is given the distinction of becoming a "Golden Shellback". This is what happened to Jim. There is an initiation ceremony at which the sailor is initiated into the realm of Neptune to become a Golden Shellback. Depending on the circumstances, these ceremonies can, again, be very elaborate – almost *Mardi Gras*-esque.

The same certificate is issued to each of the inductees. Usually, the first thing that happens is the ship stops and the "pollywogs" jump overboard and swim around in the equatorial waters to become Shellbacks. However, on this occasion, because they were on a mission, they were not able to stop the ship. They did, however, build "Neptune's Kingdom" aboard ship and those being initiated had to crawl through aircraft target sleeves. These were tubes that were pulled behind the ships and used as targets for aircraft to practice on.

As the inductees were crawling through the sleeves onboard the ship, they were beaten with socks full of wet clothing until they came out the other end. They'd then get thrown in a plastic pool and some big boatswain's mate would hold them down under water and then, eventually, pull the inductees back up by the hair to let them breath again. They had to run this circuit multiple times. All the time, there was yelling and chanting at the inductees by the rest of the crew. Everyone available was strongly urged to participate. One of the honored "pollywogs" was a second-class boatswain's mate named Sykes. Sykes was chained to the bow of the ship, leaving one arm free. Waves from the ocean would come crashing over him. He was given a short length of water hose. From the bridge of the ship, he was ordered to "blow tubes." He had to blow into the hose like a trumpet and make it sound, over and over. Every ship and every captain run their ceremony a little differently, as timing and circumstances allow.

It was still October 1941 and Jim and the *Northampton* were back at Pearl Harbor. Life got back into a routine. Not that Jim minded. The *Northampton* went through its drills and exercises and Jim did his regular job and helped resupply the ship. Again, Jim was able to get some leisure time, go to the movies, read, swim at the beach, and generally enjoy himself.

Jim, far right, on Waikiki Beach

On one occasion in October, while Jim was on the beach near the Royal Hawaiian Hotel, he found that one of the people sitting near him was the swimmer and soon to be actress, Esther Williams. She had hoped to compete in the 1940 Olympics, but they had been cancelled because of the war that Japan was involved in. Ms. Williams had been in the Aquacade Show, but it had closed a year earlier. She had married Leonard Kovner in June of 1940. It appears that she was in Hawaii for an impromptu vacation. Her presence, when discovered, caused quite a stir. Jim thought she looked swell in a bathing suit, all 5'9" of her.

On November 28, 1941, under orders from Admiral Kimmel, the USS *Enterprise* Task Force 8, under Rear Admiral Halsey, and which included the *Northampton*, was sent to deliver Marine Corps fighter planes to Wake Island. The distance from Pearl to Wake Island is approximately 2,300 miles. On December 4, the group delivered the aircraft and was on its way back to Pearl Harbor. Task Force 8 was due to arrive in Pearl Harbor on December 6, what would have turned out to be just 23 hours prior to history being made. By this time, the rest of the U.S. carriers were not in Pearl Harbor, either. On December 5, Admiral Kimmel sent the USS *Lexington* and a task force to deliver 25 scout bombers to Midway Island. The last Pacific carrier, USS *Saratoga*, had left Pearl Harbor for upkeep and repairs back on the West Coast.

During the return trip to Pearl, the *Northampton* was dispatched to refuel several of the task force's destroyers, an operation that had been carried out many times before without a mishap. During the particular refueling, however, a section of eight-inch line somehow became entangled around one of the ship's screws (propellers), thus forcing her to stop until the line could be removed.

While the crew went about the task of untangling the wayward hemp from the prop, all the men vented their anger and frustration at the possibility of missing a weekend of liberty in Honolulu or lounging around the beach at Waikiki. Finally, during the early morning hours of December 6, the last strands of line were removed from the *Northampton's* screw. Resigned to the fact that no matter how fast they pushed the sleek warship, liberty would have to wait for until another time. Very disappointed, the crew settled down for another night at sea.

On the morning of December 7, 1941, approximately 6:15 a.m., the *Northampton* and the *Enterprise* were approximately 215 miles due west of Oahu. At approximately 8 a.m. that fateful morning, each ship's General Quarters Alarm went off and their speakers blared, "General Quarters! General Quarters! This is no drill! Pearl Harbor is under attack!" Everyone aboard the *Northampton* was shocked by the alarm. The General Quarters Alarm is loud and disturbing. It is meant to be that way. It is designed to shake you out of a sound sleep. The alarm simultaneously is accompanied by an announcement which is made loud and clear. When this happens, all hell breaks loose. All crew members are supposed to drop whatever they are doing and report to their stations and immediately start preparing. This includes off-duty crew members or those who are sleeping. Security is increased, watertight doors are shut, and the engineering rooms and bridge are guarded. It's basically a lockdown, a state of full readiness.

On the other hand, when "Battle Stations" is called, everyone reports to his station and gets ready for combat. Crew members wear their battle gear, ready the guns and prepare to engage in combat. The announcement then says, "General Quarters. General Quarters. All hands man your Battle Stations."

There is a "route" a sailor follows aboard a warship which must always be adhered to, without exception. It must become second nature for times like this, when "General Quarters" or "Battle Stations" is sounded. In order to keep things organized when all hell is breaking loose, a sailor must travel forward and up on the starboard side, and back and down on the port side. This means if you are on the right-hand side of the ship as you are facing the bow (or front of the ship), you must travel up the ladders and toward the bow of the ship. If you wish to go toward the rear of the ship(stern) or down a ladder, then you must do so on the port or left-hand side of the ship.

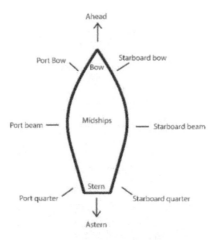

So, in the heat of the moment of General Quarters, sailors need to be able to follow these routes instinctively. There are literally hundreds of men rushing to get to their stations all over the ship. This route or plan was universally put into place by the Navy so that it could be done quickly, efficiently, and safely.

The CXAM radar system was the first production radar system deployed on United States Navy ships, operating in the mid-high VHF frequency band of 200 MHz. The first six units RCA produced (delivered in 1940) were denoted "CXAM" and were a fusion of two different radar technologies. These were installed on only six ships, the *Northampton* being one of them.

Jim now was assigned to a five-inch, anti-aircraft gun platform on the port side. And his role had changed to what was referred to as a "JR Talker." A JR Talker stands next to the operator of the anti-aircraft guns and directs the direction of fire. Jim was supervised by a gunnery officer. The talker wears a helmet equipped with a headphone and a microphone. A radar operator in the radar room provides enemy contact information to the talker, who in turn communicates that information to the gunnery officer or gunner.

Example of a JR Talker helmet with microphone and Kapok life jacket.

Jim's gunnery officer had made a survivor's kit early on in his enlistment. He had taken a tin can and filled it with things he might need in case he had to abandon ship. It included chocolate bars, cigarettes, chewing gum, matches, first-aid supplies, and a sewing needle and thread. The gunnery officer waterproofed it by wrapping it in multiple condoms and secured a line around the can so he could wear it around his neck or around his wrist. He kept it with him every time he went to Battle Stations. All the guys gave him the business about it, a good-natured ribbing, but he didn't mind. One day he might have the last laugh.

For Jim, the announcement and alarm on December 7 was one of those rare moments that instantly changed his life forever. He was 19 years old and now he was at war. Like so many of the sailors aboard, he was in shock. He couldn't believe that Pearl Harbor, the place that he had called home for the last eight months, was under attack. He was angry, frustrated, and ready to fight. But there wasn't a lot he or anyone else on board could do at that moment. They were too far away to get into the action. He wished he was at Pearl Harbor, but it turned out to be a blessing that the *Enterprise*, the *Northampton* and the entire task force was 200 miles out to sea. The *Enterprise* Task Force was a significant part of all that was left of the Pacific fleet. If they had been in port at Pearl, they likely would have been destroyed or heavily damaged as well.

SOC Seagulls from the *Northampton* flying
over the Hawaiian Islands in early 1941.

Doing what they could, the *Northampton* sent two SOC Seagull scout-planes out. Like those on the *Cincinnati*, these planes were generally used for scouting and rescue. They were not fighter planes, although they were equipped with machine guns. Occasionally, the machine guns aboard these seaplanes proved effective. While out scouting, the planes of the *Northampton* came upon a damaged Japanese Zero heading back to its carrier. In a 20-minute running gun battle, the Americans managed to bring it down. Pilot Lt. Baxter and gunner Ensign Perry were given credit for shooting down the enemy plane. Although it was only a small incident, it gave great pride to the task force crews, particularly those aboard the *Northampton*. From this point on she was lovingly referred to as "Fighting Nora."

Photo # 80-G-32548   USS Northampton enters Pearl Harbor, 8 December 1941

As Jim described it, when the *Northampton* pulled into Pearl Harbor on December 8, 1941, it was on "a river of tears." The only words he could use to describe what he saw were "smoke, fire and devastation." Even 65 years later, when recounting that day, Jim had to take time to collect himself. The emotions were still strong from what he witnessed. One of the first things they encountered as the ships were first coming into Pearl Harbor was the sight of the *Nevada* run up on the beach in the channel, nearly closing it down. During the attack, the *Nevada* had tried to get out of the harbor to open sea. It was attacked by several Japanese planes and heavily damaged. The *Nevada* had enough sense to know that they couldn't make it out and they would likely block the channel and bottleneck any efforts for other ships to get in or out of Pearl. So, the ship's captain ordered the ship to be run up on the beach.

Those aboard the *Northampton* had to swallow their anger and get to work helping out, doing all they could to assist in the rescue and recovery operations. They helped put out fires, rescue people and transport men to the hospital, all while getting their ship prepared and ready to head out. As time went on, they realized there were fewer people to rescue and save. The men were tired to the point of near exhaustion. Anger turned to desperation.

The captains of the available ships and vessels were involved with planning groups and meetings, assessing the damage, protecting the remaining fleet and planning what do in the short run.

The *Northampton* crew was ordered to remain at Condition 2, a modified General Quarters used in large ships to permit some minor relaxation among personnel. Instead of being at your Battle Station continuously, they worked a "four-hours on, four-hours off" schedule, around the clock. The command staff wanted the ships fueled and provisioned as soon as possible and returned to sea. It was safer to have the remaining ships in the fleet at sea, rather than anchored in port like sitting ducks. They feared a secondary Japanese attack and there wasn't any time to waste. The ship was a blur of activity.

As an assistant storekeeper, it was part of Jim's duties to help get the ship resupplied and ready to get back out. For Jim, Charlie Fortier and the rest of the storekeepers, this involved working at double time. While the ship was being refueled, they inventoried the supplies and recruited every available man to help get the stores restocked without delay. To say there was a sense of urgency is an understatement.

On December 9, as soon as it was ready to go, Task Force 8 was back out to sea to search for the Japanese. By the next day it saw its first action as planes from the *Enterprise* sank a Japanese submarine, I-70, the first of many enemy ships that would fall victim to the carrier's air group. Indeed, as Japanese Admiral Yamamoto famously said, "I fear all we have done is to awaken a sleeping giant and fill him with a terrible resolve." For the men of the *Northampton* that's exactly what the attack had done. And it wasn't long before the giant showed how mad and angry it was.

1942 One Hell of a Year

Lionel reported for duty on January 2, 1942, at Naval Air Station Squantum in Quincy, Massachusetts. Essentially, he was going back home, as the station was less than 50 miles from Lowell. During the Second World War, NAS Squantum served as a maritime patrol and training base. Regular Navy squadrons flew anti-submarine patrols over Massachusetts Bay and the Gulf of Maine using Grumman Ducks, Consolidated PBY Catalinas, Vought-Sikorsky Kingfishers, Douglas Dauntlesses, and Curtiss Helldivers, on what were referred to as inshore patrols.

Prior to 1929, Squantum was a seaplane-only base, though occasional naval landplane operations were conducted using the airfield at the nearby Dennison Airport. Throughout the 1930s, Squantum was greatly improved and expanded due, in large part, to the ingenuity of Executive Officer John J. Shea, a man who knew how to leverage and make the most out of volunteer labor, salvaged materials and Depression-era public works programs like the Works Progress Administration. The greatest expansion efforts on the base took place between 1939 and 1941 when, among other things, three "proper" paved runways were built, and the old Victory Plant Shipyard buildings were razed. On March 5, 1941, the base at Squantum was re-designated as a Naval Air Station, or NAS.

On January 13, 1942, Lionel was assigned to inshore patrol Squadron VS 1D1. Flight orders were issued, allowing Lionel to be a member of the crew. Although still not training to be a pilot, his stock continued to rise in the Navy. On April 1, Lionel was advanced in rating to aviation machinist mate first class.

According to Navy records, on June 20, 1942, Lionel had completed three years net service for pay purposes, and on July 19, 1942, his enlistment expired. Records showed that there was no time lost and he was recommended for a good conduct medal. He was now otherwise entitled to an honorable discharge but, instead, sought a two-year extension. On July 20, 1942, he was examined and found to be physically qualified to extend enlistment for the two full years.

Because he was now a member of the crew, he needed to be certified on the aircraft's weapons. Weapons aboard these types of aircraft usually involved .30 caliber and .50 caliber machine guns. He looked forward to practicing, but with his eyesight, he would have to wear glasses.

Lionel had been lucky enough to be assigned to duty stations stateside, many of them in New England. He took advantage of any leave or furloughs he could and returned to visit his family and his girlfriend, Claire Brennan.

Claire had attended Lowell High School with Lionel's younger brother, Jim, graduating in 1939. She was both smart and pretty and looked a little bit like the actress Donna Reed. She had been very active in school activities and was a fine athlete as well. In fact, she was on a girl's baseball team, the Grove Belles, that beat the boy's team, the Hudson Tigers, in a 3-0 shutout in September 1938. As one can imagine, that caused quite a stir. She was mentioned in the article written in the *Lowell Sun* describing the game. She was quite a catch, and Lionel knew it. On August 10, 1942, Lionel and Claire announced their engagement.

Claire Brennan.

On October 21, 1942, Lionel qualified for weapons certification as an aircraft machine gunner. His rating as a machine gunner was average. In other words, he could hit the broad side of a barn with a .50 caliber machine gun, which was good enough for government work.

On November 23, Lionel was transferred to NAS Quonset Point, Rhode Island[5], Fleet Air Wing Nine, Headquarters (HEDRON) Squadron VS 1D1. The Headquarters Squadron (HEDRON) and Patrol Service Units (PATSU) had recently been formed on July 12 that year. NAS Quonset Point was commissioned the same day and encompassed what was once Camp Dyer. Quonset Point became a major naval facility throughout World War II. The war was in full swing and he knew that it was not likely he would stay in Rhode Island much longer.

Like the Turcotte sisters, Claire wanted to be a Navy nurse. Lionel and Claire were young, in love and had their whole future ahead of them. The only thing in their way was a small detail – WWII.

Bob wrote his dad a letter dated February 3, 1942, on USS *Cincinnati* stationery:

At Sea

It seems that it has been quite some time since last writing to you. My topics are closely restricted as you may know. My work even though in the same line cannot be discussed. Many have the occasions occurred where your knowledge and advice would sure have come in handy.

---

[5] The name for a Quonset hut comes from the site of their first manufacture at Quonset Point at the Davisville Naval Construction Battalion Center in Davisville, Rhode Island.

Bob with his father in Lowell, Massachusetts.

You can be sure that the last line would have made his father proud and made him feel that the time spent with his children was well-spent and that his son respected him and his opinions on matters of great importance. Bob knew his father was a good mechanic and knew planes. So, he asked his father:

Dad if possible I would like to have you send me a few books. Preferably those on ignition and carburation. All the data available to me at present is not as thorough as could be. Those issues you gave me when I was home I reviewed M-27-1A, 1B&1D. The one covering carburation M-27-1C (it) is the one I did not get. If possible I'd like to have one covering more deeply. Different types, adjustments and trouble shooting. Things here as I have said do not cover items that are overhauled in the A&R shops.

You spoke of those mags you had at home. I regret that I haven't had a chance to get home and learn a little more. If it is possible for me to get advance mech school I wouldn't ask for anything more.

Excuse the handwriting for it was done in a hurry. I'll be waiting for those books. You'll hear from me again in the future.

#2 son

Bob

The first offensive World War II naval battle in the Pacific was at the Island of Wotje, part of the Maloelap Atoll in the Marshall Islands. After World War I, the island came under the South Pacific Mandate of the Empire of Japan. From the end of the 1930s, Wotje was developed into a major Japanese seaplane base. It also had an airfield with two runways for land-based aircraft and several hundred support buildings. Once the war started, the atoll was garrisoned by the Japanese and the coasts were heavily fortified with artillery and anti-aircraft batteries.

This first operation by task forces of the U.S. Pacific Fleet took place just eight weeks after Japan's attack on December 7, 1941, at Pearl Harbor. The intervening period had been one constant success after another for the enemy – Pearl Harbor was virtually destroyed, Manila and Cavite fell on January 2, 1942, Bougainville in the Solomon Islands succumbed on January 22, and Ribault and Balikpapan fell the very next day.

The wins were the result not only of a matured and well-implemented campaign plan but also were due to Japan's ability to exploit the advantages it gained from its initial Pearl Harbor surprise attack. In addition, neutrality patrol commitments in the Atlantic contributed to the defensive role which was forced upon America's Pacific Fleet. The Navy simply did not have the offensive capability immediately after Pearl Harbor.

Nevertheless, enemy movements were carefully monitored, scrutinized and their relative strengths considered in order that offensive action might be launched at the earliest moment. During the first days of January 1942, the pattern of these movements began to indicate that such a moment was soon approaching.

On January 9, based on the best intelligence available, Admiral Nimitz directed Admiral Halsey to raid the southern Marshall and northern Gilbert areas. Further details of the plan, as they developed, required that the *Enterprise* launch the main air attack on Kwajalein Island on February 1, as near to 15 minutes before sunrise as practical. Simultaneously, the bombardment group, composed of the *Northampton*, the *Salt Lake City*, and the *Dunlap*, was to shell Wotje and the *Chester*, the *Balch* and the *Maury* would shell Maloelap. Fighter planes from the *Enterprise* were to support the bombardment groups by strafing prior to bombardment. Attacks were to be repeated and other objectives attacked as developments warranted.

At 6:30 p.m. on January 31, the task group consisting of the *Northampton*, the *Salt Lake City*, and the *Dunlap*, with Rear Admiral Spruance commanding, proceeded toward Wotje Island.   As   a result of intelligence, it was believed that all Japanese shore installations would be found on the island of Wotje and that enemy vessels inside the atoll would probably be in anchorage immediately to the westward of that island. This did not, however, preclude the possibilities that shore batteries might be located on outlying supporting islands and that ships might be found anchoring using other area atolls or attempting to leave or enter the lagoon.

During the early morning hours on February 1, the ships were turned into the wind for launching aircraft. All cruiser planes were catapulted into the air by 6:16 a.m. It was anticipated that Wotje would prove the most fully developed from a military viewpoint. For this reason, the main attack was built around bombardment beginning at 7:15 a.m. The task force's presence was signaled to the shore by a rocket fired from a small Japanese patrol boat.

The *Dunlap* was tasked with sinking the Japanese boat which went zigzagging away. Only the bow gun of the destroyer was in a position to fire, so she had some difficulty hitting the fleeing, small, low-profiled target.

The first Japanese fighter attack against the American task force was unopposed but did no damage and the second was met by anti-aircraft fire. The enemy planes had left the island before the beginning of the naval bombardment by U.S. forces.

Upon completion of the task force's aircraft launch, planes from the *Salt Lake City* and the *Northampton* rendezvoused as a unit and proceeded to the north of Wotje Island. At 6:53 a.m., the anti-aircraft guns on the island opened fire on the fighters from the *Enterprise* and a few minutes later shifted fire to the spotting planes. These are aircraft sent up to provide up-to-the-second information to the gunners aboard ship to help direct their fire. These planes station themselves above and away from the targets to avoid enemy fire. This area is referred to as a spotting station. In this case, the spotting station was taken up north of the island.

At about 6:55 a.m., the ships of the task group sighted land on the starboard bow, consisting of numerous low-lying islands with the island to the extreme right, Wotje, having what appeared to be two radio towers of medium height and various fire control and lookout masts. Upon closer observation, one large ship was seen in the lagoon and, within a few minutes, the stacks of about five others came into view. Many of the ships were showing black smoke, indicating that they were starting their engines and preparing to flee. An initial report of "three ships and no shore batteries" was received from the reconnaissance aircraft. Subsequently, it was learned that actually eight ships and five batteries were present. Such initial incomplete information could have resulted in disaster for the American forces.

When the range from the U.S. ships to Wotje was about 24,000 yards, three large freighter-type ships could be seen. The left-hand ship was clearly visible and was the chosen target for the *Northampton*. The *Salt Lake City* control officer designated the right-hand auxiliary ship for his target.

At the commencement of the bombardment at 7:15 a.m., 13 minutes after sunrise, the cruisers were in column with the *Dunlap* screening ahead and having under fire the Japanese patrol vessel. Thereafter, the *Dunlap* operated independently, sinking the patrol vessel and then searching to the west for two submarines reported to be moving out of the lagoon. It finally followed the cruisers on a northeasterly course, bombarding Wotje Island.

U.S. warships are built with many forms of armament, with the larger ships featuring multiple gun turrets with each containing multiple gun barrels.

Whether he was a 19-year-old, wide-eyed with excitement, or the ripe old age of 92 and given the perspective of time, Jim always described the sights and sounds of battle the same. As each salvo was discharged, flames shot from the gun barrel and smoke bellowed from the muzzle. There was a concussive force that hit you in the belly, especially from the eight-inch guns, which had a loud sound that was sometimes disorienting. At times, you couldn't tell exactly where the shot had been fired from – forward or aft, below you or behind you. It was something that was repeated with every successive volley. There were times you couldn't tell if it came from your ship or from another. Because the ships were generally moving when firing, as each salvo went off, the smoke would drift downwind aft of the ship. Every man on that side of the ship would get enveloped in smoke as it passed. In addition, each turret and gun deck were firing at a different rate. So, it seemed that you were always in a cloud of acrid gun smoke, burning your nose and making your eyes water. It was a smell that Jim would never forget. He always joked that he breathed in so much of that smoke that the smell became embedded in his brain and probably killed most of his brain cells.

When the order to commence firing was given, the men of the *Northampton* remembered what they saw on December 8 when entering Pearl Harbor. As the flagship, they were going to send a direct and clear message to the Japanese. The *Northampton* opened fire with a full salvo, firing all its armament. Near simultaneously, all nine of her eight-inch guns and all eight of her five-inch guns exploded with fire shooting out the end of each barrel. The eight-inch guns used a silk bag filled with powder to send a 260-pound projectile at a velocity of 2,800 feet per second in on her enemy. Each five-inch gun fired a 54-pound projectile at a velocity of 2,100 feet per second to land on Wotje. Likewise, the *Salt Lake City* followed suit and opened with a full salvo. There could be no misunderstanding of the message. It was sent loud and clear. Thereafter, the *Northampton* and the *Salt Lake City* slowed firing to single turret salvos to economize ammunition. They continued to fire their guns onto the hillside of Wotje. This quickly quieted the Japanese batteries except for the explosions of their ordinance when the American shells found their target.

After initially striking at the island, the next targets for the U.S. cruisers were the Japanese vessels in the lagoon. Target designations against the enemy ships initially proved a difficult problem for the ship's control officers. The enemy ships in the Wotje harbor were partially hidden by high spots of land, with some of the ships getting underway and all of them changing their relative positions. In addition, the American ships also were moving, changing their relative position to the targets. To complicate matters, U.S. air spotters had trouble attaining good spotting positions because of clouds and their efforts to avoid incoming enemy anti-aircraft fire. This frustrated the gunnery crews on the *Northampton* and the *Salt Lake City*. It was like shooting blindfolded with one hand tied behind your back. The problem of locating target designations was finally solved by giving the plane spotter the best possible description of the target in order to identify it. The gunners hung in there and worked through the issues and this proved to be the answer. Grit.

91

The USS *Northampton*: A view of port side 5"/25-caliber guns in action against Japanese-held Wotje Island, February 1, 1942. Jim's battle station was on this port side and he may be one of those in the photo.

As described by Jim many years later, there was one enemy transport that kept sticking its nose out from behind an elevated position in the harbor. Every time it did so, the Americans would open up on it with their five-inch guns, but the transport would duck back to cover. Shortly after 8:00 a.m., the *Salt Lake City* and *Northampton* reversed course and the enemy ship came into clear view. Also, by this time, the plane spotter had obtained a good position over the lagoon and sent in satisfactory information on the target maneuvers and spots. Control ordered full ten-gun salvos but maintained slow fire.

The gun range was 15,900 yards. The first salvo landed just over the spot and to the left. The next was a perfect straddle. In other words, the shots hit on both sides of the target, having aimed and led the shots correctly. The next salvo was a similar straddle. The enemy ship was extremely fortunate to survive those initial two attempts. The plane observers later reported that it was unbelievable that she was still visible when the splashes cleared away. The next salvo landed to the right. The next was another perfect straddle and the ship started to go down by the bow. She then appeared to steady and hold her own, however, so the *Salt Lake City* control officer ordered, "Give her another good one." After the salvo fell slightly off to the right in deflection, control ordered, "One more and make it good." No spot was made when this final salvo landed, but the target was perfectly centered in the splashes. Just before this salvo hit, the ship began going down rapidly by the bow. When this last salvo landed, a great flash appeared in the superstructure just below the bridge. The enemy ship was sunk at 8:12 a.m. With word that they got their target, everyone, including Jim, gave a rousing cheer.

At this point, the *Northampton* and *Salt Lake City* shifted their fire back to shore objectives on Wotje. The extent and perfection of the camouflage used by the Japanese on their shore installations made spotting from the ships very difficult. Gasoline tanks were painted green and were covered on top with sod. Other installations, such as buildings, were often painted to resemble sand dunes. Many of the buildings were discovered only because of the shadows they cast in the sunlight. Both ships fired repeated salvos at the island. During this time, there was return fire from shore batteries, but their shots landed short of the U.S. vessels.

Surviving Japanese guns of the three-inch and five-inch variety began responding from the hills. Jim described how the *Northampton* continued to make numerous "battle runs" against these installations, as well as other targets on the island. This amounted to steaming back and forth, firing many salvos. The more they fired, the more smoke Jim saw rising from the island. They were hitting their intended targets – the gun installations, gas tanks, fuel depots, and munitions stores. Jim knew their intended message was getting through to their enemy and the crew's morale was cautiously elevated.

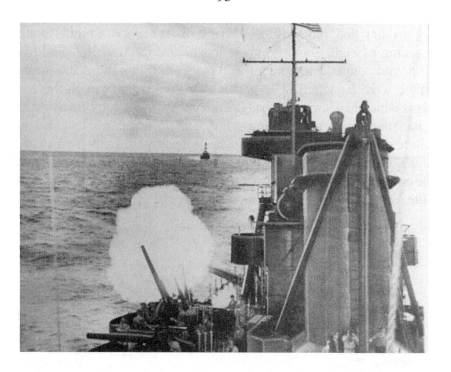

The USS *Northampton* firing her eight-inch guns during the raid on Japanese-held Wotje Atoll in the Marshall Islands on February 1, 1942. The photo is taken from the ship's forward superstructure, looking aft on the starboard side, with five-inch guns and the ship's smokestack in the foreground. The USS *Salt Lake City* (CA-25) is behind the stern.

Just before 9:00 a.m., the flagship ordered "cease firing" by the *Northampton* and the *Salt Lake City*. The planes from both ships were ordered to attack the remaining objectives with the two, 100-pound bombs each plane carried.

By 10:00 a.m., the task group withdrew and began recovering their aircraft. Even this routine procedure was not without risk. During recovery, one plane from the *Salt Lake City* crashed into the side of the ship. The *Dunlap* rescued the unidentified pilot and his radio man, then sank the plane with machine gun and rifle fire, so as not to have it fall into enemy hands.

Later that morning, at 11:16 a.m., a second aircraft group, consisting of eight scout bombers, each carrying one 500- and two 100-pound bombs, and nine torpedo planes carrying three 500-pound bombs, were launched. The planes delivered an attack on the few targets which had survived the Naval bombardment, looking to put an exclamation point on their message. The Japanese airfield and its facilities on the atoll were completely destroyed. Only two of the original eight or nine enemy ships in the harbor could be seen. Every time one of the 500 pounders was dropped and found a target the crew of the *Northampton* reacted with a rousing cheer.

Wotje Atoll on February 1, 1942. Seen burning are
a Japanese ammunition depot and fuel dumps. Note the
seaplane (L) flying over the island.

Jim and his crewmembers were ecstatic and could barely contain themselves. They took great pride in being the first American naval force to offensively take on the Japanese. This was the first time the Americans had retaliated against a Japanese target in an organized fashion. When they returned to Pearl, they sought permission from Fleet Headquarters to fly broomsticks from the *Northampton*'s mast, indicative of a "clean sweep." A "clean sweep" for a naval vessel refers to having "swept the enemy from the seas," during a completely successful mission. Permission was granted and the ship came into port with brooms crossed on its forward mast to the cheers of the other sailors stationed at Pearl Harbor, as well as from their own. The U.S.

Navy had its first success and, most importantly, at the moment, morale was very high.

Upon returning to Pearl, the *Northampton* was anchored in cruiser row, just perpendicular to Ford Island. The entire fleet stationed at Pearl was still on Condition 2 status (with crews working four hours on and four hours off). Everyone was still on edge from the attack of December 7. After December 7 and the Battle of Wotje, the men took their preparedness and vigilance during these shifts a lot more seriously. After giving the Japanese a taste of their own medicine at Wotje, the Navy was concerned about retaliation.

During regular shift hours, Jim and the other storekeepers took inventory and got the *Northampton*'s provisions resupplied and stored aboard ship. During his shift at Battle Stations, he was back at the port-side elevated anti-aircraft platform.

As the JR Talker, he was always the first to receive a warning from the radar shack if any planes were inbound. Standard procedure called for returning American aircraft to give the code of the day. As a result, if the pilot appropriately responded, the incoming plane would not be seen as a threat. One Sunday, Jim was at his assigned battle station and he received a warning there was an unidentified plane coming in from the port side and heading toward cruiser row. The plane had not responded to the repeated requests of the radar shack to provide the code or otherwise be identified. Jim immediately notified his gunners of the potential threat approaching. Only seconds later, Jim heard the plane and then looked to the rear port quarter. He immediately saw that "there was some kind of a plane, coming right into Pearl Harbor toward the cruiser division, and it was wobbling like blazes." All the ships in the harbor sounded General Quarters ("General Quarters! General Quarters! Enemy Attack!"). The alarm sounded and men who were off duty scrambled to their stations. What Jim saw amazed him, and he said he would not have believed it if he hadn't seen it with his own two eyes.

A Bell P-39 Airacobra, Henderson Field, Guadalcanal.

Here's how he described it years later:

Here was this lone plane up there weaving back and forth, the wings dipping and wobbling all over the place. Lo and behold, when it got close enough to me, I noticed a pilot's chute was caught on the tail and he (the pilot) was out trailing behind this American P-39 Bell Airacobra fighter. The pilot was an Army pilot. He couldn't have been any more than 500 feet off the water. He's coming right at the stern of the Northampton. Well, all the ships in the harbor trained all their anti-aircraft guns towards this plane, fearing it was a Japanese plane. Thank God they held their fire. They later found that it was an American pilot that had bailed out of a faulty plane and he was hanging off the tail. Just as he got close to the Northampton, and thank goodness no one had fired, the plane peeled over to the right and headed down and went into the water just off our starboard quarter. Thank goodness, when the plane turned, it went upside down, and his chute flew off. He could not have been more than two or three hundred feet from the water. He braced his legs and hit the water. By this time, it was like a caravan of boats going around in a circle. And two seconds later a rescue boat pulled him out. He stood up on the boat and waved his hands to show he was OK to the crew and maybe even thanking everybody in the harbor for not shooting him down. But when that Bell Airacobra hit the water, I watched it hit the water just off our starboard quarter, it was a needle-nosed fighter, it hit the water and went right down. It must have hit the bottom. There was not a bit of debris on the top. It was like a bullet. He was the luckiest man in the world and I never knew what his name was. I would still like to find out.

Military men, especially sailors during WWII, had a lot of superstitions. They strongly believed in "good luck" and "bad luck." Some carried a good luck charm, like a rabbit's foot, a lucky coin, a picture of their wife or girlfriend, or a religious artifact. Others performed some sort of a good-luck ritual. Some believe that luck of all types, good or bad, could rub off on you. In battle a sailor wanted all the good luck he could get. At that moment, Jim hoped that some of that pilot's good luck would rub off on him and the crew of the *Northampton*.

Only a couple of weeks after the Wotje battle, the Enterprise Task Force was given its next opportunity to test its luck against the Japanese. This time, the target was Wake Island, located about 2,000 miles west of Hawaii and 600 miles north of the Marshall Islands. Wake Island impressed American naval planners as an ideal site for an advance defensive outpost. Wake is actually an atoll with a couple of smaller islands – Peale Island and Wilkes Island – connected by bridges.

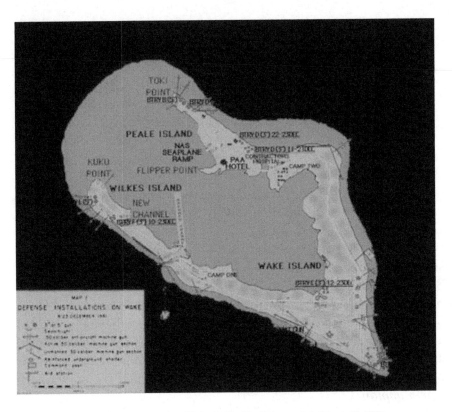

Map of Wake Island, early raids in the Pacific, February 1 to March 10, 1942.

As background, in January 1941 a group of civilian firms called Contractors Pacific Naval Air Bases (CPNAB) began construction of military facilities on Wake. Unfortunately, by December 1941, while they had more than 1,100 construction workers toiling there, they had not completed work before the outbreak of war between Japan and the United States. A garrison of 449 U.S. Marines, several dozen Navy personnel, and a handful of army radio operators also were stationed on Wake Island. American strategists determined that they needed nearly 2,100 more troops to properly defend the atoll.

These defenders were equipped with six five-inch (127-mm) coastal artillery pieces, 12 three-inch (76-mm) anti-aircraft guns, 12 F4F Wildcat fighter planes, and an assortment of machine guns and small arms. Forty-five Guamanian men, employed by Pan American

Airways as part of its trans-Pacific Clipper service, rounded out the atoll's population.

With a wave of tactical bombers launched from the Marshall Islands, the Japanese first struck Wake Island at noon on December 8, 1941. The atoll's defenders had received word of the Pearl Harbor attack several hours earlier (Wake and Hawaii are separated by the International Date Line), but heavy cloud cover and the absence of radar facilities nevertheless allowed the attackers to achieve total surprise. The Japanese were able to catch the bulk of the island's fighter squadron on the ground and killed or wounded nearly two-thirds of the aviation personnel. Wake was bombed on an almost daily basis for the next two weeks. Once Wake became a battlefield, 186 CPNAB employees volunteered to fight alongside the Marines, and another approximately 250 workers found other ways to support the embattled garrison – from building bomb shelters to delivering hot meals to gun positions and other battle stations. Despite their best efforts, Wake came under Japanese control as of December 22, 1941.

On February 11, 1942, orders were issued for the task force to raid the island. Much information regarding the Japanese presence on Wake was provided and later corroborated by new photographs taken by an Army plane. Due to limitations in technology at the time, these photos had to be developed and printed in Oahu, and then flown to the task force at sea by a PBY Catalina amphibious boat plane. The one-way trip alone was over two thousand miles.

The group was specifically ordered to seize any opportunity to destroy important enemy forces. Photographs were to be made and provided, if possible, but not to such an extent as to impair the scale of attack. Any fishing boats or other small craft encountered were to be regarded as enemy and sunk as quickly as possible. Aircraft were instructed to avoid being sighted by such boats or observed from the islands.

The first group of the task force left Pearl Harbor on February 14. The second group followed two days later. Proceeding westward toward the attack areas, both groups engaged in target practice and other exercises. Meanwhile, the situation in the southwest Pacific had deteriorated even further. Singapore fell to the enemy on February 15, and there now seemed no likelihood in halting the advance short of Australia.

On February 16, 1942, Admiral Halsey received orders that the second group of the task force was to be detached and instructed to proceed to the area of Canton Island in the Phoenix group. The first group was ordered to execute the attack on Wake.

The bombardment group remained with the task force until late in the afternoon of February 23, when it broke off and began working its way westward. No contact was made with the enemy during the night, but at 5:05 a.m., local time, a Japanese voice transmission was intercepted, possibly from a patrol craft reporting the presence of the U.S. ships.

In accord with the plans, the bombardment group continued to proceed southwest in column, the order of ships being the *Maury*, the *Northampton*, the *Salt Lake City*, and the *Balch*. The ships maintained a distance of 1,500 yards from each other. At 6:41 a.m., the column assumed a speed of 21.2 knots and, during the bombardment, pursued a generally easterly or northeasterly course, with Wake and its two satellite islands to starboard. The cruisers refrained from launching their planes until the last minute out of concern that the flash of the catapulting might be seen from the shore and thus compromise the surprise of the *Enterprise*'s planes, which were scheduled to arrive over the islands at 7:08 a.m. (ten minutes before sunrise).

This proved a needless precaution as bad weather delayed the launching of the *Enterprise* air group for a full half hour. Three Japanese reconnaissance seaplanes were the first to be sighted at 7:07 a.m. Having the advantage of a land-based take-off, they got into the air first and subsequently dive-bombed the *Maury* and *Northampton*, but their bombs fell wide and did no damage. At that time, the ships were about 18 miles from Wake.

View of the deck of the USS *Enterprise* (CV-6). The USS *Northampton* (CA-26) is visible, back left, with an unidentified ship astern as well.

Now engaged in his second battle, Jim felt more comfortable as a JR Talker, gaining information from the radar operator and providing it to the gunners. Jim's job was more complicated than it sounds. The operator always provided the information to the JR Talker in code, and the codes changed daily. In the heat of battle, it was crucial that Jim knew the codes cold and be able to instantaneously translate them, so as to provide the information in a timely fashion to the gunners. They had been practicing this task non-stop since he got aboard the *Northampton*. Jim told himself this day was no different – except that it's always different when it is no longer practice and it's the real deal. He had to make sure that his five-inch guns were ready for bombardment of the island and, just as importantly, that his anti-aircraft men were ready for any incoming air attacks.

102

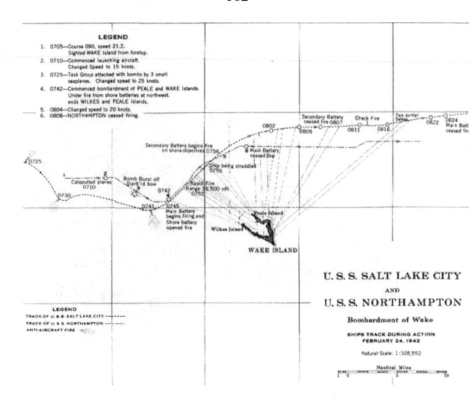

U. S. S. SALT LAKE CITY

AND

U. S. S. NORTHAMPTON

Bombardment of Wake

SHIPS TRACK DURING ACTION
FEBRUARY 24, 1942

Natural Scale: 1:328,592

Nautical Miles

Although the Enterprise was delayed in launching her aircraft, between 7:10 a.m. and 7:22 a.m., the *Northampton* launched four planes and the *Salt Lake City* two for reconnaissance and spotting purposes. At 7:42 a.m., when the range of Peale Island had come to within 16,000 yards, the column opened the bombardment. Although the weather was good, a heavy mist covered the islands and it was difficult to see the target, especially since the approach was from the west, looking directly east, with the rising sun shining in the eyes of the director pointers, trainers and range-finder operators. Throughout the bombardment, the U.S. ships maintained a range of between 14,000 and 16,000 yards of distance from the atoll. This was at the outer-range limit of the shore batteries, as shells from their guns landed, at times, within just 100 yards of the ships. The *Maury*, the lead ship, usually kept 1,000 to 1,500 yards inside of the cruisers, putting itself in harm's way.

The bombardment of Peale Island lasted about half an hour before the *Northampton* ceased fire, having expended her allowance of main battery ammunition at 8:08 a.m. The three other ships ceased fire a few minutes later. Peale Island had been subjected to extremely heavy fire by the U.S. Naval forces and it showed. In the bombardment, the *Northampton* expended 264 rounds of eight-inch ammunition and the *Salt Lake City* 261 rounds. The *Balch* used 995 rounds of five-inch shells and 199 rounds of anti-aircraft ammunition firing at shore objectives. The *Maury*, the guide ship, expended only 348 rounds of five-inch shells at shore objectives. The *Maury*'s expenditure was materially reduced by the necessity of alerting gun battery and because of having to fire at enemy scout seaplanes which attacked the ship bombardment group. In all, more than 2,000 shells of various sizes were hurled at the tiny atoll. Fortunately, no U.S. damage or casualties were suffered during the exchange of gunfire. The shelling from the *Northampton* was so intense that its radar went out of commission because of the collapsing of the antenna array from the shock of the ship's own guns. With the radar being out of commission, Jim became a spotter, using binoculars and calling in the action. He had to be on the lookout for enemy planes looking to do damage to the Northampton, as well as monitoring the activity on the island. Being that the *Northampton* was the only ship of the group that had radar, this was of major concern for the task force.

Throughout this long, relentless pounding, Jim could see smoke and flames everywhere on the island. Because of their accuracy and the sheer volume of projectiles raining in on the enemy, many of the buildings and installations suffered significant damage. Each of the projectiles from the *Northampton*'s eight-inch guns that struck the island blasted a car-sized crater into the atoll and set buildings on fire. One structure, apparently a gasoline storage facility, burst into flames, shooting fire hundreds of feet into the air. When that happened, many of the sailors instinctively cheered. As the battle raged, numerous smaller fires also were visible. Thick, black smoke could be seen curling up from the crescent-shaped atoll as the shells continued to fall. A large dredge in the lagoon near the seaplane ramp also was hit and set on fire. Despite this effort, the Japanese shore batteries along the northern shores of Peale and Wake Islands were not completely silenced and continued to try and strike back at the U.S. forces, but without much success.

Following the bombardment, the planes attached to the cruisers were directed to bomb the islands. Previously, they had rendezvoused and climbed to a spotting station about 5,000 feet up and north of Peale and Wake Islands. At 8:30 a.m., in accordance with orders, they delivered a dive-bombing attack on buildings located on the northwest tip of Wake, dropping eleven 100-pound bombs. "Dropping our little, puny bombs with our obsolete aircraft was more a gesture than anything else," one of the participating pilots remarked. During the course of this attack the SOCs (Scout Observational Craft) were themselves attacked by a Japanese seaplane of the same type. As Jim looked on, he noted that it took on the look of a vintage WWI dogfight. Although the enemy plane was, by all accounts, superior to the U.S. aircraft both in power and speed, the cruiser planes escaped undamaged. During the next half hour or so, the *Northampton* and the *Salt Lake City* recovered their six scout planes and the column set a course with a speed of 25 knots.

At 10:54 a.m., an enemy patrol boat was sighted approximately six miles away. The *Balch* was ordered to sink it with gunfire and, shortly after, the enemy craft sank and an underwater explosion was heard, believed to have been made by depth charges aboard which had not been set on "safe." By 11:30 a.m. the *Balch* picked up four Japanese survivors, three of whom had superficial cuts. All men were searched, given medical treatment and placed under guard as prisoners of war.

As the ships started their return, heading eastward, an enemy patrol plane was seen to be persistently following them, although always remaining just beyond gun range. The plane "shadowed" the group until sunset. The rest of the day was uneventful except for the frequent sighting of the "shadowing" enemy plane, which called for constant manning of the anti-aircraft guns. A request was radioed to the *Enterprise* for fighter planes to drive the shadowing plane away, but the *Enterprise*'s planes failed to locate both the ship group or its "shadower."

The *Northampton,* in the distance, being attacked by Japanese fighters. Note the bomb hitting the water to the front right of the ship and the bursts of anti-aircraft fire above the ship, trying to fend off Japanese attackers.

At 5:43 p.m., when it was becoming dark, the Japanese patrol plane, or another like it, was seen to be approaching somewhat closer. All attention was centered on this threat when, much higher and from another part of the sky, two twin-engine Japanese landplanes appeared and almost immediately released their bombs. Anti-aircraft fire could not be effectively developed before the planes dropped their ordinance. The bombing was accurate enough to put the fear of God into the men, with three bombs landing near the *Salt Lake City* and one near the *Northampton.* Fortunately, no damage resulted, and all three planes disappeared. Without its radar, the *Northampton* was unable to prepare for the incoming attack.

Jim noted throughout his life that the whistling sound of an incoming bomb will send a chill down your spine, especially if you can't pick up where it's coming from. Often times, because of clouds or sun glare, he said it was hard to see an incoming bomb.

The *Enterprise*, after having recovered their attack group of planes and heading to the northeast, was forced to launched three fighters to attempt interception of the enemy plane reportedly trailing the cruiser *Northampton*, which was then about 100 miles to the southwest. Because of changing winds and rain squalls, the fighters were unable to locate either the *Northampton* or the "trailer" plane. Their return to the carrier also was complicated by the weather, a lack of upper air soundings and a subsequent change of course of the *Enterprise*, the latter which was not transmitted to the planes. Much time was consumed before the planes were able to contact the *Enterprise*. As a result of this 5-hour, 20-minute flight, Ensign Joseph R. Daly ran out of gas and was forced to make a downwind landing in water close by the carrier. The plane sank almost immediately, but the pilot was picked up by a U.S. destroyer.

In the after-action reports there are distinct differences of opinion as to the effectiveness of the bombardment of the Wake Atoll. One officer said, "Shore batteries present poor targets and firing at them with cruiser eight-inch [guns] is, in general, considered wasteful of ammunition for the results obtained."

The destroyers' officers, however, appeared satisfied with the result of their gunfire, one writing, "Five-inch gun fire was again apparently effective in silencing shore batteries of the character installed in these islands."

Regarding this engagement Admiral Spruance, commanding the bombardment group, wrote:

At the time of the attack cruisers were in line of bearing approximately normal to the sun, to best cope with an attack from that direction. It is interesting to note, however, that in this case the planes made their approach along the line of bearing, in which direction the least effective anti-aircraft fire could be developed. The fact that the sun was low (45 minutes before sunset) may have convinced the enemy of the advantages of approach from a direction where least concentration of fire might be expected, rather than from the direction of the sun. Also, both cruisers could be bombed on the same run. The inoperative status of Northampton radar was sorely felt at this time. The approach of these planes undetected may have been caused by too much attention being concentrated on the tracking patrol plane, which was in plain sight. This emphasizes the serious consequence of lookouts and others being distracted from their assigned sectors by such a diversion.

Recounting his experiences at Wake, an officer of the *Enterprise* air group said:

It was just a matter of going in and unloading your bombs. We found no surface ships at all and no airplanes except three four-engined big boats, and one of the Japanese destroyers which was probably damaged in their attack on Wake and which they had beached. Also, they have removed the guns and installed them on the island. The only difference that we noticed in Wake from the photographs taken before it was captured by the enemy was that they had dug a trench all the way around the three islands. It appeared that they had planned to put their guns in there and use it as a trench to defend themselves against any attack that we might try to make.

Another officer of the same command said, informally,

We made our attack and, in my opinion, made a mistake in not staying there to repeatedly attack them. We have found that you only do real damage when you make a second and third attack. But we knew that an air group was flying up to take possession of the airfield that day around 12 o'clock, and also the Japs made a statement that they had 300 American war prisoners still in the construction camp area.

On this same point, Captain Zacharias, commanding officer of the *Salt Lake City*, wrote:

The carrier fighter planes left the scene before all enemy planes (particularly four-engine patrol planes) had been destroyed. This left the heavy ships vulnerable to shadowing and later bombing, which should have been prevented. It is, therefore, recommended that the carrier be sufficiently close to the heavy ships to send fighters to destroy shadowers when notified of their existence. It is noted that as a result of this shadowing, in addition to the bombing attack made near dark, the persistence of the enemy enabled them to fix the position at dark and provide for a systematic search from that point the next day. The radius of search was just short of finding us. There appears to be a special technique used by the shadower after his bombing planes have arrived in the area. In this case, the shadower, after remaining on the horizon all day and at times invisible, suddenly started an approach as if to attack. This had the effect of centering attention on himself. Meanwhile the bombers at very high altitude approached the release point unobserved until just as they were about to release. Observed at this time proper avoiding action was taken and heavy bombs fell where the ship would have been. It is therefore recommended that in the presence of a shadower a special overhead 'release point' lookout be established in a reclining chair on the bridge, particularly when cloud formations exist as in this case.

The raid was another success. Fortunately, the bombing and shelling of Wake Island caused little harm to any of the American Marines, sailors, and construction workers. The civilian workmen (Contractors Pacific Naval Air Bases) remained on the island to continue work on defenses.

Shortly after Wake, the *Enterprise*, the *Northampton*, and the *Salt Lake City* had one more errand to run on Japanese-controlled

Marcus Island, which was not much more than an airfield surround by water.

The attack was arranged to take place before sunrise on March 4 in the expectation that the full moon would provide sufficient light for the launching of planes and for rendezvous. Early in the morning of March 4 the *Enterprise*, in company with the *Northampton* and *Salt Lake City*, speed 24 knots, was nearing Marcus. Because it was desired to include fighters in the attack, launching of planes was delayed until the ships were about 125 miles from the island. At approximately 4:30 a.m. the *Enterprise* changed her course into the wind and a few minutes later the first plane was launched. The attack group consisted of the air group commander with 14 scout bombers, 17 bombers, and 6 fighters. Strong southerly winds prevailed, with an overcast of heavy cumulus clouds extending from 4,000 to 8,000 feet. The moon was full.

At 6:30 a.m. the island was sighted through a break in the clouds, "nestling in the moonlight," and the order to attack from an altitude of 16,000 feet was given. The surprise was complete. At least four bombs were dropped before any anti-aircraft fire was noticed. The various planes began their bombing missions. Although no enemy aircraft was encountered in the air or sighted on the ground or water, the anti-aircraft fire, coming presumably from 3-inch guns located on each point of the island, was sufficiently heavy to prevent close inspection of the damage done. The spotting plane, however, witnessed a hit on and subsequent fire in what looked like a fuel storage tank. Several buildings or hangars on both sides of the field were on fire and several explosions at short intervals occurred in one group. Two large fires visible from 20 to 30 miles were still burning fiercely at 7:00 a.m., as well as numerous smaller fires. Unfortunately, considerably fewer objectives were found than had been anticipated.

One plane failed to return from the attack. At 7:05 a.m. the pilot reported that his plane was on fire and that he was about to land in the water. Another pilot stated that he saw the burning plane land in the sea about 10 miles east of Marcus, and that the pilot and gunner manned their rubber boat, waved and gave a "thumbs up" signal before he departed from the scene. By 8:00 a.m. the planes had returned to the *Enterprise*, which, with the *Northampton* and *Salt Lake City* was already steaming eastward to Hawaii.

After these two battles, Jim said that he and all the young sailors started to feel like veterans. They headed back to Pearl Harbor. The good news was they were going to be allowed liberty.

The *Cincinnati* made a pit stop back in the States. On July 5, 1942, Bob received orders to take charge of five men and proceed and report to Floyd Bennett Naval Station in Brooklyn, New York, for temporary duty. Transportation would be by truck. According to the orders, all records and accounts for Bob and the men under his charge would be retained on board the *Cincinnati*. For Bob, it was nice to be ashore for a little while, but with the comfort of knowing he was definitely going back to the *Cincinnati* as soon as the assignment was over. This gave Bob an opportunity to relax a little and see the city. He had just turned 22 in June. You can be sure that he, like most young sailors, wanted to blow off a little steam.

Even though he had responsibilities to the Navy, he had a lot more free time than when he was aboard ship. When aboard ship, there was only so much he could see and do. In New York City, the world was his oyster. As soon as work was over, he could go out on the town with his buddies. Unfortunately, it didn't last very long and they were back on board the *Cincinnati* a few weeks later. By July 21, the ship headed back to the South Atlantic.

Bob didn't waste any time getting back into the swing of things. As a result of his efforts, he had a good couple of months in the Navy. Effective August 1, 1942, he was appointed aviation machinist mate first class. [AMM1c]. With the promotion, this meant not only a few extra bucks in his pocket, but also that he was only one promotion away from aviation chief machinist mate. Earlier, on July 24, one of the scout planes of the *Cincinnati* capsized on landing. Bob jumped in and saved the plane from sinking. The scouting and reconnaissance planes aboard the *Cincinnati* and other ships like it are situated on a catapult mechanism mounted on the deck of the ship. On take-off, the pilot revs the engine and an explosive charge on the catapult launches the plane outward, over the sea [See photo]. When the plane returns, it lands via its pontoons on the ocean and is recovered by a crane mechanism, also mounted on the deck of the ship. With the help of the crane, the crew mounts the plane back onto the catapult for its next flight. Occasionally, on return, the planes had what the Navy called "a casualty." As a result of pilot error, weather or sea conditions, the plane may capsize and/or sink.

As a result of Bob's quick actions, on August 6, he received a commendation at Meritorious Mast. Meritorious Mast awards are used as official recognition for a job well done. They are used in the United States Navy to recognize enlisted members who have performed above and beyond their usual requirements of duty or have displayed exceptional judgement or initiative.

The citation of meritorious mast read as follows:

On July 24, 1942 on the occasion of a casualty to a USS Cincinnati plane, number 5903, which resulted in it being in a capsized and sinking condition in the water, Robert, without hesitation or regard for his own safety, dove in the water, went underneath this plane and secured a line by which the USS Humboldt was able to hoist the plane on board. It was considered that by Robert Turcotte's prompt and skilled action, the plane was saved.

The Commanding Officer takes pleasure in commending you for your action on this occasion, which is in keeping with the best traditions of the Naval Service.

Signed

E.M. Senn,

Captain, U.S. Navy

The same day Bob received his commendation his father wrote him a letter on a booklet from U.S. Army Air Forces Training Detachment at the New England Aircraft School in Boston, which was located at 20 Overland Street in downtown. Overland Street was a small side street off Brookline Avenue, just around the corner from Fenway Park. Herman was an instructor there.

Hi Rob,

I started this letter by dating it with my pen but the darned thing ran out of fuel so here goes with the pencil. I am right in the middle of a night class in B4 (Basic Electricity) my class is taking a test. Boy I've had to work like hec [sic] since I got back from my vacation and it seems now like I'd never had one. I spent my vacation rather quietly. Only went on two trips. One to Lake George, N.Y. and the other up to Lewiston Maine to see Lionel. Mom, Em and Claire came with me. Lionel is now back at Squantum and I suppose you have heard the big news by now. Lionel and Claire are engaged to be married. I don't think the date is set yet, though I wouldn't really know. I had an idea that you and Helen would beat Lionel to it, but it doesn't look so now. By the way, I haven't seen Helen since the last time you brought her up, altho [sic] I think mom & Mary ran into her down town [sic] one day. Nothing much new around here. My classes are larger and more of them, but the training program is much the same. I've sure been waiting a long time, to hear from you boy. I haven't heard from Jim in a long time either. I hope everything is O.K. with you. Write when you can & I hope much more that you will be putting into some nearby port soon so you can get home. Got to quit now son. But remember we are thinking of you constantly.

Good luck & loads of love from the gang and your Dad

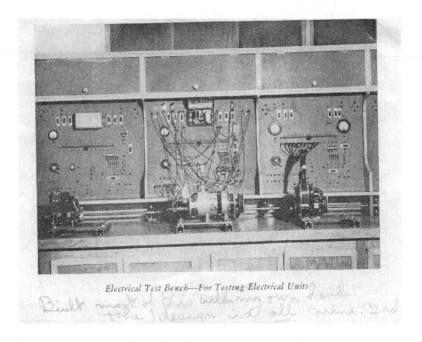

Electrical Test Bench—For Testing Electrical Units

Inside the booklet, there was a black-and-white photo of an electrical work bench used for testing electrical units. There was a note from his father under the photo. "Built most of this with my own two hands. The design is all mine."

In a letter, written in pencil and dated August 26, "At Sea,"

Bob responded to his father:

> *Hello Dad,*
>
> *Your pen may have gone dry but believe me the pencil served its purpose. I am sorry that my reason cannot be similar.*
>
> *I have again broken a bone; this time my right wrist. It is difficult and quite tedious to do it left handedly but here goes.*
>
> *That was a pretty nice booklet on the school, quite an original idea. I took special notice of that test board I had*

heard so much about. Surely wish I could see the original. I imagine that spending a few weeks in that school would really better my knowledge. R-1340 & 985 are the only ones that I have occasion to work. And I do know that my knowledge of ignition and carburetion can easily be widened.

Say Dad that was more of a surprise to me about Lionel, one I won't get over for a long time. It may have been a surprise to you, but a wallop to me. Here's hoping that I am in the territory when the marriage takes place.

By the what [sic] gave you the idea that Helen and I would beat them to it. Not while I am doing sea duty.

Well Dad I'll have to bid thee Au' Revoir for this left hand has been doing double duty all day.

Give my regards to the gang. As you may already know I am once again on even status with Lionel - $\frac{1}{2}$

#2 Son

Bob

Bob never mentions to his father that he was promoted, that he had heroically saved one of the ship's planes or that the Navy officially recognized him and he received a commendation for his actions.

In April 1942, the *Northampton* was called upon for another secret mission. Each man took an oath of secrecy. It was known to all as "Doolittle's Raid on Tokyo" and, later on, sometimes referred to as "Shangri-La." This was perhaps the most daring naval mission of World War II. Conceived in January 1942, in the wake of the Japanese attack on Pearl Harbor, the joint Army-Navy mission was to bomb Japanese industrial centers to inflict both "material and psychological" damage upon the enemy. Planners hoped that the former would include the destruction of specific targets "with ensuing confusion and retardation of production." Those who planned the attacks on the Japanese homeland hoped to induce the enemy to recall "combat equipment from other theaters for home defense," and incite a "fear complex in Japan."

Additionally, it was hoped that the execution of the raid would improve the United States relationships with its allies and receive a "favorable reaction [on the part] of the American people." Originally, the concept called for the use of U.S. Army Air Force bombers to be launched from, and recovered by, an aircraft carrier. Research disclosed the North American B-25 Mitchell to be "best suited to the purpose." Tests aboard the aircraft carrier *Hornet* (CV-8) off of Norfolk and ashore there soon proved that while a B-25 could take off with comparative ease, "landing back on again would be extremely difficult."

The attack planners decided upon a carrier transporting the B-25s to a point east of Tokyo, whereupon she would launch one Pathfinder to proceed ahead and drop incendiaries to blaze a trail for the other bombers to follow. The planes would then proceed to either the east coast of China or to Vladivostok in the Soviet Union. However, Soviet reluctance to allow the use of Vladivostok as a terminus and the Stalin regime's unwillingness to provoke Japan compelled the selection of Chinese landing sites. At a secret conference at San Francisco, Lieutenant Colonel James H. Doolittle, USAAF, who would personally lead the attack, met with Vice Admiral William F. Halsey, Jr., who would command the task force that would take Doolittle's aircraft to the very gates of the Japanese Empire. They agreed upon a launch point some 400 miles due east from Tokyo. However, if discovered, Task Force 16 (TF-16) would launch planes at that point and retire.

Planes drawn from the 17th Bombardment Group, USAAF, were prepared for the mission, with additional fuel tanks installed and "certain unnecessary equipment" removed. With everything not deemed essential stripped from the planes, the *Hornet* loaded 16 B-

25s on board and sailed to rendezvous with the carrier *Enterprise* to form part of Halsey's Task Force-16.

The Japanese, monitoring U.S. Navy radio traffic, deduced that a carrier raid on the homeland was a possibility after April 14, and prepared accordingly. Task Force-16 approached to within 650 miles of Japan on April 18, 1942. Lacking radar, the Japanese "early warning" capability lay in parallel lines of picket boats – radio-equipped converted fishing trawlers – operating at prescribed intervals offshore. One of these little vessels, No.23 *Nitto Maru*, discovered the task force on the morning of April 18 and radioed a sighting report. Although Halsey had initially agreed to take Task Force-16 within 400 miles of Japan to ensure maximum success, the admiral recognized he had a potential threat to the whole mission. Too much planning and preparation had gone into the mission to risk it. The exigencies of war dictated that Halsey order the *Hornet* to launch the 16 Mitchells earlier than planned.

Jim was aboard the *Northampton*, which was acting as an escort to the USS *Hornet* and had a ringside seat to history. As Jim described it, the *Northampton* was just off the starboard side of the *Hornet* with Admiral Spruance aboard. The weather had taken such a turn – cold and damp – that Jim was wearing his winter long johns.[6] A decision was made to take off a day early. Jim indicated that this was in part due to the weather and in part due to the Japanese boat in the immediate area. They feared that the Japanese vessel had a radio and was going to notify Tokyo of the American presence. The success of the mission relied on the element of surprise and secrecy. The USS *Nashville*, which was astern of the *Hornet*, pulled out of position and headed flank (full) speed and sank the Japanese picket boat. In addition, because they were taking off a day early, they had to strip any and all excess weight from the bombers and load them up with extra fuel. The planes were slightly heavier than was anticipated, given the need for the extra fuel.

---

[6] What he was doing with long johns in the Pacific in April I could never understand.

An Army Air Force B-25B bomber takes off from USS *Hornet* (CV-8) at the start of the Doolittle raid on April 18, 1942. Note the men at right watching from the signal lamp platform.

As described earlier by Jim, when carriers plow through the ocean they pitch forward in an up and down manner. Due to their design, carriers do not generally rock from side to side. Admiral Nimitz and the other Navy commanders knew this and used it to their advantage. The carrier *Hornet* steered herself directly into the wind. The bombers needed to time their take-off with the pitch of the ship. The bombers would rev their engines full throttle and as the ship was at the lowest point, they would release the brakes and travel headlong down the carrier hoping that the ship would be at its zenith of pitch when the planes reached the end of the ship.

This would allow a little more lift, almost catapulting the planes up into the air. Jim said the planes were so heavy with fuel and munitions that even with the little extra lift, each would drop off and nearly hit the water. Although some came very close to going into the ocean, thankfully, none did. Jim watched all 16 Mitchells take off and literally held his breath as each one rumbled off the deck of the *Hornet*. "My heart was in my mouth," he said. Col. Doolittle circled back over the *Hornet* and corrected his plane's compass by using the ship's known bearing. The other bombers corrected their compasses off of Doolittle's. Jim always joked that it took the Navy to show Doolittle how to get to Tokyo.

Jim had a sense of excitement and exhilaration during the whole time the planes were taking off and for hours afterward. Just as soon as the last bomber was off, the task force turned around and steamed out of the area as fast as it could. Jim knew it would be a little while before they heard any news about the success or failure of the mission.[7]

The Japanese, expecting the Americans to approach within 200 miles of Japan as they had done in the raids in February in the Marshalls and Gilberts, and at Wake and Marcus, launched 29 medium bombers equipped with torpedoes from the Port of Kisarazu to locate Task Force-16, but were unable to do so.

The unexpected deployment of long-range U.S. Army bombers, however, took the Japanese by surprise. Taking a little over an hour to launch, Doolittle's B-25s, carrying high explosive and incendiary bombs, flew on and hit targets in Tokyo, Yokosuka, Yokohama, Kobe, and Nagoya, against negligible opposition. One B-25's ordnance damaged the aircraft carrier *Ryuho* while it was being repaired at Yokosuka. After successfully completing their mission, of the 16 B-25s, however, 15 crashed in occupied China, where the Japanese inflicted brutal reprisals against the Chinese populace in Chekiang province for harboring surviving crew. One B-25 landed intact at Vladivostok, where the Soviets interned it and its crew.

Although the material damage inflicted by Doolittle's raiders proved relatively light, the psychological effect on the Japanese capital itself was enormous. Admiral Yamamoto Isoroku's fear of a

---

[7] While working the flight deck, Seaman 1c R.W. Wall was blown into the propeller of an airplane. It struck his left shoulder and so cut it as to necessitate amputation of the left arm.

U.S. carrier strike against the homeland, deemed "unreasonable" by the Imperial Naval General Staff, had occurred completely unimpeded.

When Jim and the other sailors heard about the success of "Doolittle's Raiders," they were excited that the mission was successful and proud that they had played a small part in it. Even into his 90s, Jim read any article or newspaper clipping on Doolittle, his Raiders or Shangri-La. He even obtained a signed photograph from a navigator who was aboard one of Doolittle's bombers.

When the attack on Tokyo took place, no one knew where the American bombers had taken off from. Although there was a great deal of speculation about a secret base in China or elsewhere, no one imagined the big heavy bombers had flown from the deck of a carrier as it had never been done before. The use of land-based bombers also confused the Japanese. When asked by reporters where the attack had originated, Roosevelt replied, "They came from our secret base at Shangri-La." The entire task force was sworn to secrecy until the U.S. government released the information in April 1943.

Due to its participation in the Doolittle raid, the *Northampton* was not directly involved in the Coral Sea Battle, which occurred at the same time. The ship was just returning from the raid on mainland Japan and hung on the outskirts of the battle, using it as a "cover" from their true purpose for being in the area. They did not want the Japanese to know that the U.S. fleet had come that close to their mainland, or that they had the capacity to fly bombers off their carriers. During the Coral Sea Battle, the Japanese seriously damaged the carrier *Yorktown*, actually believing they had sunk her. They would soon be surprised.

Photo # NH 97808   USS Northampton refueling at sea, April 1942

After Doolittle's Raid and Coral Sea, the task force headed back to Pearl Harbor, where Jim enjoyed some time off to swim, go to the movies and see Honolulu. The *Northampton* and other members of the task force continued their defensive patrols of the Hawaiian Islands and surrounding areas. They went about their usual activities, although the regular area patrols actually helped in killing two birds with one stone.

On occasion, a ship needs to be demagnetized or degaussed. The ship's hull, made of steel, acts like a large floating magnet. When the ship moves through the water, the magnetic field moves along with it. This was of concern to the Navy because when a ship would come near a magnetic mine or a magnetic torpedo, the magnetic field of the ship could actuate the firing mechanism and cause the mine or torpedo to explode. Thus, degaussing systems were installed to counteract the ship's magnetic field by cancelling the changes in earth's magnetic field around the hull of the ship. This would help prevent naval ships from being damaged or destroyed by the enemy magnetic mines and torpedoes. Prior to the installation of degaussing equipment aboard ships, the Navy used other methods.

According to Jim, one of the ways in which the *Northampton* degaussed or demagnetized the ship was to travel around an island in the same direction multiple times as it dragged a large electrical cable along the side of the ship. The cable would have a pulse of about 2,000 amps flowing through it. This was called wiping, inducing the proper field into the ship in the form of a slight bias. To avoid magnetization in the first place, captains were instructed to change direction as often as possible to avoid this problem. Nevertheless, the bias did wear off eventually and ships had to be degaussed on a schedule. Smaller ships continued to use wiping throughout the war. While at Pearl Harbor, the *Northampton* did it by repeatedly circling around the Island of Molokai.

Molokai, nicknamed "The Friendly Isle," is the fifth largest island of the eight major islands that make up the Hawaiian Islands. It lies east of Oahu across the 25-mile-wide Kaiwi Channel. As the *Northampton* repeatedly circled Molokai, torpedo boats, also known as P.T. boats, would practice and drill using a large sleeve towed behind the *Northampton* as a target. One thing all the sailors talked about on these trips was the fact that in 1942 Molokai had an inhabited leper colony on it.

In the 1800s, the government established a leper colony located on an isolated peninsula on the northern side of Molokai that operated from 1866 to 1969. It was called Kalaupapa.[8] Despite its appearance of untouched beauty, over the course of more than a century, more than 8,000 victims of leprosy lived and died there. The disease was introduced to the Hawaiians, who had no immunities to it, from visiting outsiders. There was no prevention or treatment for the disease, at that time, so unlike treatments readily available today, quarantine and isolation seemed like the best solutions to stop its spread. This law was carried out by King Kamehameha V. Many of

---

[8] The colony has since been turned into Kalaupapa National Historic Park. It requires some preplanning and a permit to visit.

123

the victims of the disease were transported to Kalaupapa by boat, in a cattle pen, after being forcefully taken from their homes. The colony was located on an isolated section of the island, at the bottom of one of the steepest sea cliffs in the world. There was no way to leave the colony, except by boat, or by scaling the 1,700-foot-high sea cliffs. Supplies only came to the island once every year. This was always a topic of conversation when the Navy ships cruised around the island.

The next major confrontation the United States had with the Japanese was at Midway Island in the central Pacific Ocean. The Battle of Midway was one of the most important of World War II and proved to be the turning point of the war in the Pacific. The battle took place over four days between June 3-6, 1942.

As Jim described it many years later, the Japanese intended to attack Midway Island, a lookout outpost for Pearl Harbor, which they deemed to be a "sentry for Pearl Harbor." Unbeknownst to them, however, U.S. Navy "code-breakers" had broken the Japanese codes and knew they were going to attack the island. U.S. submarines had picked up the Japanese fleet of ships heading to Midway. Despite the damage done to the *Yorktown* during the Coral Sea Battle, to the surprise of the Japanese it was still very much involved in the mission. The *Enterprise, Hornet,* and *Yorktown* traveled west of Honolulu. Aircraft patrols spent 24 hours looking for the Japanese armada. Just after midnight of June 4th, night-flying PBY patrol planes reported the Japanese main body was 574 miles from Midway. Only hours later on the morning of the 4th, search planes took off at 4:15 a.m. At 5:45 a.m., the patrol planes reported seeing "many planes heading for Midway." These planes were only 150 miles from Midway. At 5:52 a.m., a PBY Catalina notified the task force the sighting of two Japanese carriers. By 6:00 a.m. all Midway planes were in the air ready to intercept enemy bombers.

U.S. forces used three carriers and the island of Midway as a fourth place to launch planes to destroy the Japanese fleet. This plan was a very risky gamble. They were putting all their eggs in a single basket. If the Americans were badly beaten it would be a huge loss to the U.S. Pacific Fleet which, in turn, would open up the whole Pacific, including Hawaii, and perhaps the U.S. west coast, to Japan.

"We are actively preparing to greet our expected visitors with the kind of reception they deserve," Admiral and Commander in Chief, U.S. Pacific Fleet, Chester W. Nimitz wrote to Admiral and Commander in Chief, U.S. Fleet and Chief of Naval Operations, Ernest J. King on May 29, 1942, "and we will do the best we can with what we have."

A massive force was consolidated in one place for this battle. Task Force SUGAR, commanded by Rear Admiral Raymond A. Spruance, involved the aircraft carriers *Enterprise* and *Hornet*; six cruisers; five heavy cruisers – the *Pensacola*, the *Northampton*, the *Vincennes*, the *Minneapolis* and the *New Orleans*; and one light cruiser, the *Atlanta*. Also involved were nine destroyers – the *Balch*, the *Benham*, the *Phelps*, the *Worden*, the *Aylwin*, the *Monaghan*, the *Ellet*, the *Maury* and the *Conyngham*.

Task Force FOX, commanded by Rear Admiral Frank J. Fletcher, included the aircraft carrier *Yorktown*; two heavy cruisers – the *Astoria* and the *Portland*; and five destroyers – the *Hammann*, the *Morris*, the *Russell*, the *Anderson* and the *Hughes*. In addition, there was an armada of submarines, including the *Cachalot*, the *Grenadier*, the *Pompano*, the *Cuttlefish*, the *Grouper*, the *Porpoise*, the *Dolphin*, the *Growler*, the *Tambor*, the *Drum*, the *Gudgeon*, the *Tarpon*, the *Finback*, the *Narwhal*, the *Trigger*, the *Flying Fish*, the *Nautilus*, the *Trout*, the *Gato*, the *Pike*, the *Tuna*, the *Grayling*, the *Plunger*, the *Greenling*, and the *Pollack* – some 25 in all.

Despite the huge size of the U.S. Navy force, the Japanese had superior numbers. However, the Navy felt it had the element of surprise on its side. It also was decided that it was imperative to strike at long range at the Japanese carrier force.

During the battle, planes from four Japanese carriers, all of which were among the ones that had attacked Hawaii six months before, pounded Midway. Heroic Marine Corps fighter pilots, some of whom had only recently earned their wings, fought to defend the island. Still, damage to Midway was severe, with nearly all structures above ground being destroyed or badly damaged. The powerhouse had been hit, the hangar destroyed and, perhaps worst of all, the gasoline system had been so severely damaged that subsequent plane refueling had to be done by hand. This involved a tremendous amount of labor which, for a while, badly handicapped air operations. Fortunately, the Japanese spared the runways, apparently for their own anticipated use in the future.

Brave but piecemeal attacks by Midway-based planes threw off the tempo of the Japanese carrier operations as best they could, although torpedo attacks by planes from the undiscovered U.S. carriers were repelled with heavy losses. On June 4, the providential arrival of the *Yorktown* air group and *Enterprise* dive bombers, however, changed the course of battle in just five minutes, as U.S. bombs turned three Japanese carriers into floating infernos. Two strikes from the Japanese carrier that survived the initial onslaught damaged the *Yorktown* and forced her abandonment, but planes from the *Enterprise* disabled the fourth enemy carrier before the afternoon was out. Action over the next two days claimed a Japanese heavy cruiser. A Japanese submarine sunk a destroyer and further damaged the *Yorktown*, which sunk on June 7. The loss of four Japanese carriers prompted the defeated enemy to retire.

Even though the U.S. task forces had caught the Japanese carriers by surprise, they took some devastating losses. Of the 30 VT-8 torpedo bomber aircrew from the USS *Hornet* that participated in the Midway Battle, Ensign George Gay was the sole survivor. After attacking and probably scoring a hit on the Japanese carrier *Kaga*, he crashed near her sister-ship, the *Akagi*. By hiding under a floating seat cushion and refraining from inflating his life raft till until after dark, he saved his own life and witnessed the succeeding attacks by U.S. carrier forces. Gay had been in the water less than an hour when the *Enterprise* and *Yorktown* groups arrived.

Jim described the Midway Battle this way: "We lived on station for four days. We ate and slept on our duty stations." U.S.

planes were flying multiple missions a day throughout the battle. Each U.S. plane was given a new code daily. As a plane returned and approached any of the U.S. Navy ships, it would have to identify itself with the code or, otherwise, be shot down. It was imperative that both the pilot and the ship's crew knew the codes to avoid a friendly-fire catastrophe.

The cruisers did everything they could to prevent Japanese pilots from hitting their targets. Jim was amazed how the Japanese kept coming, wave after wave. After 2:40 p.m. on June 7, Japanese torpedo bombers attacked the injured *Yorktown* and a series of torpedoes were released against her. The *Yorktown* avoided several through skillful maneuverings that resulted in the torpedoes passing under her bow. Two others, however, could not be avoided and they caught the *Yorktown* amidships on the port side. The two explosions at 2:45 p.m. were about 30 seconds apart. The planes which scored these hits were shot down either in passing the *Yorktown* or in attempting to pass through the fire of her escorting vessels, including the *Northampton*. It is believed that not one of the attacking enemy squadron returned to its carrier. The torpedoes had badly damaged the *Yorktown*. She had been initially injured in the Coral Sea Battle and now she took catastrophic damage on June 4 when she took a direct hit from a Japanese dive bomber after 11:30 a.m. The subsequent torpedo attacks several hours later sealed her fate.

Corpsmen treating casualties on board the USS *Yorktown* (CV-5) shortly after the carrier was hit by Japanese bombs on June 4, 1942. The dead and wounded were members of the crew of 1.1-inch machine gun mount Number 4, in the center background, who were struck by fragments from a bomb that exploded on the flight deck just aft of the midship's elevator. This view looks directly to starboard from the front of the midship's elevator. The aircraft crane is at left, with 1.1-inch gun mount Number 3 visible in the upper left corner. Note a bearded chief petty officer walking by, flight-deck clothing worn by some of those present and the fire extinguisher at lower left (80-G-312021).

By 2:47 p.m. all firing had ceased. The *Yorktown*, listing heavily to port, was losing speed and turning in a small circle to port. She then stopped and white smoke poured from her stacks. The screening vessels began to circle the ailing vessel, much like circling wagons. Inside the *Yorktown*, all lights had gone out. While diesel generators were cut in, the circuit breakers would not hold and the ship remained in darkness. The list gradually increased to 26 degrees and, without power, nothing could be done to correct it.

128

"This was an engagement of ships at a far distance, the damage being done by fleets of planes," is how Jim remembered the battle as recounted in an article in the *Lowell Sun* in 1943:

> *It was pretty hot while it lasted. The bombers dove in, the heavy bombers winged on high, the torpedo planes skimmed in and then there were our own fighters blasting away at the Japs waves. We heard afterwards that our pilots had sunk several Jap ships including three cruisers. They got direct hits on the carriers and while they didn't see them go down they were pretty certain that the flat tops couldn't get very far.*

> *We were right near the Yorktown when she started blazing. We saw her go down, and let me tell you right now the Japs threw every kind of bomb they had to sink her. They did it but they paid the price in planes for that one. Midway was the best of the lot. There was a lot of excitement and it came off during the day so we could get an idea of what was happening and who it was happening to.*

Jim was a witness to the demise of the *Yorktown*, since the *Northampton* was about 500 yards off her side. To a 20-year-old, it was clear that she was going to sink, and the crew was going to be taken off by other ships. Many of the men had gathered on the carrier's flight deck. There were injured, dead and survivors alike. From what Jim could see, the dead were separated from the injured. They were lined up, side by side and covered. The injured were in various positions on the flight deck. The more seriously injured were lying prone on their backs, receiving treatment from corpsmen. They were triaging these more seriously injured. Others were sitting up, bandaged and bleeding, many with their heads wrapped in gauze, arms wrapped in slings or legs in splints. Nearly all were smoking cigarettes. Some of the injured were mobile enough to be on their feet, mingling with the other sailors. Smoke was pouring out of the *Yorktown* from the damage she sustained. Some of her sailors were still trying to battle the fires but had difficulty given the ship's loss of power. The *Yorktown* continued to list as Jim looked on.

At one point, as he surveyed the scene, Jim couldn't believe his eyes. A bunch of awaiting sailors were sitting on the flight deck eating ice cream from the gedunk stand (a gedunk stand, or geedunk bar, is the canteen or snack bar aboard ship, the place you could get ice cream, candy bars, or chewing gum). The sailors quickly realized that now that the power was out on the *Yorktown*, the ice cream was going to melt. So, instead of letting that happen or have it go down with the ship, they raided the stand and enjoyed a frozen treat as the ship slowly foundered and they waited to be rescued. It was a rather surreal, Kafkaesque, moment in the four-day battle. While suffering the harsh consequences of battle, the sailors of the *Yorktown* shared a brief second of "normalcy." Whenever Jim related this story, he would always finish it with, "No one would believe it if you told them."

At 2:55 p.m. orders to abandon ship were given to the *Yorktown* crew. The *Hammann* picked up survivors in the water, including *Yorktown*'s skipper, Captain Buckmaster, and transferred them to the larger ships. In as much as the *Yorktown* did not actually sink, efforts were mounted to save the stricken carrier the next morning. A skeleton crew returned to board the carrier, and attempts were made to tow her to safety. The *Hammann* came alongside on June 6 to transfer a damage-control party. The destroyer then lay alongside, providing hoses and water for firefighting, power and other services while tied up next to the carrier.

The salvage party was making progress when the protective destroyer screen was penetrated by a Japanese submarine after noon that day. Four torpedoes were loosed – one missed, two passed under the *Hammann* and hit the *Yorktown*, and the fourth hit the destroyer amidships, breaking her in half. Jim watched in amazement and horror as debris from the explosion rained down and the ships lurched apart. It was apparent that the *Hammann* was doomed. Her life rafts were lowered and rescue efforts by surrounding ships commenced. The *Hammann* sank, bow first, in just four minutes. Following the sinking there was a violent underwater explosion, likely caused by the destroyer's depth charges and torpedoes going off. The explosion caused many deaths in the water, bringing the toll to 80. Survivors

130

were taken aboard two other destroyers, the *Benham* and the *Balch*. The *Yorktown* eventually sank on June 7, 1942, at which time the task force retired to safety.

Collection photo #NHF-00401: USS *Yorktown* (CV-5) burning, photographed during the Battle of Midway in June 1942.

Both Admiral Spruance and Admiral Fletcher later pointed out: "In a duel between carriers, the side which is able to strike the first blow against enemy carriers whose planes are on board wins." At Midway, the United States won in precisely this manner, and was able to do this because its forces knew of the enemy's presence, the approximate composition of the Japanese force, and it had calculated correctly the Japanese method of approach. The Battle of Midway was essentially a victory of intelligence. The Japanese, on the other hand, probably did not know of the presence of the U.S. forces until shortly before carrier planes attacked them. In attempting a surprise attack, they were surprised themselves. The placing of the U.S. Navy fleet to fall upon the enemy's flank was a piece of brilliant tactics, skillfully executed. They "closed the door behind them," as Jim described it later. The Navy's single misfortune was failure to locate and attack the fourth enemy carrier with sufficient promptness when its presence was suspected which, tragically, resulted in the demise of the *Yorktown*.

All in all, the U.S. task force downed four Japanese carriers and a Japanese cruiser and damaged others. At the end, the Japanese retired from battle and looked to escape to the Aleutian Islands. Throughout the Battle of Midway, the *Northampton* successfully protected her carrier and returned undamaged to Pearl Harbor on June 13, 1942.

Thanks to American intelligence, judicious aircraft carrier tactics and more than a little luck, the U.S. Navy had in early August 1942, the Allied forces landed troops a number of places in the area in an effort to drive the Japanese out, including at Guadalcanal, Tulagi, Gavutu, and Savo Island. As a result, over the next several months there would be a series of naval run-ins with the Japanese in the Solomon Islands and surrounding areas. The U.S. pilots and crews had won the day through courage, determination, and heroic sacrifice. The Japanese lost the four large carriers that had attacked Pearl Harbor, while the Americans only lost one carrier. More importantly, the Japanese lost more than 100 trained pilots who were never to be replaced. As a result, the balance of sea power in the Pacific shifted from Japan to one of equity between the two combatants. Soon after the Battle of Midway, the United States and its allies would take the offensive in the Pacific.

After the battle, Jim and the other sailors from the task force were exhausted. They had been living on caffeine, nicotine, and adrenaline. Jim couldn't wait to get some sleep and didn't even try to eat before he hit the rack while the ship headed back to port and was resupplied.

After Midway, morale was high among the men. They had had a few good victories in a row, with Midway being the biggest. From there, the task force headed west into the Guadalcanal area, in the eastern portion of the Solomon Island Chain. This was an area of heavy combat on the islands between the Japanese and the Allies. The fleet was called in to give support as the Americans were going on the offensive. As a result of Midway, they had learned that they could successfully fight against the Japanese, even when outnumbered.

The *Northampton* pulled into New Caledonia in early August 1942. New Caledonia is south of the Solomon Islands, just to the east of Australia. This was friendly territory for the Americans. New Caledonia was formerly a French penal colony, but still had native islanders who were supportive of the Americans. It would be out of New Caledonia that the task force would operate for the next several months. At one point, there were as many as 86 Allied ships in the New Caledonia Harbor of Nouméa. In addition, the Navy was operating some of its ships and land forces out of Espiritu Santo, an island of 1527 square miles, approximately 430 miles north of New Caledonia, in the New Hebrides Islands.

The Japanese were working out of Rabaul, New Guinea. They had taken over the island by the end of January 1942 and had built the region into a quite powerful military base. The opposing forces were in close proximity to each other. Both sides were mostly north and east of Australia. U.S. planes from Espiritu Santo and American ships, including the *San Juan*, the *Buchanan*, and the *Wasp*, were supporting the Marines and Army fighting on Guadalcanal.

The initial sea battle during this time was at Savo Island on August 9, 1942 (the *Northampton* did not participate in this battle). The Japanese Navy, in response to Allied amphibious landings in the eastern Solomon Islands on August 7-8, undertook a night surface attack on the ships screening the Allied landing force. The attack resulted in horrible losses for the Allied forces. The *Vincennes* was sunk during this battle. One of its surviving crew, Mo Shifley, was rescued and later became a shipmate and a lifelong friend of Jim's. The U.S. carriers were able to escape the onslaught and make their way back to the Port of Nouméa in New Caledonia. Despite the loss, the Navy recouped and prepared for the battles ahead.

The *Northampton* continued to escort and protect the *Enterprise* during this time. The *Enterprise* was being used for air support for troops on Guadalcanal, as well as employing its planes to attack and harass Japanese ships and bases in the area. The *Northampton* had to keep an eye out for enemy planes and enemy submarines looking to take out any of the remaining U.S. carriers in the Pacific.

Many of the naval battles of WWII were night-time battles. Jim disliked night-time battles a great deal. For him, the worst part was the darkness. The battles were intense because the darkness gave them a whole different dimension. The sea itself was black, black as ink. The only light to speak of came from the moon and the stars. If the weather was overcast, the moonlight was muted, like placing a silk scarf over the lampshade. It just made things even darker. There was no light pollution in the middle of the Pacific in the 1940s. These small islands were in the middle of nowhere. There was no "skyglow" cast from the lights of any major metropolitan cities. The darkness changed the whole feel. Noir.

As a practical matter, the darkness made it far more difficult for the spotters aboard ship to pick up the movement of the enemy ships by sight, so they had to rely on radar. The radar in use at that time was not very sophisticated or accurate. Therefore, sailors looked for flashes of light, which actually were huge bursts of flame generated by the enemy firing its guns. The American gunners took aim at those flashes. Ships on both sides would launch torpedoes in the direction they thought the enemy was heading.

The guns played a big role in the effect of a night battle. There were the great flashes of light from the nearby guns going off. No matter where you turned during battle, a gun of some type was firing. It was like having a flash from a camera continuously going off in the face, over and over again. These bright flashes of light disrupted the sailor's natural night vision. This effect could be very disorienting. In addition, the guns were horribly loud. Firing these weapons was nothing more than a controlled explosion. At that time, most sailors did not have ear protection to wear. A few guys would put cotton in their ears, but most sailors had no protection at all. There was the noise from enemy gunfire, friendly gunfire and your own ship's gunfire. To no one's surprise, gunnery personnel's ears rang for hours after a battle. Jim lost a great deal of his hearing as he aged due to repeated exposure to the high-decibel level gunfire at close range.

Then there was always the concern of submarines. They were the silent killer, particularly true at night. During day-time operations, if a ship saw a torpedo in the water early enough it could take evasive action to avoid impact or lessen the blow. Just as importantly, a destroyer or cruiser could take action to take the hit, rather than a carrier. At night, the spotting of torpedoes in the water was far more difficult. For some sailors, as scary as it was to see a torpedo coming, it was even scarier *not* seeing one coming. On top of it all, both sides were continuously maneuvering to avoid being an easy target. Task force ships were constantly moving forward and changing course, port and starboard, so as not to be sitting ducks.

In sum, as a sailor aboard ship during a nighttime battle, you never knew if your ship was going to get hit from enemy gunfire, friendly fire, or from a torpedo. It was loud, surreal and frightening. Nonetheless, these brave sailors, many still young boys, swallowed their fear, girded up their loins and did their jobs nobly.

As Jim described it, on September 15, 1942, the carriers *Wasp* and *Hornet* were at sea along with their contingents of support ships. They were in the process of supporting the 7th Marine Division and were recovering planes that had been out in support of that mission. Often times, these ships would cruise the same areas multiple times a week. The enemy would employ many different ways of determining where the American carriers were located. As you can imagine, the crews of these large ships created a great deal of garbage. During wartime, the ships weren't very worried about proper disposal of their garbage. At night the ships would just dump their garbage into the sea as they were cruising.

In hindsight, the ships should have been more careful about what they did with their refuse – and not just for environmental reasons. One of the ways the Japanese developed to locate the American ships was to keep an eye on their garbage. By tracking the refuse, if the Japanese submarines suspected that the Americans would be coming, they would set in wait for them. At one point, the *Wasp* was coming back through an area that it had dumped its garbage only the night before. The Japanese had picked up this information and set the trap. Unbeknownst to the U.S. carrier groups, nine submarines lay in wait in wait. At approximately 2:45 p.m., the *Wasp* took multiple torpedo hits. The *Northampton* was able to see the *Wasp* being attacked and sounded General Quarters.

As he came on deck, Jim was able to count at least twelve torpedoes in the water being shot at the *Hornet* and the *Wasp* as he went to his battle station. As he was running forward to his position, he saw the destroyer the USS *O'Brien* move from position and increase its speed to take a torpedo hit to its bow, protecting the *Hornet*. As a member of the aircraft carrier *Hornet*'s anti-submarine warfare screen, the *O'Brien* made an emergency turn to the right. While accelerating and swinging right, her lookouts spotted a torpedo two points forward of the port beam, only 1,000 yards away. Luckily, the torpedo missed the *O'Brien* close astern. Yet while her crew's attention was concentrated on the first torpedo, another torpedo hit her in the extreme bow to the port side. The crew didn't have time to brace for impact and the ship reeled as a shock wave undulated down to her keel. It was like being in a high-speed car accident. The force of the impact sent men flying. Many were thrown into bulkheads, against equipment and onto decks. A lot of sailors ended up with bumps, bruises, and scrapes. Fortunately, no one on the *O'Brien* was killed or even seriously hurt. The entire crew counted their lucky stars as the explosion did very little obvious damage.

Due to the heroic actions of ships like the *O'Brien*, neither the *Hornet* nor the *Enterprise* was hit. The *Wasp*, however, could not be saved. Struck by three torpedoes, she suffered catastrophic damage and was on fire and listing. The *Wasp* lost approximately 193 sailors, killed or missing, and more than 300 were injured.

Jim watched as the *Wasp* turned in order to place the wind on the starboard bow. This was to keep the wind blowing the flames away from undamaged portions of the ship and to clear burning oil on the water. Despite tempests of flame and a lethal rain of exploding ammunition, officers and men[9] alike courageously grabbed hoses and attempted to fight the fire.

The USS *Wasp* sinking on September 15, 1942.

Jim described what he saw in a February 20, 1943, article in the *Lowell Sun*:

> *The Wasp was a tough one to see. The sea was covered in oil and the oil was blazing when the men had to jump. Dropping from the flat-top to the sea is a mighty mean jump in the best conditions. It's a drop of about 75 feet which is a little tougher than a hurdle. Some of those guys were dropping into a flaming sea and it's a wonder that most of*

---

[9] "Officers and men" was a common phrase used during WWII when referring to commissioned officers and enlisted men together in the same sentence.

them weren't charred to charcoal. They weren't though.
There were some burns, but they weren't too tough.

The *Wasp*'s Captain Sherman later praised the captains of the five destroyers who came to the rescue of his men, noting, "Their task required the nicest judgment in seamanship and required that their ships be stopped for considerable periods while many seriously wounded casualties were laboriously taken aboard. The limited facilities of the USS *Duncan* and *Lansdowne*, in particular, were stretched almost to the breaking point in an attempt to support life in the gravely wounded and to make all others as comfortable as possible during the passage to port." The *Wasp* was scuttled by the Lansdowne later that night. Jim watched as the *Lansdowne* put three torpedoes into the doomed carrier.

A quiet peacefulness came over the *Northampton*. The sun had already set and the sea was calm after battle. They watched as the *Wasp*, like the sun only minutes earlier, slowly slipped into the sea. For Jim, it was a very sad thing to watch. He knew they lost a lot of guys and the fleet had lost one of its critically needed carriers.

As for the *O'Brien*, the impact of the torpedo strike to the ship was so far forward that it was thought that the damage was very minor. However, the undulation caused by the shock wave set up severe structural stresses throughout the destroyer's framework. Still, after taking the hit on September 15, she was able to proceed under her own power to Espiritu Santo, where temporary repairs were made. On September 21, the *O'Brien* steamed out, bound for Nouméa, New Caledonia, for further repairs. The damage in the official report was described as "severe flexural vibration of the ship girder." In simple terms, her hull had been strained like a piece of tin bent at one point repeatedly. On October 10, the *O'Brien* headed for San Francisco, making several stops along the way.

Unfortunately, she never made it to the mainland as the temporary repairs didn't hold. Stress damage to the hull began to show greater signs of weakness and it began to buckle. The rate of leakage of seawater into the ship increased and, on October 19, her bottom suddenly split open. By 6:30 a.m., all hands, except for a small salvage crew, abandoned ship. Just before 8:00 a.m., after a month and having traveled nearly 3,000 nautical miles since being torpedoed, the *O'Brien* descended beneath the waves. Thankfully, all members of her crew were saved.

In early October 1942, just after Jim was promoted to Storekeeper Second class, the "Fighting Nora," in the company of the USS *Hornet*, steamed to the Solomon Islands. At the time, the *Hornet* was the only operational U.S. carrier in the South Pacific. She was responsible for providing air cover over the Solomon Islands until October 24, 1942. Then, on October 5, an attack was launched on the Island of Bougainville, wherein the *Northampton* screened the carrier during attacks. They attempted to attack Japanese vessels but did not have much success. They were hoping for the quick return of the *Enterprise*.

Admiral Halsey took over as commander on October 18, 1942. He came into New Caledonia ahead of his flagship, the *Enterprise*. The *Enterprise* had gone back to Pearl Harbor for some work to be done on her.

October 24 became an important day for Halsey. In his cabin aboard the *Argonne* in Nouméa Harbor, Halsey met with General Vandegrift, Rear Admiral Kelly Turner, and senior Army and Marine officers. The conference would turn into a crucial meeting. Just before adjourning, ground commanders articulated the woes of the long-suffering troops on Guadalcanal. They said morale was deteriorating under constant attacks and, further, that they believed more enemy forces were massing at Rabaul and Truk. Rabaul is on the island of New Britain, part of Papua New Guinea and located north of Australia but just below the equator. Truk is part of the Caroline Islands, north of New Guinea and the equator. The two sites are separated by about 800 miles.

According to Halsey, the representatives of the ground forces, "began to echo the question that the public had asked in the weeks following Pearl Harbor, 'Where is the Navy?'" The meeting turned into a full-scale airing of grievances to Halsey. It was late into the night by the time the litany of complaints of the riflemen ended. Halsey asked General Vandegrift and Major General Millard F. Harmon, the senior U.S. Army officer in the South Pacific, "Are we going to evacuate or hold?" General Vandegrift responded, "I can hold, but I've got to have more active support than I've been getting." It was simply unacceptable to Halsey for the Navy to be viewed by the Marines as not carrying its end. He told Vandegrift, "All right. Go on back. I'll promise you everything I've got."

Halsey's more immediate task was deciding what to do about the threat from the Japanese carriers. Surveying intelligence and reconnaissance reports suggesting the approach of a Japanese carrier force, he concluded that "action was obviously a matter of hours." He took stock of the needs of the Marines and the capabilities of his Naval force and liked his chances a great deal better now that two carriers were on hand. "Carrier power varies as the square," he wrote in his memoirs. "Two carriers are four times as powerful as one." In a two-carrier task force, one carrier could be designated as the "duty" carrier, sending out air searches and providing combat air patrols and anti-submarine patrols, while the other carrier holds a fully armed and fueled squadron of planes on deck, ready to strike. One carrier operating alone could do none of these things very effectively, and her crews were especially hard-pressed to switch between roles. "Until the *Enterprise* arrived, our plight had been almost hopeless. Now we had a fighting chance," Halsey added.

As his Marines ashore were battling the Japanese assault and he was still getting an earful from Vandergrift, Kelly Turner and the others in Nouméa Harbor, the *Enterprise* was steaming back from Pearl into the war zone area. Halsey radioed his principal naval commanders, Rear Admirals Kinkaid and Lee. He ordered Kinkaid to ring up 22 knots and take the *Enterprise* and *Hornet* task forces northwest from their patrol position east of Santa Cruz. With all the carriers back together, it would be a reprise of Midway, a curtain-call for the Coral Sea Battle. The *Enterprise* made a mad dash and rendezvoused with the *Hornet*, ensuring a better balance of carrier power in the Pacific. During the same call, Halsey gave Kinkaid and

Lee a galvanizing message that would echo through the passageways and compartments of every ship in the South Pacific force. The four words, bereft of any operational specificity or doctrinal nuance and apropos of no particular target, placed a clean vector through everyone's mind that ordered and oriented their next moves, "Strike! I repeat, Strike!"

Since before the founding of our nation, field commanders have enjoyed the freedom to exercise their best personal initiative based upon their experience and the circumstances as they exist. Admiral Halsey was free to act on his instinct now. Halsey's two carrier groups sailed toward the suspected location of the Japanese carrier fleet.

Activity in the area of the Solomon Islands and Guadalcanal increased. The men of the *Northampton* didn't get a lot of sleep – on watch for four hours, off watch for four hours, work your regular job as well. Repeat (several times). However, according to Jim, Admiral Halsey's order of "Strike! I repeat, strike!" and his slogan, "Hit hard, hit fast, hit often," soon became bywords for the Navy. The morale of both the sailors and the soldiers on Guadalcanal were buoyed by his aggressive stance. Even though they were all tired, it rallied the men.

It was October 26, 1942, at approximately 7:00 a.m. when the Santa Cruz Battle was about to begin. Both sides had carrier groups and planes out searching for the other to see who would attack first. The *Northampton* was assigned to the *Hornet* group. The captain of the *Northampton* at the time was Captain Willard A. Kitz III, who had just come aboard the previous month. The *Enterprise* group was ahead of and not in sight of the *Hornet* group. All personnel were at their General Quarters station assignments. Jim was at the gun platform. He was getting his reports from the radar operators in the radar shack. The radar capability at the time could only look out approximately 72 miles for boats and ships. As radar technology was still in its infancy, the decision as to what type of gun should be used was based upon the radar operator's "interpretation" of what type of aircraft was coming at them (i.e., torpedo bombers, dive bombers, high-altitude bombers or fighters). The "interpretation" made by the radar operators was also in its infancy. These interpretations were often nothing more than guesswork.

The *Enterprise*, many miles in front of the *Hornet* group, was the first to see the enemy fleet and began bombing them. Word was quickly sent to the *Hornet* group. The Japanese had more than 100 planes heading toward the American fleet. Jim got word at the 72-mile mark of enemy planes approaching the *Hornet*. The carrier immediately began launching planes to rebuff the attack.

The *Hornet* believed that the Japanese planes were coming in at a relatively low altitude. But when the American pilots reached their contacts, they discovered they were high above their targets, at almost 17,000 feet. They still had a lot to learn about radar contacts. They also had thought the Japanese planes were torpedo bombers while, in fact, most were Japanese Val dive bombers, which came in with high-speed approaches to attack the *Hornet*. At this point, all hell broke loose as all guns started firing. The *Northampton* and the *Pensacola* tightened the protection knot around the *Hornet* to within 2,000 yards and kept firing upward to protect her. The *San Juan* and the *Juneau* were filling in the remaining openings. Smoke from the repeated salvos filled the air.

Japanese Type 99 shipboard bomber (Allied code name Val) trails smoke as it dives toward the *Hornet* (CV-8) during the morning of October 26, 1942. The plane struck the ship's stack and then her flight deck.

While the *Hornet* changed course and maneuvered side-to-side to avoid being struck by the bombers, the enemy seemed to be everywhere at the same time. As they came in waves, ordinance from the dive bomber were released with deadly accuracy. Bombs hit the *Hornet*'s deck adjacent to the flight deck and drilled down three decks, causing a huge explosion. Several bombs pierced the flight deck, causing secondary explosions.

143

Damage to the smokestack and signal bridge of the USS *Hornet* (CV-8) after it was struck by a crashing Japanese dive bomber during the morning of October 26, 1942. Smoke at bottom is from fires started when the plane subsequently hit the flight deck. Note the ship's tripod mast, with CXAM radar antenna at top left and the flag still flying above the damaged structure (Official U.S. Navy photograph, now in the collections of the U.S. National Archives, Catalog #80-G-40300).

In addition, an enemy bomber intentionally crashed directly into the *Hornet*. Flames and smoke were everywhere. As Jim witnessed from his battle station, there was what he believed to be a reporter or newsman with a camera on a small platform just forward of the smokestack on the carrier. Despite yelling out the locations of the incoming threats to his control officer, Jim was transfixed looking at the scene before him. The man was taking pictures of the planes as they were coming in.

Jim watched in horror as the plane came in at high speed directly at the reporter. To Jim, it was almost as if this pilot of this one dive bomber was taking deadly aim at the reporter. The man never took his camera off the incoming plane and the dive bomber careened into him at full speed, taking the reporter and the platform right down the stack into the interior of the ship. There was an immediate explosion just after impact. Smoke and flames erupted out of the crater. The crash and explosion caused major damage to the carrier.

The *Hornet* and all the ships around her were still firing, trying to keep the planes off them. The *Hornet*'s flag was still flying so she kept fighting. It was bedlam. Enemy planes were all over the place. The bombers really caught Jim's attention as they came in waves. Jim and the gunnery crew were trying to shoot down as many as they could, so he needed to know where they were. They were painted in bright colors. They had red fuselages with orange wings and the bright red "rising sun" dot on the wings. Jim later described it as a "crazy circus plane." One dive bomber, after she dropped her bombs on the *Hornet*, swung toward the *Northampton*. As it sailed by, it was just off the ocean. There was a 50-caliber machine gun just one deck below Jim. The gunners were about to fire on the enemy plane as it passed by them, no more than 50 feet away. Jim had a perfect view of the plane as the pilot looked directly at him and his fellow crew members. His plane then went into a turn and splashed into the water. They never saw him again. They didn't have to shoot him – he took care of himself.

The *Hornet* had taken terrible hits from the dive bomber and torpedo bombers. But more devastation was about to be heaped upon them as two enemy torpedoes struck the *Hornet* only 20 seconds apart. It was a one-two punch and turned out to be the ship's death blow as the torpedoes hit the engine rooms and crumpled bulkheads. The escort ships circled around the *Hornet* with their firepower concentrated on the starboard side of their own ship, firing outward. In this way, they could fire without fear of hitting the *Hornet* or any of the other U.S. ships. They were doing everything they could to try and protect the crippled carrier.

Jim said, at this point, the *Hornet* was essentially dead in the water and ablaze. He saw smoke – thick, black, and pungent – and flames everywhere. The remaining able-bodied men aboard the *Hornet* were doing everything they could to save the wounded, recover the dead, and still be ready to fight off any incoming planes. Wounded and dead were brought up to the flight deck. Many of the wounded had traumatic injuries – loss of limbs or worse. The wounded were being cared for by Navy corpsmen and medics, not far from where the dead were being placed. With loss of power, the *Hornet* also had lost water pressure and the ability to fight the fires on her own. Two destroyers came alongside, one on port and one on starboard, to help try to put out the fires. For Jim, this was déjà vu all over again. He couldn't help but be reminded of the loss of the *Wasp* only months earlier. Once the fires on the *Hornet* were put out, the *Northampton* came to her aid in an attempt to tow her back to port.

As she was doing so, a lone Japanese Val bomber came over the scene, releasing a bomb designed to finish off the *Hornet*. Tensions were temporarily relieved when the bomb landed 25 yards off the carrier's stern. The enemy bomber had come in so fast that none of the guns from the ships could get at it. It just swooped low over the water and got away. This caused the *Northampton* to break away. It then circled the *Hornet* and returned to take her in tow for a short time at three to four knots.

Note the numerous crew members on the flight deck of the *Hornet.*

Unfortunately, the line parted and the ships surrounding the *Hornet* began to take the wounded off. The *Northampton* again attempted to put the *Hornet* under tow. This time they got up to about three knots, while the *Hornet* attempted to get power on one of her shafts. They got word of approaching enemy aircraft, which were pointing at the *Northampton,* looking to knock out both ships. The captain of the *Hornet* prepared to abandon ship. Two Japanese bombers approached, with one planting a bomb near the *Hornet* and the other near the cruiser *San Diego.* The *Northampton* eventually abandoned its efforts to tow the carrier and concentrated on evading her attackers.

Orders were given to scuttle the *Hornet.* U.S. Navy destroyers fired five-inch guns and multiple "friendly" torpedoes into the *Hornet* and sank her. All of the crews witnessing this were sick about it. For

Jim, it was a day he would never forget – October 27, which was Navy Day in the United States in 1942. Navy Day was a tradition started in the late 1800s. Even though it was last celebrated in 1949, Jim always made a special effort to either fly the American flag or wear his U.S. Navy hat with pride every October 27. He always remembered that day and always remembered watching the sinking of the *Hornet*.

As all this was taking place with the *Hornet*, over the horizon another battle was taking place with the *Enterprise*, as the carrier also was being attacked by Japanese fighter aircraft. Simultaneously, U.S. planes were attacking the Japanese carriers, scoring direct hits on them as well. One of the escorts for the *Enterprise*, the USS *Porter* was damaged when a U.S. plane ditched into the ocean just near the ship. The impact jarred the torpedo loose from the plane, thereby engaging it. The torpedo hit the *Porter*, resulting in severe damage. After the *Porter*'s crew was recovered, the USS *Shaw* fired on the crippled boat and sank her, as the Navy never wants one of its ships and its technology to fall into enemy hands. The battle had gone on into the night and into the next day, October 27. As darkness fell, the *Enterprise* was able to break away into the cover of night to fight another day.

After the sinking of the *Hornet*, the remaining members of its task force set course for Espiritu Santo. However, as the *Northampton* proceeded into early darkness, a lone enemy scout plane could be heard. Jim was at his battle station and could hear the plane droning overhead, several thousand feet in the air. They didn't dare fire at it as they would have given their position away. If they fired and missed, the scout plane was sure to radio their location to either a submarine or a Japanese ship. Jim theorized that the plane was trying to follow the fluorescent wake of the ships as they departed the battle area to see where they were headed. Eventually, they lost the scout plane and made it back without any additional losses or damage.

In 1943, Naval Intelligence prepared a detailed after-action report about the Santa Cruz Battle. As summarized, it concluded that the *Hornet* underwent a well-coordinated dive-bombing and torpedo attack from several directions. The 5-inch batteries and automatic weapons of the Hornet and screening ships threw up a heavy anti-aircraft curtain, but it was ineffective in preventing many planes from coming in on the Hornet. One of the first Japanese dive bombers scored a hit with a bomb on the starboard side of the back end of the flight deck. Next, a dive bomber came in with machine-guns blazing and crashed into the stack, spraying gasoline over the signal bridge, and plunged part way through the flight deck about where the initial bomb hit. This suicide plane demolished the signal enclosure, causing many casualties, and partly destroyed the stack and causing a large fire there and in the compartment below. This fire on and under the flight deck burned for nearly two hours.

Almost simultaneously a torpedo attack developed from the starboard quarter resulting in two hits which disrupted all power and communications and caused a 10½° list to starboard. At the same instant two 500-pound bombs landed on the rear part of the ship, one penetrating to the fourth deck before exploding, and the other detonating on initially piercing the flight deck. A third heavy bomb reached the third or fourth deck and exploded near the front dining compartment, starting fierce fires and killing a number of personnel.

By 10:21 a.m. the *Hornet* was dead in the water, with several large fires burning, many of her personnel killed, many more injured, and power and communications so disrupted that all efforts to reestablish them failed. At this point preparations were made for the *Northampton* to leave her defensive position in the screen and make ready to tow the Hornet. As she prepared to do so, she was almost immediately interrupted by an attack from a Japanese bomber. No damage ensued and the plane got away, despite being fired upon by many of the U.S. ships. The *Northampton* again attempted a tow, but her line snapped.

Just before noon, the Juneau intercepted a message from the Northampton to the returning *Hornet* aircraft, saying "Go to Enterprise." Unaware that the message was intended for the planes, the *Juneau* proceeded to join the *Enterprise* resulting in the *Hornet's* anti-aircraft protection being diminished when she was most vulnerable. At approximately 1:00 p.m. Admiral Murray and his staff were taken from the *Hornet* and transferred to the *Pensacola*, which became the flagship for the Hornet group. The *Russell* then went alongside the *Hornet* and removed wounded and some uninjured survivors. A total of 500 men were taken aboard the *Russell* by means of cargo nets stretched from the *Hornet's* deck. The *Hughes* also took off some of the *Hornet's* personnel.

It wasn't until 2:30 p.m. that the *Northampton* had secured another line to the *Hornet* and commenced tow. Efforts were still being made to remove more injured. By 3:40 p.m. all seriously wounded and excess personnel had been transferred to destroyers. The *Hornet* was being towed at a speed of 3 knots, and there was a faint hope that the persistent efforts of all engineering personnel might be successful in partially restoring her power. However, a group of Japanese planes came in and attacked. One or two targeted the *Northampton*. She promptly abandoned her tow efforts and avoided damage or destruction by taking strong evasive action with a hard left rudder.

Of the two or three Japanese planes targeting the *Hornet*, one struck a hard blow to the starboard side, causing extensive damage and worsening her list. As a result, about a hundred men abandoned ship by sliding down lines into the water. The *Mustin* was sent in, in order to torpedo and sink the *Hornet*.

For several hours after, the Force was shadowed by Japanese patrol planes which hovered just outside anti-aircraft range but took no offensive action against the task force.

Years later, Jim remembered that when the *Northampton* returned to Espiritu Santo, they found that the USS *Calvin Coolidge*, a transport ship, had hit mines as it had come up the channel into Espiritu Santo. The skipper intentionally ran the ship aground and kept it from blocking the shipping channel and all crew were evacuated from the ship. When Captain Elwood Joseph Euart, 103rd Field Artillery Regiment heard that some his troops were still aboard, trapped below decks, he went back and led a rescue party to save them. Tying a rope around his waist, he had himself lowered down into the now seriously listing ship via a sea door. The remaining men were able to scramble up the rope that Elwood held the end of, deep in the ship's interior. However, as the last of them made it to safety, the ship began to roll and slip toward the deep shipping channel. With arms aching and energy spent, Elwood was not able to make it up the rope before the *Coolidge* sank, taking his life with it. For extraordinary heroism in action, Captain Elwood J. Euart was awarded the Distinguished Service Cross, the second-highest award for valor in America, in addition to the Purple Heart and the Rhode Island Cross. It was a tragic loss. While it sounds somewhat callous almost 70 years later, also lost with the ship was a large shipment of cigarettes intended for the troops on Guadalcanal.

The sailors felt almost as bad for the Marines because of the loss of their cigarettes as they did for the loss of the army captain. They knew that these guys had very few luxuries and cigarettes were one of them. It would be a while before any of them would smoke their next cigarette, only adding to their misery.

During this time in the war zone area, it was Condition 2 for the sailors of the *Northampton*. They would be at their Battle Stations four hours on and four hours off. During those four hours off the sailors still were expected to do their assigned duties, get a meal and get some sleep. Most of these young men, in their late teens and early twenties, had stamina and grit. Nonetheless, it was exhausting. Despite the exhaustion, Admiral Halsey's words still rung in their ears. They felt a sense of appreciation that their conditions aboard ship were better than those of the Marines and Army personnel on Guadalcanal. There was a sense of urgency about those infantrymen's conditions. They knew that conditions for them were extremely bad. They were low on food and medicine. The soldiers were under constant attack by the Japanese ground forces as well as Japanese aircraft. Henderson Field was always a prime target for an attack by the enemy. The Japanese wanted to prevent Allied forces from landing supplies for their troops and prevent American planes from attacking Japanese forces. Jim and all of the other sailors wanted to help protect and support the American ground forces. Many of the guys on Guadalcanal were friends and neighbors they grew up with. Jim's soon-to-be brother-in-law, Gerry O'Connell, was there fighting with the 182nd Infantry, Yankee Division. While fighting on

Guadalcanal, Gerry took a bullet to the shoulder and earned a Purple Heart. It seemed like everyone knew one of those guys on Guadalcanal. The sailors didn't want to let them down. It was personal.

The *Cincinnati* continued to run patrols out of Recife, Brazil, during the fall of 1942. Recife is one of the farthest points east on the South American continent and, as such, was at a crucial narrow between Africa and South America for stopping blockade runners.

October 1942 was a relatively quiet month for the Neutrality Patrol as far as enemy raiders were concerned. No actual sub contacts were reported by ships of the South Atlantic Force, and both commerce and convoys moved freely. All that was about to change.

The USS *Milwaukee*, the *Cincinnati* and the *Somers* departed from Recife on November 8, 1942, on a search mission to the south of the equator, clear of Ascension Island and eastward. They were looking for U-boats, other submarines and blockade runners. Four days later, information came from the commander-in-chief of the Atlantic Fleet regarding the possible appearance of the blockade runners, the German vessel *Anneliese Essberger*, the Japanese boat *Kota Nopan*, and the possible route of advance of others along a middle Atlantic route south.

The task group maintained a screening line for blockade runners which reportedly could be advancing from the north at 10 to 15 knots. All steps were taken to conserve fuel in order to remain at sea for as long as possible. Likewise, aviation gasoline was used sparingly but, nonetheless, scout planes from the task force, including Bob's, made air searches for several days. On November 16, word came that the *Anneliese Essberger* and *Kota Nopan* might arrive in the equatorial area around November 19. Later, a dispatch from the U.S. Atlantic fleet's commander-in-chief warned of the possible arrival from the south of a blockade runner with an accompanying submarine. While it was estimated the two might enter the equatorial area on or about November 19, that day came and went without any contact with the targets.

Two days later, during the early morning hours of November 21, the task group was in position traveling at a speed of 15 knots. The ships were sailing toward the point of the day's search. The *Somers* led, followed by the *Milwaukee*, with the *Cincinnati* bringing up the rear. At 5:31 a.m., the *Cincinnati* reported a radar contact. Five minutes later, a high-position lookout aboard the *Milwaukee* sighted a suspicious vessel and the ship went to General Quarters. By 5:45 a.m., only 14 minutes after the first contact, the distance with the unidentified vessel had closed to 11,500 yards. Next, the task group commander ordered an emergency turn of all ships to the right of their current course and directed the *Somers* to investigate the stranger, while the *Milwaukee* and *Cincinnati* maneuvered at a distance to cover the destroyer's activities.

153

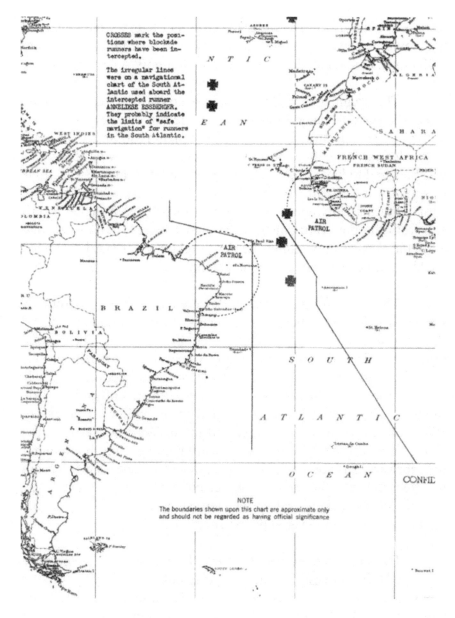

As the *Somers* drew near, she challenged the crew of the suspect vessel to identify itself. Using a blinker signal light, they made repeated inquiries as to its identity. The vessel was slow to respond but did so eventually, with the ship sending the letters "L-J-P-V," the international call sign of the steamship *Skjelbred*, a Norwegian freighter. The vessel, however, did not seem to make its response willingly, and an order to repeat her letters went unheeded. She could be seen clearly now and proved to be a freighter of about 5,000 tons, painted medium gray with a light gray superstructure.

The freighter carried two small cargo masts at the break of the forecastle deck, a heavy foremast, two large cargo masts just forward to the bridge superstructure, and a heavy mainmast. She had a boom rigged forward to a 40- or 50-foot motorboat, which by its appearance was believed to have been a small torpedo boat. A little later, a four-inch gun was seen aft. By the time the *Somers* had closed to 4,000 yards astern, a Norwegian flag could be seen at the freighter's staff, and from the port yardarm flew the signal letters L-J-P-V. At 6:40 a.m., the *Somers* drew alongside the freighter's starboard side while the latter turned sharply to port and stopped.

The crew of the freighter lowered two lifeboats from the starboard side and, when a door on the bridge suddenly opened, flames could be seen enveloping the pilot house. The *Somers* repeatedly flashed the international signal "A-J," meaning "you should not abandon your ship," but this accomplished nothing. The *Somers* armed boat party was then ordered to go onboard, and the salvage party received orders to stand by to follow, if necessary. While the armed boat party traversed the distance between the two ships, three heavy explosions were heard coming from the freighter, one forward and two aft. These explosions blew debris several hundred feet into the air and the surrounding waters. Immediately after the blasts someone raised the German Merchant Swastika at the mainmast, and then lowered the Norwegian flag.

Evidently the explosions blew the bottom out of the now-identified German vessel, as the ship was sinking rapidly by the stern before the boarding party could reach it. The armed boat party went alongside one of the survivors' boats, of which there were now four in the water, and took a German junior officer, the coxswain, back on board the injured ship. With him went two officers and six men of the armed boat party. Heat from the fire prevented any thorough search. Nevertheless, a lieutenant managed to reach the bulletin board to rip off the ship's Watch, Quarter, and Station Bill. He then went into the room of an officer, from which he retrieved a notebook and several propaganda booklets. The remainder of the boarding party scoured the parts of the ship they could reach, mainly the after part of the main deck, and picked up several items, including a swastika, a Norwegian flag, a machine gun with ammunition, and a four-inch, high-explosive shell.

By 7:14 a.m., the ship had settled astern to such a degree that the armed boat party received the order to leave. A few minutes later, the *Cincinnati* reported sighting what appeared to be a periscope, which sent the *Somers* at 25 knots to take position for an attack. It turned out the object was not a periscope but a piece of debris. As a result, the *Somers* returned to pick up the boat party. In the meantime, at 7:22, the German ship sank at 00 degrees-54 minutes North and 22 degrees-34minutes West. Given the real concern that submarines might be lurking in the immediate area, the *Somers* went on with her search. The *Milwaukee* and *Cincinnati* drew off a bit to launch aircraft and to carry on a hunt for another blockade runner thought to be in the vicinity. At this time, Bob was most likely aboard one of the scouting aircraft from the *Cincinnati*. Neither a surface ship nor a submarine was ever located. On returning to the *Somers*, the armed-boat party handed over the few objects retrieved and made several observations about the sunken vessel.

In addition to the armament already noted, on board the German ship there was a motor torpedo boat rigged on a boom for instant lowering. The Watch, Quarter, and Station Bill, taken from the bulletin board, showed there was a crew for manning the torpedo boat, with one officer in charge. The *Somers*, *Milwaukee*, and *Cincinnati* spent most of the day searching for a submarine. The *Milwaukee* took aboard the prisoners from the four German lifeboats. Altogether, they numbered 62, including 12 merchant marine officers, a naval doctor, a naval warrant gunner, and 22 enlisted men. The task group soon departed from the operating area for Recife, as it had been at sea for nearly two weeks and was running short of fuel and aviation gasoline.

From the preliminary investigation conducted aboard the *Milwaukee* there seemed no reasonable doubt that the scuttled ship was the *Anneliese Essberger*. Whether she was intended to act as a supply ship for U-Boats or was bound again for Japan could not be decided. The fact that she carried a large quantity of provisions, diesel oil, as well as hoses, indicated that the supplying of submarines was certainly part of her mission. Even so, interrogators of the German prisoners believed that the main object of the ship was to run the Allied blockade. On arrival at Recife, the prisoners, all Germans, were turned over to Brazilian authorities.[10]

During this time, the *Cincinnati* refueled, restocked her supplies and the men recharged their batteries. According to Naval records, Bob had completed three years of net service for pay purposes on December 10, 1942.

The Battle of Guadalcanal was November 12-15, 1942. This was one of the few major Pacific battles in which the *Northampton* was not directly involved. The ship was ordered to remain south of Guadalcanal in support of, but not directly involved in, the battle. During the battles, many destroyers were lost or damaged. The USS *Juneau*, with the five Sullivan brothers aboard, were lost during that confrontation, as was the *Atlanta*. The area of the Battle of Guadalcanal became known as Iron Bottom Sound, for the sheer number of ships that were sunk during this time. The loss of the Sullivan brothers was a huge loss to the country and tough on morale.

---

[10] The *Kota Nopan* was never located during this incident. It was, however, later intercepted and scuttled, while homebound on March 10, 1943, by the USS *Eberle*.

For Jim, it was a point of reflection, as he originally had a transfer to be with his brother, Bob, when he enlisted, as did his brother, Lionel. He now wondered if it wasn't a blessing in disguise that he never connected with his brothers on the transfer. He thought about his own mother and how she had three boys in the service. What would it be like for her if she lost her boys? He had to put it out of his mind. He didn't know what dangers his brothers were facing. He didn't want to speculate. The ways in which a guy could "buy it" were endless in war. He knew he had to stay focused on his mission, and let his brothers focus on theirs.

1942- The Year Ended In Near Disaster And Quiet Celebration

The Battle of Guadalcanal delayed but did not stop the later reinforcement of Japanese troops on Guadalcanal. The U.S. task force's mission was for the final destruction of the Japanese forces on and around Guadalcanal. The Japanese were putting up tremendous resistance to the American and Allied efforts to rid them from the island or force a surrender. The Army and Marine forces were having a terrible time of it. The Japanese tried all types of means to supply their troops, including physically landing supplies and troops, filling large oil drums with rice and barley and floating them to shore, and even using midget submarines to ferry supplies. The U.S. fleet aimed to put an end to that. Time and time again during the month of November, the fleet had small skirmishes with the Japanese around Guadalcanal trying to prevent them from resupplying their ground troops. The U.S. Navy decided that a major offensive against the Japanese was necessary. This became known as the Battle of Tassafaronga (often referred to as the Fourth Battle of Guadalcanal or the Fourth Battle of Savo Island).

The Battle of Tassafaronga occurred on November 30 and December 1, 1942. Tassafaronga is a spot on the northwestern shore of Guadalcanal. Savo Island is north of Guadalcanal. Florida Island is just to the east of Savo Island and Lengo Channel is a body of water that runs between Guadalcanal to the south and Florida Island to the north.

On November 30, 1942, Task Force 67 headed out Lengo Channel with the intent of arriving just off Tassafaronga by 11:00 p.m. in order to intercept a Japanese reinforcement group of eight destroyers and six troop transports. Recent intelligence suggested that on this evening, the Japanese wanted to deliver food, supplies and soldiers to Guadalcanal. It was the U.S. Navy's plan to stop them.

The Task force consisted of:

Heavy cruisers: **Light cruiser:**   **Destroyers:**

Heavy cruisers:	Light cruiser:	Destroyers:
Minneapolis	*Honolulu*	*Drayton*
New Orleans		*Fletcher*
Northampton		*Maury*
Pensacola		*Perkins*
		Lamson
		Lardner

SG radar was the latest technology when introduced in 1942 and was the first microwave radar system put into service in the U.S. Navy fleet. The radar was used primarily for detection of surface craft, but also was useful for night navigation.

It turned out the radar was instrumental in preventing the U.S. Navy from being swept aside during fierce night battles. However, at this point in 1942, not every ship had this tool. Ships in Task Force 67 lacking SG radar were the *Northampton, Pensacola, Maury, Lamson,* and *Lardner*

The plan directed the destroyers to concentrate two miles ahead of the guide ship *Minneapolis* before entering Lengo Channel. In the interim, between clearing the channel and encountering the enemy, the destroyers were to maintain the same two-mile distance. The cruisers were to form on a line and maneuver by turn movements so as to pass about six miles from the Guadalcanal coast. As the ships approached Lengo Channel, their order was the *Fletcher, Perkins, Maury,* and *Drayton,* followed by the cruiser column of the *Minneapolis, New Orleans, Pensacola, Honolulu,* and *Northampton.* This was referred to as "The Approach."

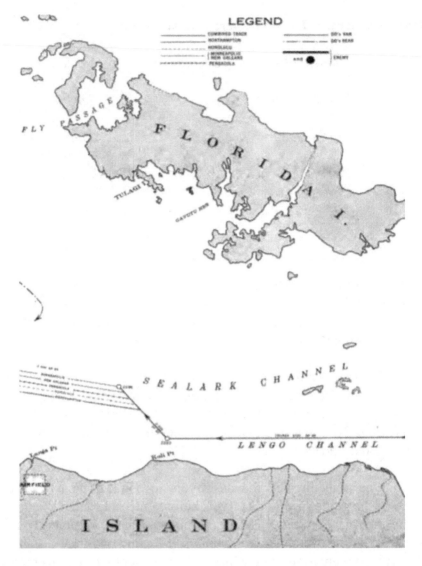

Area of Guadalcanal Island (bottom), Lengo Channel, and Florida Island.

One of the things that stuck out for Jim was just how dark this night was. The sky was completely overcast, with no moon or stars visible. Surface visibility was under two miles. It was hard to pick up the outlines of the islands and nearly impossible to see your fellow ships in the task force, never mind the enemy. Just after 11:00 pm., the *Minneapolis* and other members of the task force picked up multiple enemy contacts by use of SG radar. However, no one was sure exactly how many enemy ships were present. And, of the contacts made, no one could be sure which ones were transports and which were warships. Since the *Northampton* was last in the column, and had no SG radar, it had to depend on reports from the other ships. Despite all these issues, the battle was on.

The battle occurred in two action phases. The first was one-sided, in favor of the United States. At approximately 11:20 p.m., having received authority to launch a torpedo attack, the *Fletcher* fired ten torpedoes in two half salvos. Simultaneously, the *Perkins* launched eight torpedoes. Barely a minute after the torpedoes were launched, Admiral Wright ordered all ships to open gun fire, and the destroyers began firing their five-inch shells and star shells, the latter of which are designed to hang in the air and illuminate the area to aid U.S. gunnery positions and help those ships without radar to locate targets. In the pitch dark, the battle was like a thunderstorm. The sky would be lit up by the star shells, followed closely by multiple explosions from the five-inch salvos. Each of the salvos would send a bright flash, like lightning, into the night. The sound of the guns rolled across the ocean like repeated peals of thunder. The *Fletcher*, having SG radar, selected the rear enemy ship as her target, which was approximately 7,500 yards away. After firing about 60 rounds in two minutes, the *Fletcher* lost her target from the radar screen. The enemy vessel was presumably sunk. The *Fletcher*, therefore, ceased firing and retired to the northwest around Savo Island, followed by the other three destroyers astern.

Assisted by star shells, the main battery of the *Minneapolis* fired four salvos at what was finally identified as an enemy transport. The first salvo was somewhat over the target, but the next three were directly on. After the fourth salvo, the transport "violently disintegrated," sending up a huge ball of fire. One minute after the *Minneapolis* initially opened fire, the *New Orleans* began firing her main battery, directed entirely by radar at an enemy destroyer. Sailors on the *New Orleans* noticed that its target, moderately illuminated by star shells from the destroyers, was receiving fire from other cruisers as well. The enemy destroyer blew up, lighting up the sky, after a hit

162

from the *New Orleans'* fourth salvo. Initially, the *Pensacola*, without SG radar, had difficulty in locating a target. But after some searching, it soon picked up an unidentified object. Tracking began just as Admiral Wright gave the order to fire. With the aid of star-shell illumination from either the *Honolulu* or *Northampton*, the *Pensacola* opened fire on what her officers believed to be a Japanese light cruiser off the port bow. Because the first three salvos proved to be only near hits, the *Pensacola* resorted to her own star shells for better illumination. Additional U.S. ships also fired at the same target. The light cruiser met its fiery demise when the *Pensacola*'s fourth or fifth salvos landed on her target.

Initially frustrated that she couldn't find a target, the *Honolulu* – assisted by star shells from U.S. heavy cruisers which lit up a Japanese destroyer and through the use of their FC radar – commenced firing. Thirty seconds of rapid fire produced several hits and, after an additional minute of concentrated fire, observers on the *Honolulu* saw the enemy destroyer break up and sink.

Without an SG radar, the fifth and last cruiser, the *Northampton*, experienced great difficulties in locating the enemy. The darkness and land background of Guadalcanal blocked its efforts to pick up an enemy ship. Finally, her main batteries, as well as her anti-aircraft (AA), were trained toward the fall of shots being fired from the other cruisers and the *Northampton* promptly located an enemy destroyer target. Shortly after, the main, eight-inch battery opened fire. The target, a Japanese destroyer approximately 11,500 yards away, could not be seen until the third salvo landed. Despite frequent hits, the target ship just would not go down. To the *Northampton*'s great frustration, the danger of collision with cruisers ahead forced her to change course before sinking her target. She apparently ceased fire about 11:30 p.m. and steered out of column astern of the *Honolulu*. She did not return to the base course as soon as the latter ship. Instead, she steamed north. She was still occasionally attempting to engage her first target. While the *Northampton* apparently was firing haphazardly, after a few minutes she noted hitting her target. The *Northampton* began to come left and steamed for nearly ten minutes looking for another target.

The second target of the *Minneapolis* was as an enemy destroyer to the right of her first target. Both the *Minneapolis* and the *New Orleans* were firing on this ship. When the fourth salvo from the *Minneapolis* struck the enemy destroyer, both her bow and stern rose as though she had broken in two and a few seconds later she disappeared under the water.

As for the *Pensacola*, within a few minutes she detected another Japanese ship to her right, scarcely 8,000 yards away. As the *Pensacola* fired her first salvo, the Japanese vessel emerged from the smoke and became clearly visible. Virtually all the shells of the *Pensacola*'s second salvo landed directly down the ship's stack. A great explosion followed, after which the ship disappeared both from sight and from the radar screens.

At this stage of the battle, the *Pensacola* apparently ceased fire, the *Honolulu* still was engaged with her target, and the *Lamson* and *Lardner* could not locate the enemy, so the U.S. destroyers withdrew around Savo Island. On their retirement course around Savo Island, the destroyers noticed shells dropping astern and enemy gunfire also was directed at the U.S. cruisers. At this point, two things caused considerable concern for the American ships. First and foremost was the uncertainty regarding the composition of the Japanese forces. They were not sure exactly how many enemy ships were engaged in the battle. Second, the night was so dark, visibility so limited, and flashes and smoke in the target area so confusing that it was impossible to obtain a clear idea of what was taking place. It was critical that the U.S. warships made certain they weren't firing at each other.

Despite the concerns at the end of this one-sided first phase of the battle, U.S. commanders were very happy with the outcome thus far. Results of U.S. gunfire furnished ample cause for optimism as there was reason to believe that several enemy ships had been sunk. U.S. ships with radar capabilities seemed the most effective and the task force apparently had surprised the enemy, a prime advantage in any night action, and disrupted the Japanese retaliatory power. Most

importantly, not a single Japanese shell had struck any U.S. ship. For
a brief, shining moment, U.S. victory seemed to be a certainty.

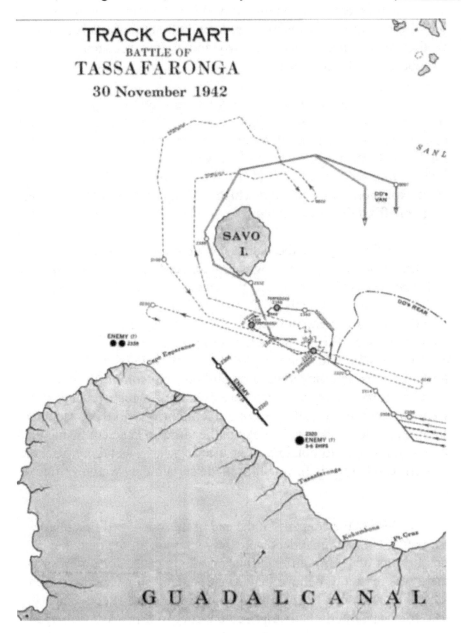

TRACK CHART
BATTLE OF
TASSAFARONGA
30 November 1942

In the second phase did not go as well for the Americans. As witnessed and later described by Jim, the U.S. ships were all in a row heading through Lengo Channel just off the coast of Tassafaronga. The Japanese destroyers were coming in from the northwest. It wasn't long before the Japanese engaged the American forces. Once the battle began anew, it felt like all hell was breaking loose. As it was any night battle, it became very disorienting. The eight-inch guns began firing, the five-inch guns began firing, area ships were firing their heavy weapons and the Japanese destroyers were firing their guns as well. Their percussion was reverberating over the ocean's surface all around Jim in a cacophony of sound. In the dark of night, with no moon, there was a host of bright flashes and explosions. The sky continuously lit up with every salvo. Jim could feel the boom of the salvos in his gut. It was difficult to say who was who, and who was firing at whom and from where. Time seemed to slow down. Actions appear slower than they were actually occurring. It felt like a complete sensory overload. It was hard to take everything in all at once. It was like being in a pitch-black room with bright lights flashing and multiple huge ear-splitting bass drums banging away over and over.

The Japanese began firing torpedoes. They had very accurate long-lance torpedoes. Jim knew it was only a matter of time before the Japanese would unleash the long lances. Once they started firing, it was disastrous for the American ships. Because it was so dark, so completely black, Jim couldn't make out the torpedoes in the water. He remembers the *Minneapolis* as the first to get hit, right in the bow and forward of turret one, abreast the aviation gasoline department. A second torpedo struck almost simultaneously, to the point that most heard and felt only one explosion. The percussion was jarring. The flames lit up the sky. Jim didn't know exactly how bad it was, but he knew it meant death and destruction for a lot of guys.

The second ship to get hit was the *New Orleans*. It was struck in the bow as well, from the number two turret forward. The ship's entire bow blew off from explosions in the ammunition magazines and fuel storage tanks when the torpedo hit it. The bow sheared off and went overboard with a lot of men still on it. It was like a dull paper-cutter ripping through a load of construction paper. It was jagged but did the job. It happened so fast and so definitively that the men aboard the *New Orleans* did not have time to react. Thank goodness, Jim recalled, that the *New Orleans* had followed procedures and had closed all the hatches between compartments. Despite the heavy damage, additional life was not lost, and the *New Orleans* was able to remain afloat and be salvaged.

The *New Orleans* on December 1, 1942, after the Battle of Tassafaronga.

The *Northampton* and the other ships in the dark were maneuvering to avoid the onslaught of Japanese torpedoes. It was like a shooting gallery in a carnival where ducks all move in a line and the player tries to shoot them down, one after another. Only here, the Japanese were the shooter, and the ducks were the U.S. ships. The USS *Honolulu* was next in line and was able to turn to starboard to avoid getting hit and went off to find another target. Next was the *Pensacola*. She wasn't as lucky as she was hit in the stern and suffered a great deal of damage. Oil-fed flames engulfed the *Pensacola*'s main deck aft where the ammunition was stored. Because of the fires, the ammunition began to explode. Only supreme effort and skillful damage control by her men saved the ship. The fire was punctuated by the repeated, frightful explosions of eight-inch projectiles in her Number 3 turret. It was like popcorn going off, on steroids. After a while, the explosions gradually subsided. The *Pensacola* pulled out and made steady progress toward the safety of Tulagi. When she arrived in Tulagi she was still burning. After 12 hours the last fire aboard was quenched. Her dead numbered seven officers and 118 men. One officer and 67 men were injured.

The next in line was Jim's ship, the *Northampton*. Amazingly, at 11:48 p.m., despite the level of darkness, lookouts from the *Northampton* noticed two torpedoes close aboard on the port bow, traveling very close together. One ran about 10 feet below the waterline, the other almost on the surface. One of Jim's fellow storekeepers Dick Lynott, from his lookout station in sky control, heard the cry, "Torpedoes! 300 degrees!" Dick leaped to the edge and looked over the side. The torpedoes streaked through the water leaving a wake behind them heading straight for the *Northampton*. He was one of the lucky ones. He saw them coming and had time to react. He grabbed the rail and waited for them to hit. For one fleeting second, he thought they had missed. He leaned over and looked down at the water, just in time to see the tremendous explosion.

Capt. Kitts barely had time to order hard left rudder before the torpedoes struck so close together that many in the *Northampton* felt only one explosion. The force sent sailors flying, arms and legs akimbo. Violent vibrations followed for several seconds. Fuel and diesel oil ignited and sprayed in flames over the mainmast structure and the boat deck, detonating the five-inch ready ammunition. The explosions from the torpedoes blew out the ship's port side leaving eight feet of skin plate protruding over the side. Parts of the main and second decks were torn away.[11] At first, the *Northampton* listed to

---

[11] One of the men killed was 27-year-old Ensign Arthur Dionne of Walpole, Mass. He had been commissioned just six months earlier. Dionne was in the engine room

port 10°, then, notwithstanding all efforts to lessen it, the angle increased to 20°. Capt. Kitts stopped the ship in the hope that she would right herself, but when the list reached 23°, he ordered the bridge abandoned, the firerooms secured and all personnel brought topside.

At 1:30 a.m., all hands except the salvage crew were ordered over the side. Twenty minutes later, the *Fletcher* and *Drayton* (which had rounded Savo Island in company with the *Honolulu*) received orders to rescue the *Northampton*'s officers and crew and, shortly thereafter, started picking them up. The cruiser's fires increased as steadily as her list and the water supply at the fire mains fell off ominously. At 2:40, when the list reached 35°, Capt. Kitts and the salvage party abandoned ship. On the morning of December 1, just after 3:00 a.m., the *Northampton* turned on her beam, rolled over and sank, stern first. An hour later, the *Fletcher* and *Drayton* completed their search for survivors, rescuing 57 officers and 716 men. By 4:35 a.m., no more men could be found in the water, so the *Fletcher* and the *Drayton* decided to make for Espiritu Santo. The ships arrived at Espiritu Santo at 10:00 a.m. on December 2, 1942. In all, the *Northampton* lost 55 men.

According to a U.S. Navy after-action report specific to the sinking of the *Northampton*, the two torpedoes did actually hit the ship nearly simultaneously. The survivors had only felt a single shock and only saw one geyser. The report noted that the night was intensely dark with no moon. The sky also was completely covered by a heavy overcast of clouds. Surface visibility was good. A light southeast breeze barely ruffled the surface of the water.

Both of the torpedo detonations were in the area of fuel oil tanks and oil was thrown throughout several second-deck spaces on the mainmast structure. Within seconds, fire broke out and spread quickly, fed by oil from the ruptured tanks bubbling up to the surface

---

at the time of the explosion and was killed instantly. The Navy named a ship in his honor. The USS *Dionne* was christened by his mother.

in the damaged area. The oil thrown over the topside was quickly ignited with the entire mainmast structure serving as a huge torch.

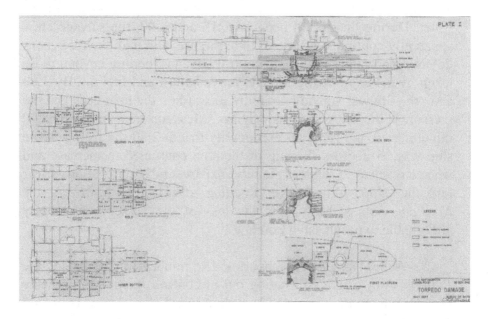

Diagram of the torpedo damage to the USS *Northampton* [War Report 41].

A considerable quantity of oil was carried up through the openings in the decks and thrown well over topside structures. Vapors from this oil apparently ignited almost immediately as it was reported that within about two seconds following the initial shock flames shot skyward.

This fuel oil, and some diesel, were thrown up and over the mainmast structure and throughout the second-deck spaces between bulkheads 90 and 150. Apparently, oil vapors in this area were ignited and the fire spread rapidly until the mainmast structure was engulfed in flames. Eventually, the five-inch ammunition in the ready-service boxes for the two after-port guns was ignited and began to go off singly with low-order detonations. Efforts to control the fire were not described beyond the statement that, at times, it was somewhat subdued but was never entirely controlled.

At 1:30 a.m. all personnel except the commanding officer and a salvage crew were ordered to abandon ship. Two U.S. destroyers arrived at about 1:55 and commenced picking up survivors in the water. During the period between 1:15 and 2:00, the salvage crew apparently continued efforts to fight the fire, although the references do not report any measures to control list and flooding beyond those taken by the engineering force to move ballast and fuel oil. By 2:00 a.m., the fire was spreading rapidly forward on the boat deck and the pressure at the fire plugs was very low. Measures taken in the next 40 minutes were not reported except only that at 2:40 the listing of the ship was 35 degrees. Listing of the ship continued to increase and when it reached 55 degrees the salvage party and commanding officer left the ship. Progressive flooding eventually destroyed the *Northampton*'s stability, and the loss of the vessel was entirely attributable to progressive flooding.

At 3:04 a.m., some 3 hours and 15 minutes after being hit, the *Fighting Nora,* fires still raging out of control, lurched to port, the bottom came into view and the ship rolled completely over and plunged by the stern with the bow making an angle of about 60 degrees with the surface as she slipped under.

Jim described what happened to him during the *Northampton*'s demise in a taped statement in 2006:

> *Before I knew it, the loudspeaker came up loud and clear, 'Stand by for torpedo starboard quarter, near the after mast, the after firerooms and engine rooms. And 20,000 tons just came up and hit me right in the ass. My division officer looked down in the dark and grabbed me by the arm and pulled me up and asked me if I was OK. I survived and stood right up. I kinda rubbed my fanny and seemed to be OK. The Northampton, being the last cruiser in line tried to maneuver to get out of the way of any more lance torpedoes. We managed to get away safely. We did get power under one screw, I think, and managed to take off out of the area called Iron Bottom Bay. [After that] We were dead in the water for some time.*

It is hard to describe, of course, the devastation that is going on around you in the dark – the dark of night, no moon, no stars. Guns firing all over the place. Torpedoes bursting, fires on deck. It was just horrendous.

All the American cruisers that had been hit, all found a safe haven mostly, I guess, in some little port around Savo Island and most of them up in Tulagi, except for the Northampton. The Northampton, like I said, did get underway then lost power, dead in the water. No chance of saving her.

The after-engine rooms were flooded. Three of our four shafts had ceased turning. We had heeled ten degree to port. So, we were losing her. Japanese guns on Guadalcanal, once we went dead in the water, began to fire from the shore, but the shells were short, thank goodness.

The ship began to list very heavily to port. They shouted over the loudspeaker, 'Abandon Ship! Abandon Ship!' I said goodbye to my watch officer. Headed for my quarters where we had to take inventory and get orders to abandon ship. I ran down the ladders on the foremast, got to the well deck and we assembled there. The S Division, there were several [guys] there. Took our orders from the division officer there to abandon ship. Made sure all hands had their lifejackets, kapok life jackets, on.

As I was about to head for the lifeline to abandon ship -- the ship was listing quite badly now-- a motor mech came running up to me near a tall ladder that leads to the after-gun deck and handed me a hose and asked me to take it up there. I took it up. Water came on. There was the motor mech and me with two hoses throwing water into the fire, up aft. I didn't know it, but I became part of the salvage crew.

The motor mech and I fought the fire for quite a little while. Some ammunition in nearby turrets started popping into the air. I think they were anti-aircraft fire, 1.1 bullets, that were assembled around a gun turret, that started popping off. A Marine captain, I have forgotten his name, came up, because we had heard a young boy yelling for help on the after mast. We were just forward of the after mast on the gun deck. I could hear the young boy yelling. I later found out that this young boy had two broken legs. The pharmacist mate had given him shots, but there was no way to get him off the after mast, so I guess they had abandoned ship and left him there. So, the Marine officer came up and we asked him to help us maybe get to that young boy on the after mast. So, the captain gave me his 45. I put it in my waist for a little while, then thought better of it, afraid of losing the family jewels, so I put it down on deck. We poured water onto him, somewhere in the smoke and darkness, we couldn't see him. Then after, I don't know how long, the water stopped. They had shut the water off down below, somewhere, because they had been pumping water to the ammunition magazines to stop them from exploding. I think they were five-inch magazines.

So, the water was now shut off on my hose and the motor mech's hose. And as soon as the water stopped that captain came sailing out of that smoke and the darkness back to where we had walked over to the starboard side, which was now quite high. We were standing at, at least a thirty-degree angle, on deck. Some of the Marines were there, getting ready to go over the side. As I was about to grab several little first-aid kits out of a locker on deck, and shove them under my kapok life jacket, the Marine officer came up to me and said, 'where is my pistol?' And I pointed back to the deck and said, 'I left it on deck, back there.' He went back to the deck to get his gun. I never saw him again. But later I found out he received an award, a Navy award. I have forgotten which one, it was quite high, for making an attempt to save the boy. He never did save the boy, but he made a good attempt, I guess, with our help.[12]

I started sliding down a gasoline hose with Marines, above and below me. [We] started sliding down this gasoline hose on the starboard side and into the water. One Marine dropped from above me into the water, he had full gear, because they were afraid they might have to swim to Guadalcanal and fight with the soldiers over there. I watched him in the dark enter the water. Even though he had a life jacket on, he vanished. He went out of sight. And when he did come to the surface again, he didn't have his helmet, he didn't have a gun or anything. He dropped all his heavy gear and came to the surface.

Now we attempted to swim away from the Northampton, which is listing very badly. Out in the water I could hear voices, meaning that there were men on rafts out there. These big rafts that used to be tied up to the eight-inch gun turrets. They had released those and put some of the wounded men in those rafts. I didn't want to go near the rafts because of possible shark's attention due to the wounded men being in the rafts. So, I stayed out alone. I was a good swimmer. I stayed out alone in the dark. I never saw anybody else. All of a sudden, I heard a voice behind me. 'Shark! Shark!' It was over near the rafts somewhere in the dark. I could hear the voices, but I couldn't see anything. And at that time, I became aware of everything around me. My shoes were gone. My socks were gone. My bare feet were down there. I immediately whipped my feet up top to the surface as much as possible. I realized that all the first aid

---

[12] The marine captain was later identified as 24-year-old William S. McLaughlin. He was awarded the Silver Star for his actions of November 30-December 1, 1942. After WWII he served as a judge on the Japanese war crimes tribunal. He later served in the Korean War and as awarded the Bronze Star for valor with oak leaf. He retired as a Lt. Colonel in 1961. William passed away on June 2, 2006, four days shy of his 88th birthday. When I spoke with his son, he was not aware of his father's heroism. Like many of his generation, his father never spoke of it.

gear that I had shoved under my life jacket was gone. My helmet was gone. I had gone over the side with my helmet on, but it was much too heavy. My wallet was gone. I reached down, the top of my 14" knife that I had made was broken off . . . I kept swimming around, just treading water, trying not to make any attention.

I don't know how long it was after I had gone over the side. I turned to the left and I saw the Northampton twist over to her port side, her bow way up in the air. An astounding thing happened, somebody on the bridge lit a headlight, a big strong light, and it went right onto the jack, which is the flag that is flying at the bow. And that light remained there. I don't know if it came on automatically, but I think somebody must have turned it on. He must have gone down with the ship if he did. The ship rolled to its port side and sank by the stern. I could feel the rumble of different machinery on the ship under the water. I could feel the vibrations as things went through bulkheads and everything.

I continued to swim or just tread water for I don't know how many hours. I could hear small arms fire from Guadalcanal. There was no moon, no stars. It was very quiet. The water was really calm. It was amazing that it was so calm.

Finally, I saw the USS Honolulu, came through the dark, it went right through all the injured men on the rafts and through us that were swimming individually. It went right through and couldn't stop for fear of being torpedoed. She kept going. The next thing I knew, I don't know how many hours or minutes or whatever – who was keeping time, I had no watch anymore, treading water – all of a sudden, I realized that I could hear voices to my port side, my left side, and I looked in the dark over there and I could see the outlines of a destroyer. I didn't know it at the time but it was the USS Fletcher. And being such a wonderful swimmer and everything, I found myself . . . on the starboard side and everybody was being picked up on the Fletcher on the port side. I had to slowly swim around and not call attention to any sharks. I swam around the bow, all the way around that bow and down the port side to the midships, where an officer reached over the side grabbed me and pulled me aboard. Thank goodness. [At this point in the taped statement, more than 60 years later, Jim became very emotional and stopped the tape to gather himself.]

Just as he was pulling me aboard, a man behind me yelled 'Shark!' and a big boatswain's mate, a big blond boatswain's mate, I never knew his name, he had a rope tied to his waist, he dove off the Fletcher and headed for that kid. Probably saved him.

Jim's days at St. Rita's Church had instilled in him a great abiding faith in God. He never lost that faith throughout his entire adult life and particularly relied on it during the morning hours of December 1, 1942. Jim prayed the entire time he was in the water. He prayed the "Our Father," he prayed the "Hail Mary," he prayed the "Glory Be," over and over again. He prayed that he would survive the night, he prayed that he would not be taken by a shark and he prayed that he would be able to see his family again. Throughout the rest of his life, he was sure that God heard his prayers while he was alone in the dark waters of the Pacific.

Jim had been swimming for almost two hours in an ocean mixed with fuel oil. All of the men looked like they were covered in an oil slick. Many of the men suffered burns to their skin as a result of the long-term exposure to the fuel oil. Because Jim had stayed on board to fight the fires and attempt to save a fellow shipmate, he was in the water 1 ½ hours less than the other sailors. Jim believed that because he had less exposure, he wasn't bothered as much by the oil. Once on board the *Fletcher*, Jim and the rest of the survivors were almost immediately hosed down and decontaminated:

I was immediately directed by the officer to go a washroom on the main deck and then proceed to an after compartment in order to balance the ship because so many men were

176

being taken aboard. They had to balance the Fletcher. As I proceeded down the ladder to the after compartment, lo and behold, the person that greeted me at the bottom of the ladder was my gunnery officer. He offered me a cigarette that he took out of that old survivor's kit that he had, which was a can which was made waterproof by condoms.

The gunnery officer always told his guys, something to the effect of, *"Just you wait, if we go over the side, I'll be the only guys with dry cigarettes."* He was right. When his men came aboard the *Fletcher*, he greeted every one of his guys with a dry cigarette and a big smile. It looks like he had the last laugh, after all.

Having that smoke, Jim reflected on his luck. He felt that he had been so very lucky to have made it unscathed through so many battles in 1942. He recognized that the *Northampton*'s luck had just plain run out. But not his. He still felt lucky and blessed. In battle, everything can go sideways in the blink of an eye. After getting hit, the ship started blazing right away and there was no way to control it effectively. The ammunition on deck started exploding all over the place. Jim had to swim in shark infested waters for some time. There were so many ways he could have been killed. He lost track of the number of prayers he said while he was in that water. So many guys weren't as lucky. He thought about the "daring and courage of every one of those lads, living through months of actual combat and then ending up by being shot out of the water." Jim knew his prayers had been answered. He was very grateful. He felt very lucky indeed.

After all the surviving crewmen were picked up, the *Fletcher* proceeded in the dark to the port of Espiritu Santo.[13] The sailors were all put aboard a transport and inventory was taken of the crews that

---

[13] It is interesting to note that future actor Jason Robards was assigned to the *Northampton* as a radioman when it was sunk. Robards, like all the others, found himself treading water until near daybreak when he was rescued. He went on to serve throughout the war.

were left. Interestingly enough, some of the men of the *Northampton* were put aboard PT 109 and taken into port. [14]

PT 109 with USS *Northampton* survivors, December 1, 1942.

After the battle, the *New Orleans*, despite having had its bow blown off, made it to port. Repair crews put on a makeshift bow and the ship was able to eventually sail back to Seattle, where they put a new permanent bow on the ship. It would not be the last time Jim saw the *New Orleans*.

For an article in the *Lowell Sun*, Jim spoke to reporter James F. Droney, giving some highlights about the Battle of Tassafaronga. Here are some excerpts from Droney's article: First, Droney makes some commentary,

"...In his mind and body and heart is imprinted with bloody ink the full story of the war in the Pacific. He has gone through every sort of naval warfare, air bombings, close ship to ship combat and the combination of both.

---

[14] At the time, John F. Kennedy was not yet PT 109's skipper. On April 23, 1943, the future president would take over command of the 109.

He has seen decks awash with blood, his pals killed and maimed. He has seen the Japs driven back again and again, and knows they paid terrible prices for slight gains..."

Then Jim provided some observations:

Our Waterloo came in the same area a few nights later. It was the same kind of battle, and for the same purpose, to prevent a Jap landing on Guadalcanal. They didn't manage it that night either. The entire task force was wiped out. We took 'em by surprise, just like at Midway. They were caught with their kimonas down.

A short time after the battle started there was a terrific blast on our ship. They think it was a torpedo. And I think they are right.

The ship started blazing right away, and there was no way to control it effectively. The ammunition on deck started exploding all over the place and the ship started to list over. Then came the call to abandon...

I was only in the water a couple of hours. The oil slick bothered me more on deck than in the water. A lot of the fellows reported burns from it, but I wasn't bothered much.

And that's about all there was to it. It happened so quickly, and I was rescued so rapidly...

Finally, Droney makes some concluding commentary,

"That's about all-except the daring and courage of every one of those lads. Living through months of actual combat and then ending up by being shot out of the water. Quite a tale, this Turcotte lad tells, and he tells it as though it was nothing at all. Like going for a loaf of bread..."

After Jim was picked up on the morning of December 1, 1942, by the *Fletcher* and brought into Espiritu Santo, he was quickly assigned to the USS *President Hayes*, a troop transport. He was transported from Espiritu Santo to Nouméa, New Caledonia, where he arrived approximately December 7. The Red Cross was there to greet him and his fellow sailors. All he had was the oil-covered dungarees he was wearing and the knife on his hip. He had lost everything else. The Red Cross gave him a canvas ditty bag with personal hygiene items, including shaving gear, toothbrush, toothpaste, and soap. Jim had that bag until the day he died and kept keepsakes from the war in it. The surviving sailors were assigned to a large tent encampment 25 to 30 miles from Nouméa, up the Dumbea River. Each tent held about ten guys and there were about 1,000 or so men assigned to the camp. In addition to survivors from the *Northampton*, there were survivors from other ships as well.

Due to conditions of the camp – overcrowding, sanitary lapses, poor design, and construction – many of the men came down with dysentery and malaria. Those with malaria had to be flown to Australia and New Zealand to be treated.

As Jim described it, the bathroom, referred to in the military as the latrine, was nothing more than a long chute or trough with running water in it. The latrine had been built on a hill and, due to the tropical weather, the rains caused the latrine to flood often and run down into the camp. Flies carried contamination around the camp, only making matters worse. More and more men became sick, suffering from illness and dehydration. Jim came down with a bad case of dysentery. He practically lived in his skivvy shorts, running up the hill repeatedly, with the hope that he would make it to the latrine before an accident. That wasn't always the case. That's the way he lived for many days. He was miserable. On top of it all, it was hot and uncomfortable and there were plenty of mosquitoes to add to the misery. The three weeks he spent in the camp were etched in Jim's mind forever.

In camp with Jim were a set of twins, the Wente brothers. They had served together aboard the *Northampton*. Jim was friends with Louie Wente. Jim and Louie decided to get out of camp and take a trip on foot to try and get into Nouméa. They knew it was 25-30 miles away, but they had had it with the conditions in the camp and needed to get out. So, very early one morning, they proceeded out through the woods in the direction of Nouméa. Other sailors had told Jim about cannibals and headhunters that lived on these islands. He believed they did that just to put a scare into him. Jim didn't pay it much mind. As they proceeded a distance, they ran across a large, native-looking black man, stripped to the waist, wearing only a loin cloth. He had a large hatchet over his shoulder. Jim started to have second thoughts about their trip. As you could imagine, Jim, being only 20 years old, was more than a little apprehensive, especially after what the older sailors had told him. As he approached Jim and Louie, the local gestured to them that he wanted a cigarette. The native put his hands up to his mouth gesturing and said, "cigarette, cigarette." He didn't appear to speak very much English. Jim now believed him to be a French-speaking native of the island. Jim accommodated the man with a couple of cigarettes. They waved good-bye and high-tailed it out of there, much to Jim's relief.

By noon or so, they ended up in a Seabee camp. The Seabees were a Naval Construction Battalion. Most of these Seabees were older, experienced construction guys. The average age of a Seabee was 34. The average Marine rifleman was 19. The Seabee camp was between 12 and 15 miles from the survivor's camp alongside the Dumbea River. When those at the camp found out their visitors were survivors from the *Northampton*, they were well-received. The Seabees gave them a fantastic meal. It appeared to Jim that not only could the Seabees build a swell bridge, but they could also cook a great lunch. Jim said it was one of the best meals he ever had in the Navy and he very much appreciated their hospitality.

The Seabees asked Jim and Louie a lot of questions about the battle and the sinking of the *Northampton*. Jim was more than happy to regale them with the story. Jim thought the Seabees treated them royally. When it came time to go, the Seabees gave them directions into Nouméa and sent them on their way. Jim and Louie were having a wonderful day. It was great being out of that hellhole of a survivor's camp. They were enjoying the sunshine, breathing fresh air, getting some exercise and had a great meal to boot. What more could they ask for under the circumstances?

They went down river another 15 miles or so to Nouméa. They were hoping to contact George Allen, an old buddy of Jim's, who also had gone over the side on the *Northampton*. When they were transported to New Caledonia, George was given quarters in Nouméa. He was assigned to an old rickety building to use as a make-shift office. George Allen had a very important job – he kept all the pay accounts and records for the *Northampton*. Amazingly, he was able to get all the pay records and crew lists off the ship before it went down. George's job was to try to figure out where each crew member was and how much was owed to them. That made him an extremely important man to both the officers and crew. He had to reconcile who had been killed, who had been injured, who had survived, where they were transferred to and so on. Jim knew all too well the downside of having no pay records. At that time, it was all paper records. There were no computers. Copies of the pay records were kept on board and a second copy was kept in a centralized location back in the States. If the records were lost at sea or damaged, it could take months to reconstruct. Jim wanted to make sure that George saw his smiling face and secured his pay file.

When they reached Nouméa, Jim and Louie asked around to see if anyone was able to point out where George was. Eventually, they found him, sitting on a low porch of a building, on a dirt road, drinking a bottle of wine. "Tough work," Jim joked. George had a big smile. For more than a week, Jim was in that survivor's camp living out of a tin cup, suffering with dysentery, and here was George drinking wine and relaxing. Nevertheless, they greeted each other warmly, catching up on how the other was doing and what had happened to them during the battle and the aftermath. They hung around and talked most of the afternoon away. They joked and laughed. Jim felt it was good for his soul. It was a great break from the routine and the conditions of the camp.

Before they knew it, it was time for Jim and Louie to get back to the survivor's camp. They had a long trek ahead of them. George gave them directions and wished them the best but told Jim it might be a little while before he saw his pay. He assured him that eventually, it would catch up with him. Ugh. They followed the Dumbea River most of the way back. They knew they would have to hike it double-time to get back before dark. When they got about 15 miles from camp, they were picked up by two officers in a command car who took pity on them. Jim and Louie sat in the back. Lo and behold, in the back of the car with them was a case of beer. The officers offered them a can of beer. Despite the fact that he had certainly earned it, Jim declined. Not that anyone cared, but Jim wasn't even of legal drinking age. Louie Wente helped himself.

It was now dark. They were traveling on an old dirt road that came in on the left-hand side of the camp. As they approached the survivor's camp, they heard a command, "Halt! Put out your lights." The officer who was driving the car had had a few beers and didn't hear the order. Jim looked ahead and saw the outline of a soldier, now with the sight of his weapon raised to his eye and the weapon pointed toward the car. He was ready to shoot out the headlight of the car, or worse. Jim was afraid the soldier would miss the headlights and hit him. Jim and Louie yelled to put out the headlights. Fortunately, the officer driving immediately put out the headlights. After some tense discussion with the sentry, they were permitted to proceed up into the camp. Despite the close call, they thanked the officers for the ride. It seemed like danger was always just around the corner. It just depended on how much luck you had to avoid it.

It was back to the camp and the poor conditions. Jim continued with the problem of dysentery and trying to make it up the dreaded hill to get to the make-shift latrine in time. He struggled to stay hydrated, and it seemed that no matter what he ate, it went straight through him.

Boredom was a big problem for the men. After you started your day with a cold shower, cleaned up your area and had something to eat, that was pretty much it. There were no activities to speak of, and no phone, no radio, no movies. There wasn't a village or town for 25 or 30 miles. The guys would mingle around and shoot the breeze. Some would play touch football, play cards, or write a letter, if they could find any paper. But most ran out of things to do pretty quickly.

Throughout his life, Jim never forgot the miserable conditions in that survivor's camp. Yet, at the same time, the experience made him feel very grateful for the small comforts of life. He always said that he wished he could find the SOB that set up the camp. Amazingly, years later, he did!

As his son, for many years I listened to him describe the camp. The survivor's camp was up the Dumbea River, a French Cavalry Camp on one side, an American camp on the other. Fast forward nearly 60 years. In late December 2001, I was a prosecuting attorney in Meriden, Connecticut. As I was discussing the cases for the day, into court came a dashing older attorney, Israel Rosenzweig. Everyone called him Izzy. He truly was a gentleman in every sense of the word. He was kind, polite, respectful, and yet very self-assured. Izzy had recently turned 85 years old and was still practicing law in nearby New Britain. Izzy walked with a cane and wore a snazzy little cap. I assumed, based upon his age, that Izzy might be a WWII veteran. "Izzy, were you in the Second World War?" I asked. Izzy acknowledged that he was. I inquired as to where he served and what he had done in the war. He told me he had been in the Army, in an engineering company, and had fought in some of the tough battles early on in the Pacific. His unit had suffered some heavy casualties – nearly 100 percent wounded or killed. As a result, he was reassigned to set up survivor's camps in the Pacific.

We were sitting at a table, across from each other and I sat forward in my chair, leaning on my elbows, and asked, "Did you set up a survivor's camp near Nouméa, New Caledonia, up the Dumbea River, French Cavalry Camp on one side and an American camp on the other?"

Izzy literally sat back, dumbfounded. "How did you know that? How could you know that?" he asked.

"My father was in that camp," I said. "If he finds you, you are a dead man!"

Without skipping a beat, he asked, "Malaria or dysentery?"

"Dysentery," I replied, smiling. We both laughed and spoke for a while about the war and this amazing coincidence. He gave me his contact information and said he wanted to meet my dad, Jim. That evening, I couldn't wait to tell my dad the story about how I had found the person that set up the survivor's camp. "Hey Pop, you know how for the last 50 years I've had to listen to you complain about the survivor's camp during the war?" I grinned.

"Yeah?" he replied, in a tone of questioning skepticism.

"You know how you always said that if you found the SOB that set up that camp, you'd kill him?" My grin kept getting bigger.

"Yeah?" he said, now grinning as well.

"Well, I met him today at work!" I exclaimed.

My dad couldn't believe it. I told him details of our conversation and gave him Izzy's contact information, adding that Izzy said he'd like to meet him. The very next day he reached out to Izzy and they set up a lunch date for just after the new year. As a joke, Jim drafted a fake lawsuit complaint. The faux lawsuit asked for millions of dollars in compensation for 60 years of pain, suffering, and humiliation for having contracted dysentery in the camp in 1942. Jim gave it to Izzy when they first met at Izzy's office. Izzy got the biggest laugh out of it. They hit it off from the start. They went to lunch and talked for hours about each other's experiences before, during and after the war. Their paths had crossed in 1942 and now they were crossing again in January 2002. Jim had closed the circle of that episode in his life. They promised to have lunch again in the near future. Unfortunately, that would be their only meeting. On May 31, 2002, Izzy passed away.

Back at the survivor's camp, every day, the captain would try to bolster the spirits of the crew. He would stand on the hood of a Jeep and tell the crew that he was doing his best to get the men back stateside and/or assigned to a new ship. He made sure that he kept the men apprised of everything going on. The men appreciated that. After a couple of weeks, it was getting close to Christmas and the captain had some big news. He gathered the men of the *Northampton* around the Jeep. To the cheers of the men, he announced that most of them were being sent stateside immediately. "Boy, what a wonderful feeling!" Jim thought as he was thrilled to be heading back to the States. He couldn't wait to pack up and get out of there.

It wasn't long after his captain's announcement in camp that Jim was in his tent packing up what little gear he had. The next day he was trucked back to Nouméa and boarded a transport to head stateside. Jim, Louie, and George were excited to be back aboard ship. The men were treated well aboard the transport. The conditions were a lot better than at the camp. He had a warm, dry place to sleep and the food was a lot better. There were no flies and with the dysentery resolving, he felt like a new man. He was free to walk the decks and get some fresh air whenever he pleased. And there were no mosquitos. Periodically, there was even some entertainment. The military people aboard would put on shows. The guys would go down in the hold of the ship and be regaled by an original musical, a talent show or a musical group. After most of the men were situated, they would announce that they needed to be quiet as they brought in soldiers, sailors, and Marines who were "shell-shocked." They would come in single file, silently, holding on to each other's shoulders. They would be escorted into the front seats. Many of these guys had been on Guadalcanal. They had suffered near-constant air and ground attacks from the Japanese. These men had what they now know to be "severe PTSD" from weeks or months of heavy fighting, some of it hand-to-hand. Jim's heart went out to these guys. He never forgot how traumatized they were and how young they were. The show couldn't start until these soldiers were seated and calmed. They weren't the only troubled guys aboard ship.

In addition, there were two Marine officers locked in a wardroom with bars on the window for fear that someone might get injured by them. They were both suffering from extreme mental illness as a result of what they experienced during battle. One of the officers would clean incessantly. When he finished, the other would urinate all over the wardroom. They would get mad at each other and physically fight. They'd get separated and start the process all over again. This went on for most of the trip. There was no real treatment aboard ship for men in this condition. They were just kept isolated from the other passengers. Food was brought to their quarters at mealtime. Jim thought it was quite pitiful and really felt bad for these guys. He recognized that these two had given everything of themselves for their country and they would never be the same.

The sailors aboard were surprised when they first went through the chow line aboard ship. As they waited in the long line, there was a hatch that was roped off, but they could look down. The men were shocked to discover there were Japanese prisoners aboard. They were being brought to the mainland to either be interrogated or imprisoned until the war was over. The prisoners would look up into the open hold and see the Americans two or three decks above them. As you can imagine, many of the Americans did not have warm feelings for the prisoners, especially considering the effects they witnessed on some of their fellow Americans aboard ship. The prisoners would yell something in Japanese and the Americans would yell and curse back at them and would throw some of their food down on them. It was not an act of kindness.

In a timely coincidence, the boat passed Christmas Island on Christmas Day, 1942. Christmas Island is in the Indian Ocean, around 220 miles south of Java and Sumatra and around 960 miles northwest of the closest point on the Australian mainland. As they passed the island, Jim reflected on the blessings he had. He knew there were guys on that very ship who had it much worse off than he did. He was alive, safe and heading back to the west coast. He had come through 1942 relatively unscathed. Luck.

187

They proceeded unescorted, without incident, all the way back to San Francisco and disembarked on Treasure Island, a man-made island in San Francisco Bay, built in the late 1930s for the Golden Gate International Exhibition. A survivor's camp had been set up for those returning from the Pacific who had lost their ships. When Jim was first told that he was to reside in another survivor's camp, his heart sank. "Oh no, not another one," he thought. But, as it turned out, it was not a tent city. They were assigned to a dormitory style building. Jim was assigned a bunk and a locker and settled in.

From Left, Dorothy Maguire, Jennie Chamberlin, Claire Brennan (Bride), Lionel Turcotte (Groom), Fred Turcotte, and Walter "Bud" Turcotte.

There was some additional good news for one of The Three Turks at the end of 1942. On December 26, 1942, at 4:00 p.m., Lionel Turcotte married Claire Brennan at St. Rita's rectory in Lowell. The Rev. Dennis J. Maguire, pastor, performed the ceremony. Lionel was dressed in his Navy uniform. Claire was wearing a white taffeta gown with a sweetheart neckline and fingertip veil. She carried a white shower bouquet of roses and sweet peas. Her aunt, Jennie Chamberlin, was maid of honor and her friend, Dorothy Maguire, was a bridesmaid. Walter "Bud" Turcotte, Lionel's youngest brother, was best man. He was just 16 years old. Lionel's Uncle Fred Turcotte was usher. Following the ceremony, a small quiet reception was held at the home of one of Claire's aunts. For her going away, Claire wore a white jersey dress with matching accessories.

Bobby Turcotte Goes Missing, Lionel Turcotte Goes To Dutch Guiana, and Jim Turcotte Goes To Harvard

On February 11, 1943, aboard the USS *Cincinnati*, Bob was recognized for meritorious conduct by saving two more planes:

> *On January 18, 1943, on the occasion of a casualty to the Cincinnati plane number 5760 resulting in the capsizing of the plane and again on February 8, 1943, on the occasion of a casualty to the Cincinnati plane number 5341 resulting in its capsizing, Robert Turcotte, without hesitation and without regard for his own personal safety, dove into the water and secured a hoisting line to the hub of the propeller of each plane, thereby enabling the personnel of the Cincinnati to salvage the plane in each instance. It is considered that Turcotte's intelligence, initiative and prompt action on each of these occasions enabled the Cincinnati to save important strategical equipment which might otherwise be lost. The Commanding Officer takes pleasure in commending you for your action on this occasion, which is in keeping with the best traditions of the Naval Service.*

> *E.M. Senn,*

> *Captain, U.S. Navy*

Bob was being recognized for a second time. On this commendation, he was acknowledged for diving into the water on two different dates, saving two planes. He had now singlehandedly saved three planes for the U.S. Navy during wartime. Planes were in high demand and short supply. He had saved the Navy thousands of dollars and repeatedly kept the *Cincinnati* from losing its scout planes.

He wrote to his father at the New England Aircraft School. The letter was dated February 7, 1943:

At Sea.

Hello Dad,

It has really been quite a lengthy period pass [sic] from my last writing to the school. Words fail me. I have been sitting here for a full half hour and still trying.

Some time ago it was mentioned in a letter received from home that you have an additional class at Harvard. It seems that your classes are forever expanding. I would give my right arm to attend any advanced class.

Lionel it seems has already left the 985's finding himself in something larger. The school he is attending is something knew to [sic] I have no idea what it could be. He has never stayed in one place much longer than a year. Pretty fortunate I must say. Here's hopping [sic] that he never finds himself on the sea.

Yes Dad I am afraid it may be another three years before I see Jim. In more ways than one he is a very lucky kid. You by this most likely know more about it than I. Believe me for a little better than a month that fellow really had me worried. As Sis said she was just dying to see him and I know. The train never carried across the country fast enough. I explained before that I shall not be able to see him this trip so until lady luck affords the opportunity my fingers are crossed.

In this envelope you most likely found the picture. Where it was taken I cannot say. The other fellow is W.J Musso a first class radioman who is my closest friend aboard ship. His home is in Lynn Mass. Several times he has made the trip up to Boston with me while we were in N.Y. last.

Your gifts were all received and I want to thank you for them. That pipe and tobacco really came at a most opportune time.

Our birds are just about due for recovery so until this lazy right hand again yields the mighty pen I say Au' Revoir. Give Jim my regards.

#2Bob

Again, Bob doesn't even mention saving any of the planes. Clearly, he knew his father's love for planes and aviation, yet he never mentioned his heroics to his father in his letters. Either he was too humble or it was a topic that couldn't be discussed due to wartime censors, most likely the former. Either way, it looked like his summers spent swimming at Mud Pond had really paid off.

Bob followed up shortly with a letter to his mother dated February 13, 1943:

In Port

Dear Mom,

Yesterday February 12, I got the biggest surprise of my life. In twenty two years there has been none so prominent. As yet I (felt) feel that I am in no position to tell you, I want to be absolutely sure of myself. If the Captain had hit me with a baseball bat I do believe the reaction would have shown little difference. The only thing I shall say is that you had better tell Lionel to be on his toes???

He had just found out that Lionel's wife was expecting and Lionel was going to be a father. You can feel his excitement in his words:

Things here aboard the Cincy are at the present pretty much the same. I sleep plenty, eat enough and work too much but such is my life. The more work the shorter the day. Here's to hoping they all get shorter.

What does Jim look like? Has he changed a great deal? I'm sorry he was unable to see Lionel in Burbank it would have been a long waited for reunion. Myself I am afraid I (will) shall miss him, for it is an impossibility for me to get home. If you take any snap shots would you send me one. It will be three years the twentieth of this month since last having seen him or his picture. I'll bet he is no longer the little kid I remember.

Speaking of pictures, I remember one day back in June, the specific day I am no sure of. It was a weekend spent in the picturesque mountains of Vermont. Yes and I believe there was quite a number of pictures taken there. Would you send me a copy of those along with Jim's. I would really like to see him.

It seems that Helen is spending a deal more time [sic] than I do. If I am not careful I'll find her a more prominent member of the family than myself. You write and tell me what Gram and Grandad think of her. Sis wrote and told me what thinks [sic] of her and Mary also has. Your opinion is the only one not yet voiced, tell me Mom, what do you think of her. They say you profit by the mistakes of others, isn't it true.

Time I turned in on this thirteenth day so give my love to the gang and you'll hear from me again in the very near future.

Love

Bob.

It is interesting that, for the first time, Bob mentioned his girlfriend, Helen, in a letter home. Time away from home, family and loved ones takes its toll on sailors, especially when they're on sea duty. Days are long, there are only a very limited number of people encountered and they feel far more isolated. Now, with his older brother married and expecting, Bob was clearly starting to think more seriously about his girlfriend and their future. Helen was spending a lot of time at the Turcotte household and they were getting to know her quite well. Bob was interested in his mother's and grandparent's opinion of Helen. In addition to missing his girl, he hadn't seen his brother Jim in three years. It is clear by the content and the frequency of the letters, Bob missed his girlfriend, his brothers, and his family. In many ways, his service had greatly matured him, but he was still a 22-year-old kid from Lowell, far away from home.

Bob again wrote his father at the New England Aircraft School:

February 17, 1943
At Sea

Hello Dad,

A few days ago I received your letter of the twenty ninth. It seems that someone has misled you for your guess was wrong. Who was the fellow?

You spoke of several in the post. There is something rotten in Denmark for this is the first received in quite some time. Maybe I shouldn't say Denmark for we both know the answer. Ship them all airmail.

That sinking of Jim's ship sure did have me worried for quite some time. Eventually mom sent the letter telling of the phone call. So help me that was one big relief. I'm very sorry that I'll not be able to walk in the front door but seeing as I have waited for three years I can wait a little longer.

Lionel it seems is forever on the go to always return. I can't understand how one guy can have so much luck. When

194

he does get back let me know as soon as possible. There is a little something I would like to have him do for me. At present his address is unknown and I would like to have him complete this little job before he shoves off again.

I want to thank you for your compliments directed at Helen. It seems that the family know her better than I. I don't know whether to expect an introduction, whenever I do get back or not. Seriously Dad I shall have to agree with you on that score.

Everything here just as busy as hell. So help me Lionel may have called an OS a lemon but he does not know the half of it. They sure give a guy a mean headache.

Stow an extra gallon of gas away occasionally for I may be home sometime this year.

Sure wish I could see Lowell with all that snow.

#2Bob

The "OS" Bob was referring to was the Vought OS2U, the Kingfisher, which was the main shipboard observation aircraft used by the Navy during World War II. This was the plane that Bob was often in as a crew member aboard the *Cincinnati*. Some 1,519 of the aircraft were built. It served on battleships and cruisers and was a catapult-launched floatplane. The Kingfisher had several variant models and configurations throughout the war. Due to its light engine, the performance of the aircraft was modest. The purpose of the Kingfisher seaplane was largely observation and rescue, but it was also involved in anti-submarine patrols, helping battleships hit their targets, and for mail runs.

On March 16, 1943, Bob was appointed aviation chief machinist mate. He was excited to tell his dad. He wrote a letter to his father, addressed to the aircraft school. The letter is dated March 20, 1943:

At Sea

Hello Dad,

Once again I find myself yielding a humble pen. This time with a specific reason. In my last letter you may remember my mentioning the fact that the future would hold a bit of good news. It's that time I had been recommended for Chief. Now I feel safe in letting out the news for a few days ago the [illegible] came from the Bureau and I now find myself an Aviation Chief machinist. Yes another rung on the ladder is below me, how and why is a long story so rather than making a poor attempt at writing I shall save it and someday tell you all about it.

Mom tells me that you too will be making a change in your uniform. She explained that when you were asked about it you simply said "I shall be wearing two stars on my shoulders, draw your own conclusions." Well, I too find myself loaded with suppositions but they shall not be voiced until further word is received. I'm hoping for the best.

Jim it seems is still having lady luck turn the tide on him every time he has a chance to meet Lionel or myself. Him not being able to see him in Penn Station just about topped it all. That has been the closest he has come to either of us in three years. February tenth three years ago was the last time I saw him and it has been quite a bit longer since I saw Lionel. Here's hoping he stays put for a few months.

I also spoke of having Lionel do me a favor when he returned to Quonset. Now that he is not stopping there and his future address is unknown I shall have to ask you to do it for me. I was about to have him order and send me some uniforms but now my only choice is you.

He gave his father, in great detail, the various measurements, the number and type of uniforms he needed, the color, the types of buttons, the rating badges he needed, the types of ties, and the names of the two stores in Boston where he could purchase them.

Well Dad that just about covers my immediate necessity and I hope it does not inconvenience you too much.

Thank you very much Dad and do let me know of your status. The money for these you can take from my bank account.

Say hello to the gang.

#2Bob

Bob, left, and Lionel, right.

In a letter from his father dated May 10, 1943, his father told Bob that he had sent him the box of uniforms on May 3, 1943. Enclosed in the package of uniforms was a gift to Bob, a pen and pencil set. It was a congratulations gift from his dad for Bob's promotion: "I'm sure proud of you son. Someday I hope to hear about how you got it. I'm sure there is a story behind it."

Back home, things were busy for their father. Herman Turcotte was the Coordinator of Training at the New England Aircraft School at the time. With the war on, there were a lot of students attending the program. He was also teaching a class at Harvard. In addition, he had three boys in the Navy to whom he tried to write. He tried to keep the house up and in good order. And he tried to be a father to his four other children still at home. It was not easy for him. He felt that he needed to keep a brave face on and appear to be the stable foundation of the family.

On May 14, it seemed that his mother was trying to write to all her boys. She wrote a letter to Bob but mailed it to Jim. When Jim received the letter, he knew it was an error, so he wrote his brother as well and sent both letters to Bob. At that time, Jim was aboard the USS *Iowa*. His letter was short, explaining the circumstances:

May 19, 1943

Hi Rob,

You will be surprised to find a letter enclosed written by mom but I'll explain what happened. She wrote a letter to you but put your name on the envelope with my address. As soon as I saw the envelope I knew that there was a mistake somewhere.

It will be delayed a little longer than it would have been but as soon as I found that it was your letter and not mine, I mailed it right off.

I haven't anything else to say that I may still get a chance to get home for a weekend, and that I also received a letter from Davy Gerow. Have you seen him at all lately?

I'm closing in order to get this letter of mom's off to you. Best of Luck.

your brother,

Jim #3.

Bob hadn't seen Jim since February 10, 1940, after Bob had finished basic training and before Jim had joined up. A lot had happened to the "Three Turks" since.

In his mother's portion of the letter, dated May 14, 1943, it read:

Dear Rob,

It is now quarter past ten and I do not feel the least bit sleepy so I will drop you a line. I got your letter of the 3rd and Pa got your letter of the 5th today. I only hope you get the uniforms in good condition. You should the way we packed and repacked them about a hundred times.

Mary worked at the Giant Store tonight and now she has gone dancing. Bud goes down the Rex roller skating. He is bugs about it. He goes two or three times a week. When Jim was home he went with Bud a few times and enjoyed it very much. Speaking of Jim he did not get much of a break while he was in that certain city. He called every weekend but did not get home once.

Oh, say, was Dot the big shot today. The school bought a jeep with the bonds the kiddos got, so she had a ride with some other kids in the jeep. She is doing well in school and next year she goes into the seventh grade. Sunday May 23rd

*she is making her confirmation. Does it seem possible to you
that she is old enough for that? Dot is getting to look more
like Sis every day.*

*Sis is doing fine. In her work and still likes it very much
and once in a while she gets quite tired and thinks nothing
ever goes right. Just now she and another girl have 35 babies
to take care of, feed, change and keep from crying. Some
fun. Pa asked Sis where the brick was that he bought for the
new part of the hospital. She told him it must have been that
gold brick that Souzy the other nurse had yesterday. I guess
you know what I mean.*

*I am trying to answer all the things you asked about. Mrs.
Westing did not come to Lowell, but if you look closely you
will see that I addressed that Easter Card and all except the
name. She sent me a swell letter and asked me to forward
the card for her as she had lost your address. I sent her a
letter last week when I wrote you boys I sent her one.*

*Uncles Arthur Turcotte and Ernest and Henry Rouseau
and some other fellow are going to have a Victory Garden
up on Julie's farm this summer. I can just imagine the kind
of garden they will have. Not any one of them knows a hoe
from a rake.*

*Some of these days that dog of Em's is going to be among
the missing when she comes home. He went for Bud again
today but he grabbed him by his collar. After Bud went by
he came for me and I threw him out doors and that is where
he stayed until she came home. I am certainly not going to
put up with that all summer long I will tell you.*

*I think I have answered all your questions so I will say
goodnight and hit my sack as you would say in the Navy.*

*That Richard is a distant cousin of yours, but so distant
you need not mention it or he will be apt to hit you up for*

your lose change. Sis says the whole family as just as loud as he is so don't worry about Sis.

Love to all.

Ma

P.S. I have forgotten to put this in the last two letters but I won't forget this one.

Bob wrote to both his parents in a letter dated May 22, 1943. He used the new pen his father had sent him for becoming aviation chief machinist mate. The ink on the letter was dark and legible:

Dear Mom & Dad,

Some time ago Dad brought it to my attention that my letters were not specific on one certain count. It seems that I have never mentioned my health and that you were all quite concerned about it. So this second paragraph shall be devoted to that important topic.

At present one would find me in the very best of health, as a matter of fact in the past few weeks I have gained a few pounds. Visually there has been not the slightest change. Picture me as you had last seen me and you shall see your number two son as he is today. Yes I still believe my most serious illness in twenty two years has been the measles.

Lionel once again finds himself enjoying the Florida sunshine. April 15th, he wrote and from his letter he and Claire are quite happy. How that older brother of mine gets all the breaks is one thing I shall never be able to understand.

Jim has not been heard from for some time which makes me think he is once again underway. Believe me that kid has gone through a lot and I do hope he stays clear for a few months.

How is the gang doing in school. Here I am speaking of the gang in school and stopping to think about it, there are only three left. On one more month they shall be again enjoying a vacation. What is a vacation??

Dad it seems that a measurement was forgotten. It makes no difference for I can have that finished aboard. Thank you once again for sending them, I shall expect to receive them soon.

Mrs. Westing sent an Easter card from Lowell, did she drop in to see you Mom?

Tell Dot to pick up a pen one of these days for it has been a considerable length of time pass[sic] from her last writing.

I must say hello to Helen so until the near future-

Love

Bob

Before he went to bed, Bob wrote his girl, Helen, a letter. Little did they know at the time, it would be her last letter from him.

In early June 1943, the USS *Cincinnati* was steaming in the South Atlantic Ocean along with the USS *Omaha* patrolling for German U-Boats and blockade runners as well as assisting U.S. convoys with safe passage. The *Cincinnati* was approximately 1,000 miles East of Curibita, Brazil. The ship was catapulting each of its two floatplanes on two missions per day searching for enemy contacts. Bob was always on one of the two planes.

On June 4, the planes were launched at 6:45 a.m. and flew an approximately 3 ½-hour mission. This mission was uneventful and the planes were recovered and brought aboard to be refueled. The next mission that day would not be so routine.

At approximately 11:45 a.m. both planes catapulted into a second flight mission from the *Cincinnati*. Bob's plane was sent from the port side. The mission was planned to cover an area of 335 miles and would last for 3 ½ hours, with the plane traveling at a speed of 100 knots. The plane was fueled with 140 gallons of petrol which, at the specified speed, should have lasted at least six hours. At approximately 4:47p.m. the companion aircraft landed and was recovered. The crew of the *Cincinnati* anxiously waited for the second plane to return, but Bob's plane was nowhere in sight. They attempted to locate it and bring it in by homing procedure. The experience of the pilot and the conditions of the sea and wind were all conducive for a landing at sea. At 5:43 p.m., the plane radioed the ship telling them they had to land at sea. The crew of the *Cincinnati* believed it was quite possible that Bob and his pilot, Sidney Goodman, were adrift at sea. At 5:45p.m., the *Cincinnati* fired star shells, expending sixteen three-inch .50 caliber rounds attempting to signal the missing plane. They immediately began searching for it. At 7:13 p.m., a message was received from the plane, "I must land." No further contact was had. The *Cincinnati* and the Omaha searched for the men over the course of June 5-7. They covered an area of 160 miles by 160 miles daily without success in either locating the plane or establishing any contact with the crew. The Navy searched nearly 40,000 square mile of ocean looking for Bob's plane. The weather during these three days was excellent. The sea was smooth and the visibility was between 15-20 miles. Not a single clue was found – no wreckage, no oil slick, nothing. They seemed to have vanished into thin air.

It would take approximately ten days before the Navy sent Bob's parents a telegram. The telegram arrived at 113 Varnum Avenue on June 14, 1943. It was a moment that every father or mother dreads when they have sons in the service of their country during wartime. One can only imagine. It read:

"The Navy Department deeply regrets to inform you that your son Robert Thomas Turcotte Aviation Chief Machinist Mate, U.S. Navy, is missing as result of not returning from airplane flight at sea while in the performance of his duties and in service of his country..."

Missing, it said, not dead. For Herman, there was the slightest glimmer of hope. Maybe since his disappearance, he had been located. Herman heard stories all the time about guys being found, despite the odds. He clinged to hope because there was nothing else but hope. He immediately dashed off a letter to Bob:

Hi Robbie boy,

The Navy Dept. just sent mom a telegram that scared the living daylights out of the whole gang of us. It simply stated that you failed to return from a flight and were listed as missing, while in the performance of duty.

Sonny if prayers will keep you well and fit you will surely pull through this one. I know you have had some mighty tough assignments and I also know that you have put everything you have got into it from the very beginning.

You may be having a terrible time of it at this very minute but some-how I have the feeling that you will lick all obstacles and will pull through all right. Nothing in this world is going to shake my faith in that assertion.

We are all anxious to get word of your safe return you can rest assured of that, so write as soon as you can to alleviate all fears. You have been away from us for a long time Rob but even though the distance we have been mighty close to one another. We always will. No matter what is in store for us.

About a year ago this time you came home to us for a little while, Remember? Jim expects to pull into port some time near the last of this month or the first of next as I told you in my last letter. Here is hoping that you get that furlow [sic] at the same time. We sure will have a swell time even though we cant [sic] go on a trip as we did the last time.

How about those uniforms that I sent you? Did you get them o.k. Write soon son, we are anxiously waiting. The gang send you the best of everything and until I see you, loads of love from,
Your Dad

The letter was returned, undelivered.

Within an hour of receiving the telegram, Bob's father went and picked up Bob's girlfriend, Helen Viera, and brought her to the Turcotte house to be with the family. Helen took the news hard. She had spent so much time with the Turcotte family. It is hard to imagine what it must have been like for her. One minute she was young and in love, waiting for Bob's return. The next minute he's gone . . . missing in action. She had been spending a lot of time with the Turcotte family while he was away serving his country and had become very close to them, almost a member of the family. Helen couldn't get any "official" word about Bob from the Navy because they weren't married. Like Bob's mother, Helen must have hung on every possible hope she could that Bob would be found alive and be returned to her safely.

Bob's Navy record described what happened in a cold, precise military fashion:

"June 4, 1943: Missing at Sea

(1) Circumstances as follows: At 1630 zebra June 4, 1943 with *Cincinnati* in latitude 27-02 south longitude 27-37 west OS2U-2 Type Airplane BU.No 5450, with Lt. (jg) S.G. Goodman pilot and Turcotte as passenger failed to return following a routine 320 mile scouting flight. At 1733 zebra radio communications was established with the plane and lost plane procedure conducted by COMCRUDIV-TWO in the *Omaha*. At 1750 zebra having been unsuccessful in making radar contact on the plane OTC commenced homing procedure, at 1913 all attempts at locating the plane were unsuccessful, a message was received as follows: "I must land." No further messages were received from the plane and extensive search operations were conducted by *Omaha* and *Cincinnati* aircraft from dawn to dusk on June 5th, 6th and 7th in the most probable areas. Search was abandoned at darkness on the 7th of June due to a shortage of ship's fuel. In view of weather conditons in this area (sea scale 4; wind southeasterly; beaufort force 3; visibility 14 miles) it is considered possible that the plane could have made a safe landing and that Lt (jg) Goodman and Turcotte

are adrift either in the plane or in their life raft, nearest land being Brazil 810 miles due west.

(2) Circumstances:

(a)Missing at sea in line of duty

(b)Next of kin: Father-Herman Oswald Turcotte, 113 Varnum Avenue, Lowell, Massachusetts

NOT NOTIFIED BY THIS COMMAND.

(c)Pay and allowance per month totaling $236.25

(d)Beneficiary: Mother-Mrs. Helen Gertrude Turcotte, 113 Varnum Ave. Lowell, Massachusetts

(e)Holds $1,000 Government Life Insurance 20 pay life, last premium paid for June 1943 by allotment. Holds $9,000 National Service Life Insurance term policy, last premium paid for June 1943 by allotment.

(f)Effects being held on board pending instruction from next of kin as to desired disposition."

Captain E.N. Senn, the man that only months before had recognized Bob for his actions in saving three planes wrote Bob's father, Herman. The letter, dated June 19, 1943, provides only minor additional details:

Dear Mr. Turcotte,

It is with deep regret that I must inform you of the circumstances concerning the disappearance at sea of your son Robert Thomas Turcotte Aviation Chief Machinist Mate.

On the afternoon of June 4, 1943 one of the ship's planes with Lt. 9jg) Sidney George Goodman as pilot and your son, R.T.T. as a passenger, failed to return to the ship after a routine three-hundred-mile scouting flight. At four o'clock, one hour after the plane was expected to return, radio communication was established and effort was made to guide it back to the ship. Continuous effort for more than one and a half hours brought no result and at 5:45 pm. A message was received from Lieutenant Goodman, "I must land." This was just before sunset and was the last message received. Aircraft from this ship and an accompanying ship searched continuously from dawn to dusk on June 5th, 6th and 7th to no avail.

At sunset on the 7th it was necessary to abandon the search, an area of nearly 40,000 square miles having been carefully searched.

In view of the circumstances your son has been reported to the Navy Department as "missing as sea, in the line of duty."

I express my own and the sentiments of all your son's shipmates in conveying my deepest sympathy for you in your great loss.

Sincerely,

E.N. Senn,

Captain, U.S. Navy

Commanding

Bob's parents received a lot of official mail concerning Bob's death, including a letter from Rear Admiral J.S. McCain, the grandfather of Senator John McCain. In his letter dated July 9, 1943, he wrote:

My Dear Mr. and Mrs. Turcotte:

The sad news that your son Aviation Chief Machinist Mate Robert Turcotte is missing from an operational flight has been reported to me. I fully realize your anxiety and grief and want you to know that you have my sincere sympathy.

Words are of little help at such a time, but it is my fervent hope that the knowledge of your son's loyalty to our country and his patriotic participation in the essential work of the aviation branch of its defense forces will comfort you in your sorrow.

I wish to extend to you the deepest sympathy of the officers and men of naval aviation.

Sincerely Yours,

J.S. McCain,

Rear Admiral, U.S. Navy

Chief of the Bureau of Aeronautics

Brother of Naval Hero Missing

Robert T. Turcotte Believed Aboard Plane Which Crashed

LOWELL—Brother of a man who fought through seven major naval battles without injury, C. P. O. Robert T. Turcotte, 22, son of Mr. and Mrs. Herman O. Tur-

Robert Turcotte

cotte, 113 Varnum avenue, was today officially listed as missing in action.

Released by the war department as a war casualty, Turcotte, a chief aviation machinist's mate, was known to have been on a

Brother of Naval Hero Missing

Continued From Front Page

flight in the South Atlantic prior to June 14. The telegram from the war department, informing his parents, was received here June 14, and was released yesterday.

Turcotte, one of three brothers now serving in the navy, enlisted almost four years ago. His last letter home was date-marked May, and his last visit home came more than a year ago.

He is a brother of James H. Turcotte, whose battle exploits in the South Pacific area were featured in a Sun story last February, when he was home on leave. Jim survived seven major battles and in addition, although this fact was not released to the public until last month, was know nto have been aboard the navy task force from which Jimmy Doolittle and his fliers took off to bomb Tokio more than a year ago. His ship was sunk off the Solomons last fall.

A third Turcotte brother, Lionel H., is also in the navy, and a fourth brother is planning to enter this year. Turcotte's father, a veteran of the last war, is now employed as co-ordinator of flight classes for New England Aircraft, Boston.

Turcotte's mother stated today that she believed her son was aboard a two-passenger reconnaissance plane when the crash came.

Lowell Sun, June 30, 1943

On the Fourth of July, 1943, a couple, George and Blanche Kellog, wrote Bob's mother on stationary from the San Diego Club:

Dear Mrs. Turcotte-

With deep regret-We learned of your son Robert ("Turk" to us)-was reported "missing" by the Navy Dept. That word "missing" does hold out a ray of hope for you and all who knew him and until such time as some definite report is received and while there is even the remotest hope let us all believe and pray he is well and safe somewhere.

In these trying times, confusion prevails and until the last chapter of this awful war is written will we know the truth. And it is often said where there is life there is hope and that word "missing" is still your lifeline of hope.

We will still look forward to both ("our") Bill and Turk dragging anchor here in San Diego Bay some one of these days.

The *Lowell Sun*, which announced Lionel and Claire's wedding on Monday December 28, 1942, indicated that, after an extended wedding trip, the couple would live in Rhode Island.

The Navy had other plans and the honeymoon was a short one. On January 6, 1943, Lionel received orders to depart for Naval Training School, Aeronautical, in Burbank, California. It was a temporary assignment for approximately one month. He was going to spend some time at Lockheed, a major manufacturer of fighters and bombers. The Lockheed Vega factory was located next to Burbank's Union Airport, which Lockheed had purchased in 1940. During the war, the entire area was camouflaged to fool enemy aerial reconnaissance. The factory was hidden beneath a huge burlap tarpaulin painted to depict a peaceful semi-rural neighborhood, complete with rubber automobiles. Hundreds of fake trees, shrubs, buildings and even fire hydrants were positioned to give a three-dimensional appearance. The trees and shrubs were created from chicken wire treated with an adhesive and covered with feathers to provide a leafy texture. Lionel arrived in Burbank on January 13, 1943 and spent the month training on the Lockheed Ventura PV-1. As bad luck would have it, unbeknownst to him, he missed an opportunity to meet up with his brother Jim by just a couple of days and a few hundred miles. His brother was in San Francisco, having just returned from the Pacific.

On February 18, 1943, Lionel was initially ordered to report to Fleet Airwing Twelve, Naval Air Station, DeLand in DeLand, Florida.

On March 1, 1943, Lionel became part of Bombing Squadron 131, a medium bombing squadron flying the PV-1 Ventura. Most of the pilots were from PBY Catalina and OS2U Kingfisher inshore patrol squadrons and were unfamiliar with the Ventura. Lionel, on the other hand, had become quite familiar with the PV-1 from his time at Lockheed. It definitely gave him a leg up. The primary mission and training for the squadron was anti-submarine warfare (ASW).

A Ventura PV-1 Bomber hunts submarines, c. 1943.

Lionel shot off a letter to his mother and father:

May 6, 1943

Orange City, Florida

Dear Mom + Dad

How's tricks way up in Massachusetts? (as they say here) Are all the kids doing alright in school? Do you know I haven't had a single letter from them since I have been here. Boy am I going to ball them out next time I see them.

Everything is going along fine down here although a week ago I had a mighty sick young lady on my hands. But everything came out O.K. she is sitting over on the bed writing to her Mom and I'm at the desk here writing to mine.

Claire is going to go home if I have to go to boca Chica. So if you get a visitor around the last of the month don't be surprised. I hope we don't go though and we may not have to as they have stopped delivery on these planes and probably won't get any more for some time. We are having trouble enough to keep the five we have flying. They've given us more trouble than you can shake a stick at. I am about fed-up with them. I think I've got to go the Jax tomorrow with a propeller that won't unfeather. We've tried all we know and are still stumped so we bring it to the (the)prop shop. Si! So I'm elected I guess.

I said hello to Claire tonight about 4:30 on my way back from Sanford from about 500 ft. at 300 miles an hour. She said she thought we were coming right in to see her. I was on a raiding tour trying to get some tail wheel tires.

How are things going with you, Dad? Still showing the "wrappies" a thing or two? Had a P-38 and a P-40 in the other day and I still think a PV or should I say Ventura will still stay with them when it comes to speed. We did 420 the other day straight and level. Not bad huh? I never thought I'd get to go that fast in my life.

Well, folks, my little ol' sack is calling to me so I guess I'll turn in for a fast day to-morrow. Here's hoping to be seeing you someday soon.

Love to all

Lionel + Claire

P.S. I'll send the bill of sale as soon as I get it.

Lionel mentioned that Claire was sick. She was suffering morning sickness while expecting their first child.

On June 1, 1943, despite having received only four of its aircraft out of an assigned complement of 12, Lionel's squadron was transferred to Naval Air Station Boca Chica in Key West, Florida. They were being sent for intensive anti-submarine warfare training in preparation for operational deployment.

Lionel sent off a letter to his mom and dad:

June 3, 1943

Dear Mom and Dad,

This place takes the cake; all of it. Deland was a paradise in comparison to Boca Chica here. You can't sleep at night because of the mosquitoes and you can't sleep in the day because of the heat so you can see what we are up against. We don't know how long we'll here as it depends on whether or not we get the planes. When we do leave we won't be able to tell you as it will, of course, be a secret. They had quite a bit of trouble with information leaking out in some of the other squadrons so they are clamping down quite good now.

How's Claire? Has she been over to see you yet? I hope she got there all right and that everything is O.K. You keep me posted on how she is, huh Mom?

Dad, you want to watch out or I'll be as good as you on ignition one of these days. These engines we have have [sic] been giving us a lot of trouble here lately and so far I've made out O.K. But I don't know how long it will last. It's bad enough now I wonder what it will be like when we get more planes and no mechs.

I'm all set to go up for chief anytime they let me. I don't know when it will be but I'm ready right now. I'm already standing chief's watch in place of a man in the squadron who made chief. I don't know how long it will be for but I hope it is a sign of good luck.

Dad, I never have heard from those people concerning my automobile. If you could I'd really appreciate it if you could look up Commercial Credit Co. at 664 Commonwealth and see just what the score is. I think I'm getting a bum deal there or something. Anyway if you can, Dad, get the title and then sell it.

I'm going to quite now so I can go for a swim with the boys before it gets too dark. There is a swell swimming hole right at the end of the warm up mat. It's not too bad. It could be a lot worse and I'm still in the good ol' United States.

Well folks, I'll be seeing you again as soon as I can. Say hello to Claire for me too.

Loads of love,

Lionel

P.S. Hello Doty. How are ya'?

In a letter to his father dated June 27, 1943, Lionel never mentions his brother Robert. It appeared that he did not yet know that his brother has been declared missing in action. Instead, he was dealing with his own burdens, with his wife expecting and him far from home. In the letter, he wrote:

U.S.N.A.A.F.

Boca Chica, Fla

Dear Dad,

I am sorry that I am not up to date with my correspondence but as soon as we get squared away I'll try to do better.

Don't say anything to Claire just yet, but I think that tonight I'll be spending my last night in the good old U.S. I don't know where we are going but we be gone by tomorrow night. Kinda have the kids or someone watch out for Claire now and then and I will feel a lot better about her. All I want is to be back here in the states when the young one is born.

Everything is okey dokey other than the fact that we are leaving. The planes have been grounded for three days to get them in shape for the trip, other than test hops.

I've got one of the new planes for the hops and it is in 4.0 shape. Not a thing wrong with it. I don't know all there is to know about these bills of sale, Dad, but I did the best I know how. I hope that it is what you want and that it will be O.K.

How is Mom and the kids? Did Mary pass her exam for the hospital? I sure wish I was up that way again. As soon as I can I will be too.

I am going to quit now, Dad, as we have had quite a day today loading planes, etc. and will need all the sleep I can get tonight. As soon as I get situated I'll drop you a good line and let you in on all the dope I can what with the censors, etc.

Your #1 son,

Lionel

P.S. You'll find my new address on the envelope   L.T.

He enclosed a bill of sale for a 1937 two-door Chevrolet in the amount of $150.00 to his father. It made sense. Lionel sold his car to his father. A car was a luxury he and his wife could not afford. Lionel was on his way to his new assignment, he was a newlywed, and he had a baby on the way. He needed the money.

On July 1, 1943, Lionel got a big shot in the arm. Lionel's rating was advanced to aviation chief machinist mate. Although he could not be a pilot, he qualified in all other respects as plane captain in a PV-1 type plane. As a result, Lionel was assigned as crew chief of a Lockheed Ventura PV-1 Bomber. This is what he had been working for.

Lionel loved flying and he loved his crew. As the war progressed, he saw planes and men crash or not come back from missions. He and his mechanics worked tirelessly to make sure every mission would be as safe as it could be under the circumstances. They relied on each other to keep the planes and crew safe. As a unit, they had a good safety record.

Lionel, second row, second from right, with Ventura PV-1 Bomber and crew and mascot.

Aviation Chief Machinist Mate Lionel Turcotte

Later in July, Lionel found time to write his mother. By this time, he knew his brother has been listed as "missing in action:"

July 13, 1943

Dear Mom,

It was sure good to hear from you, Mom. I 'm glad to hear that Claire is doing well. I'm a little worried about her and its nice to know that you've a swell mom to look after the family while you're away.

Mom, I understand now the trouble we had with some of our correspondence. Today I received three letters, one from you, Claire and the other from Jimmy Sullivan. Claire's and yours are dated June 28 and Sully's from Feb. 15. His followed me all over the country and back again but I don't understand Claire's and yours. They must have just been in some P.O. box until they found where I was. I guess it has all been straightened out now so we'll try it and see.

Have you folks had any further word concerning Rob? I've got my eyes and ears open here and say a little prayer or two every night in hope for his safe return. If you hear anything let me know first thing, won't you Mom? Here's hoping we have some good news before too long a time.

There is nothing much I can tell you about the place here or what we are doing but we do have movies every night (old ones) and manage to play a little baseball or tennis now and then to keep in shape.

I sure was glad to hear that Mary had passed her entrance examination to the hospital. Sis ought to be about ready to sew up her R.N. degree by now, hadn't she? I hope for Mary's sake that she does as well as Sis and she'll get by O.K.

How are Dad and the Chev. Getting along? I hope he hasn't had too much trouble with it. It will be pretty good transportation if the tires hold out.

Well, Mom, I want to see the movie tonight and have to shower and shave yet so I'll leave you now. Keep me posted on how Claire is doing now and then as I don't want anything to happen to her. Take good care of yourself too, you know and let's don't have any more finger incidents.

Lots of love to the gang

Lionel

Effective July 21, 1943, Lionel, along with Bombing Squadron 131, was transferred to Fleet Air Wing Eleven (Hedron Detachment). It would be their job to find German submarines and U-Boats and take them out. They would fly patrol missions along the South Atlantic in the same general area where his brother Bob was lost.

His father wrote Lionel on the 18th of July 1943. In response, he wrote his dad a short letter on July 23, 1943:

Dear Dad,

Got your letter of the eighteenth the other day and just getting around to answering it now. As you have probably noticed by the return address I have been transferred and am no longer with the squadron. I am pretty well pleased with the swap and will tell you all about it sometime. In the meantime, I think that they'll have plenty for me to do.

We are going to take up golf in a day or two as soon as we get squared away to keep up with our

*exercises. So, you had better sharpen up your game
because one of these days----*

*I'm glad to hear that Jim likes his new ship. I only
hope that she is as good to him as his old one was. He
had quite a year on her but she brought him though
O.K.*

*I've tried to beat the lights, Dad, to dash it all out
but can't quite make it. I at least was able to let you
know the change of address though. So keep the letters
coming + I'll make mine a little longer next time.*
Love to the gang

Lionel

In September 1943, Herman and Helen heard from Captain
Senn. He wanted to relate that no further news about Bob had come
to light. It had been over three months since his plane went missing.
What little hope there was had faded. Bob's personal effects had been
shipped back to his parents at 113 Varnum Avenue, Lowell.

Meanwhile, back home in Lowell, Claire was due at the end
of November. On September 28, 1943, Lionel was temporarily
transferred to Naval Air Station Guantanamo Bay, Cuba. Almost
immediately thereafter, his unit, VB-131, detached from NAS
Guantanamo Bay to Naval Air Station San Juan for three weeks of
Anti-Submarine Warfare (ASW) training using radar for night
operations. During the entire deployment, only one submarine was
sighted, and it submerged quickly before coming into effective attack
range.

Upon completion of training in early October, Lionel and his
squadron were sent to a secret airbase, Zandry Field, in Dutch Guiana
(Suriname) in South America, for anti-submarine warfare and convoy
patrol duty. The field was shared with an Army detachment flying B-
25s, each armed with a 75mm cannon in the nose. Since the B-25s

had no radar, they flew only in daylight. Lionel's squadron, the VPB-131 crews, took the night shift.

Lionel wrote a two-page letter to his father in pencil, dated October 21, 1943. Clearly, Lionel was feeling the effects of not being with his pregnant wife, the loneliness of being away from his family, the nagging feeling of his brother missing in action, and the strain of his work:

Dear Dad,

Please don't mind the pencil as I'm doing this down on the line in a little spare time I've got. I've got all the ships in my section in good shape for a change therefore am able to get this off to you.

I am glad to hear you are over the tough luck you had are able to get back to work. I guess it's no fun to be laid up like that.

Claire told me about Jim getting his appointment and there is no one happier about it than I am. If there was any one man in this navy that deserved getting an appointment, I think it was Jim especially after what he went through in the last couple of years. He deserves every bit of it and a little more too.

Oh, I'm ok I guess, dad. Physically ok except for a little weight the sun has cut off but spiritually not worth a dam. I think you know just as well as I do what the trouble is and there isn't a thing in the world that will help out right now. Maybe before too long tho something will break and I'll get my chance and boy, when I do, watch out.

I am glad that you like the pictures, Dad. You see quite a while ago I took one from Mom and gave it to Claire so I promised them I'd send some so they could all have one. How about one of yourself? I haven't seen you in so long I've almost forgotten what you all look like. (joke)

I'm glad to hear Mary and Sis are doing so well at the hospital. You know dad, if Mary makes the grade there, that will do more for her than 50 million dollars. It would be just what she needs to make life worthwhile.

I sure wish as you do, Dad, that they'd make up their mind at the bureau just how things stand in Rob's case. Of course, I don't want to rush things any more than you do but I would like to know just the same.

No, dad I can't tell you very much about the future from this place but if I do get leave, you'll be seeing me, I promise. No one wants to get home anymore [sic] than I do this Dec. You know why too, I think.

So, the Army is still going along O.K., huh? I used to like that outfit pretty much up until a very short while ago. Now, you can have all of it you want. None for yours truly, thanks.

So Butch and Kitty are going to get married when he gets home, huh? Well, I always thought they would one of these days but it sure took a long time. Let's see, they were going together over five years ago that I can remember.

So they're still pretty hot on the gasoline situation there in the east. I'm still going to miss the ol' jalopy just the same. She used to wheeze around on a half -

gallon like nobody's business. Guess I'll have to buy a new one after this business is over.

I'll have to knock off now, Dad, as I've got some business to attend to. I'll see what can be done about getting to see you but I don't want you to count too much on it though.

Love to the gang,

Your #1 son,

Lionel

Flying in bombers was dangerous work and it would get more dangerous as time went on. As with any wartime air unit, the more missions flown, the greater the risk. The statistics start to catch up to you. On October 23, 1943, Lieutenant (jg) Byron C. Kern and crew from one of the Ventura bombers in Lionel's squadron experienced instrument failure during a night mission and flew into the sea. One crewman was lost when the aircraft sank, although the rest were able to get into a life raft and were rescued the next day.

In a letter of November 1, 1943, it was clear that Lionel has had enough of Dutch Guiana:

Dear Dad,

I'm ok all right but as usual have had no love lost for the tropics. Give me that northern duty that I used to have and I'd be a much happier man for it. I always felt better while I was up there. If I ever get the chance again, I'm going to get burrowed so deep there they'll never get me out.

What's this electronics course you are taking, Dad? I've read quite a few short adds pertaining to it in books but never enough to give me a real good idea just what it is all about. How about some first-hand information if you can, huh Dad?

My travels that you speak of, Dad, seem to be curtailed to one spot right now. I hope, though, as you do that when I do get on the move again that they take me north. That's exactly what I am hoping for.

I am looking forward to having a good bull session with you about aircraft and engines, Dad. Of course, the Army has certain different methods than us but know I can certainly pick up some good dope from you. Too bad we haven't got an old engine we could tinker with the way we used to when we had the garage. I'd like very much to be able to go to a good carburetor school somewhere and get some advanced dope on them. Then if possible, a year on a test stand somewhere where I could get some experience on overhauled engines, such as trouble shooting and so on. That, I guess will have to wait though until after we get this job over with down here.

Dad, I don't want you folks to go to any bother to send me much of anything for Christmas as things are going to be pretty fouled up for the holidays. I mean by that the mail situation. I'd be plenty well pleased with just a card to let me know how you are. I do wish though that I was in a spot where I could something to you but my hands are sure tied here. I'm going to have Claire do that for me this year.

Things here are pretty well straightened out now or should I say I'm straightened out with things here and everything is going smooth. It could be a lot worse, so I'm going to keep up my end and hope that the end will come pretty soon. Speaking of the end of things, I hear that they lifted the blackout regulations in the states now. That's good news. I can just see New

Years and Boston. I'll bet they look like a couple of Christmas trees. I bet too that it will seem funny to drive with all of the use of the headlights again.

Boy, I can remember how that used to bother me, going back and forth to Boston, in the Chev. I'll bet it's a huge relief.

Dad, I've been moving around so much in the last six months that I just can't seem to really get any special buddies to chum around with. Don't get me wrong; I never have trouble making friends or anything but I no sooner do, it seems that I'm off again to another advanced base. I get along swell here with everybody and they're all a pretty swell bunch of fellows. There is one fellow that has been with me quite some time though. In fact, he was with me when we were in the old squadron. He's a comical dude and I get a lot of laughs out of him. We call him "Colonel" as he is from Kentucky. Bowling-Green to be exact. Ever hear of it? It's in the "bluegrass" region. He is a metalsmith; and a good one too. We make out pretty good together.

I got one of the pictures, Dad. One of Claire and Jim together and they both look mighty good to me. Hope I can see them both soon.

I'm gonna leave you now, Dad, as I want to write another letter before lights out and catch a little shut-eye. I'll write again soon so don't worry about me.

Love to the whole gang,

Your #1 son

Lionel

On November 9, 1943, Lieutenant John W. Powers returned from investigating a possible submarine contact at night to find Atkinson Field closed due to rain and fog. Lacking enough fuel to proceed to another airstrip, Powers ditched the aircraft in a river near Paramaribo, Dutch Guiana. While waiting in the water for eventual rescue, the crew observed one of the search planes flown by Lieutenant (jg) Robert G. Winthers crash practically on top of the site where they had just ditched their own aircraft. Winthers and his crew of five were killed in the crash. Lieutenant Powers and his crew were rescued the following day. The odds were starting to catch up to Lionel.

On November 30, 1943, Claire gave birth to Carol Ann Turcotte. She would call her Ann. Unfortunately, Lionel wasn't home for the birth. Most likely, she was accompanied to the hospital by her mother, Hazel Brennan, with whom she was living. Tragically, Ann was diagnosed with a blood disorder and, just 18 days later, died on December 17, 1943, at Lowell General Hospital. Lionel wasn't home for the funeral, either. On getting word, he put in for an emergency furlough. He was devastated that he was never able to see his daughter. He felt guilty that Claire had to go through all of this without him. Due to the circumstances, the Navy granted a short furlough. Lionel made it home before Christmas. He spent as much time as he could with Claire and his family.

While Lionel was home on leave, luck ran out for Lieutenant (jg) Byron C. Kern from his squadron and his crew of five aboard. They crashed on takeoff, resulting in the loss of all hands onboard on January 5, 1944.

Almost everything Jim owned was lost when the *Northampton* sunk. The only things he had left were the few items he picked up in New Caledonia – one clean pair of dungarees, some tee shirts, a couple of pairs of undershorts and his personal hygiene gear. That was it. Once he got to Treasure Island, he ordered new uniforms and gear, but it was going to take a few weeks to arrive. A lot of guys borrowed uniforms from other sailors who were stationed in San Francisco or on Treasure Island. He decided to wait and make do with what he had.

Jim, like many of that generation, was raised during the Great Depression. They knew what it was like to "make do" and be thankful for what little you had. He remembered having to carry two golf bags for 18 holes and put all the money in a "meat jar" so the family might get some protein once in a while. Jim felt pretty lucky to be where he was. He was going to make the best of it.

At the first opportunity, Jim made a call home and let his family know he was safe. Although it had been over a month since the sinking of the *Northampton*, it was the first opportunity he had to contact them, and he was sure they must be worried. When he called, he told them that his ship had gone down but didn't give them any of the scary details. He described the survivor's camp, again leaving out anything unpleasant that might upset his mother. Repeatedly, Jim assured his mom that he was doing just fine. He only had three minutes on the phone to get it all in.

This was the second time Jim had been to San Francisco without any money. He wasn't sure how long it would be before the Navy would straighten things out. They were still waiting for pay accounts and records to be sorted out with his old pal, George Allen. Of course, this was his first liberty back in the States in some time. There was a lot of, in Jim's words, "wahooping," parties and the like. It was liberty at its best. For the first time in a long time, Jim was without any serious concerns. He had a dry place to sleep, three square meals a day, and no one was shooting at him. Jim didn't have any money, but he made the best of it. He rested and enjoyed the time off. He went into the city whenever he could. There was still a curfew so even if he went into San Francisco, he had to return to the base every night. Every morning he had to report to his duty officer.

Throughout his time in the Navy, Jim had been communicating back home and with his brothers and sisters by letters. Often it took months for the mail to catch up to him. Jim's mail caught up with him at Treasure Island. It was there that he found out that his brother Lionel was at Lockheed in Burbank, just a few hundred miles from San Francisco. Jim wanted to see if he could try and visit his brother. It had been a long time since they had seen each other. Lionel was only going to be at Lockheed for a couple more weeks. Jim knew time was ticking away on this opportunity, but first he had to wait on uniforms and money – especially the money. Without that, he had no chance of seeing his brother.

It was late January 1943 when the uniforms arrived, and payday came around. Finally, things were looking up. However, at the same time Jim also received orders to report to New York to help put the USS *Iowa* in commission. He was going to be a plank owner of this brand-new battleship. Being a plank owner gives a sailor a special connection with a ship, as he's put her into service, and is part of her first crew.

It was going to be a little while before the *Iowa* was actually going to be commissioned, but they had to outfit her, stock her and prepare her for launching. So, the Navy put Jim on a train headed for New York. He was hoping the train would head south in California before heading east so he could see his brother. Instead, the train headed north into California. He wasn't going to be able to meet up with Lionel. So close, but yet so far. Only a few hundred lousy miles separated them. Another opportunity lost.

As always, Jim made the best of it. Once he arrived in New York, he still had some time before he had to report and was able to head home to Lowell for a short visit before reporting to the *Iowa*. He spent time with his mom and dad and his sisters and younger brother, Bud. His mother had heard about the sinking of the *Northampton* shortly after it happened. She had been so worried and was so relieved to now have him home, even if it was for a short while. She cooked and he ate. Boy, did he eat. He didn't miss a meal. Jim loved being back in Lowell. He ran over to Stoddard's bakery and had a few Black Moons. He visited neighbors and friends. They always offered him something to eat and he obliged. He attended Sunday mass at St. Rita's Church and visited with Father Maguire.

Before heading off to Brooklyn, he gave an interview to his hometown newspaper, the *Lowell Sun*. The article ran on Saturday, February 20, 1943. It was a long article that catalogued Jim's escapades in the Pacific. He regaled them with stories of some of his battles and the sinking of the *Northampton*. The article also mentioned his two other brothers in the Navy, Lionel and Bobby. The article made quite a splash. It read, in part:

21-Year-Old Local Sailor In Seven Major Sea Battles

James H. Turcotte Present When Wasp, Yorktown and Hornet Met Gallant Ends

By James F. Droney

LOWELL—He was in Pearl Harbor the day after the Jap surprise attack. He was there when the navy planes bombed Wotje island to rubble. He was part of the naval force that revenged the Wake Island marines by bombing Jap emplacements.

If he chose to, he could wear seven pins on his chest, each signifying a major naval engagement. His record reads like a history of the war in the Pacific, Wotje, Wake, Midway, the Solomons and Savo. Especially Savo because it was there that his ship was sunk under him and he floundered for hours, oil gagged and groggy, in the waters of the South Pacific.

Has Seen It All

He has seen it all, the only big battle his boat missed was the battle of the Coral sea, and they missed that because they were busy bombing an island less than 1000 miles from the Jap mainland.

Yes, he has seen it all, this 21-year-old, slight and trim sailor, James H. Turcotte. He was there when the Wasp went to the bottom, and when the Yorktown went down, and, too, when the Hornet was bombed and battered into a useless hulk.

In his mind and body and heart is imprinted with bloody ink the

James H. Turcotte

full story of the war in the Pacific. He has gone through every sort of naval warfare, air bombings, close ship to ship combat and the combination of both.

He has seen decks awash with blood, his pals killed and maimed. He has seen the Japs driven back

Continued on Page Six

Part of the article in the *Lowell Sun* February 20, 1943.

The funny part of it is when we went into Wotje, practically the entire crew was seeing action for the first

*time . . . They were green at the start but they soon polished
up and performed beautifully as a unit . . . I think our skipper,
officer compliment and crew were the best boatful of men in
the Navy . . . I think that accounts for our being able to go
through so many engagements without getting hit. We were
never scratched until that last one, off of Guadalcanal.*

At the end of the article, the reporter wrote:

"All things considered, the Turcotte family is probably
the fightingist group in the city, considering the number of
its members taking a direct part in the war, and the amount
of actual combat the men have seen. Jim's record alone is
enough for any three men. And he will be heading back
shortly to add to that record."

The battleship USS *Iowa*.

Jim boarded the *Iowa* in mid-February 1943. He made a lot of
new friends on the *Iowa*. He met guys like Mo Shifley. Mo had served
on the USS *Vincennes*. The *Vincennes* went down in the Battle of
Savo Island on August 9, 1942. The sinking of the *Vincennes* resulted
in some 322 men missing or dead. Mo was nearly trapped as the ship

was going down. As he tried to make his escape, he opened a watertight hatch only to find the sea rushing in on him. Miraculously, Mo was able to make his way out and over the side and was eventually rescued. Since both were "survivors," Mo and Jim immediately had a special bond. Another friend Jim made was Louie Shapiro, a transfer in from another base. The three became friends for life.

The *Iowa* was formally commissioned on February 22, 1943, with Captain John L. McCrea in command. Compared to the *Northampton*, as a battleship, the *Iowa* was huge. It was 887 feet long, 287 feet longer than the *Northampton*, and weighed approximately six times as much. It had approximately 151 officers and 2,637 enlisted men. She could cruise at 33 knots, had nine sixteen-inch guns, 20 five-inch guns, and as many more anti-aircraft weapons. The *Iowa* was a sight to behold and, in battle, a thing to be feared. On February 24, 1943, the *Iowa* put to sea for a shakedown cruise in the Chesapeake Bay and along the Atlantic coast. Jim turned 21 years old on February 27, 1943, just five days after the commissioning.

Throughout his time in the Pacific, Jim had decided that he wanted to be a naval officer. It had been quite a while since he was in formal schooling. But between battles and in his spare time, Jim had hit the books and studied as much as he could. He borrowed math and science books from the ship's library to refresh his knowledge. Finally, now that he was assigned to the Atlantic Fleet, Jim decided to send in his application for Officer Candidate School (OCS). Needless to say, it was an exciting month for him.

On April 22, 1943, a second article ran about Jim in the *Lowell Sun* concerning the *Northampton's* presence at Doolittle's Raid. Doolittle's Raiders had captivated the American public's imagination for months. No one was aware of how they pulled it off – until now. The U.S. government had just released information as to how they accomplished the mission. The *Lowell Sun* printed the details of the raid the day before, on April 21, 1943. Now Lowell had one of their own to be proud of as part of that invasion force.

Local Sailor Had Part in Tokio Attack

J. H. Turcotte Aboard Cruiser Northampton at Time of Take-off

LOWELL—Sons of Lowell have been in on every major event of the war so far, and just to keep the record clear, there was a Lowell boy mixed up in the year-old bombing of Tokio.

He is 21-year old James H. Turcotte, U. S. N., who was aboard the cruiser Northampton, part of the task force which surrounded the aircraft carrier Hornet, from

James H. Turcotte

which the planes were launched to bomb the capital city of the Japanese.

Jim Turcotte's story was told in this paper last February when he was home on a brief leave after his ship, the same Northampton, had been sunk in one of the Solomon Island battles. Jim related the history of the Northampton which was engaged in

Continued on Page Eleven

Until February 1943, when Jim was home on leave, his father had no idea that Jim was part of Shangri-La, despite his father openly speculating to Jim about how Doolittle and his Raiders had pulled it off. Jim just smiled inside. He hadn't told anyone about the Doolittle mission. He finally told his parents about it, just before leaving to board the *Iowa*. He swore them to secrecy until the details were released by the military. Once the government released the information, the newspapers went to Jim's parents, who told the press about Jim's involvement. At the time the article was published, Jim was in the Atlantic Ocean aboard the *Iowa*.

Nonetheless, the whole of Lowell was buzzing about another one of Jim's escapades in the Pacific. He would take quite a ribbing from his friends and extended family when he got back to Lowell about being there when Doolittle and his Raiders took off from the *Hornet*.

On May 1, 1943, Jim was promoted to storekeeper first class and it wasn't long before the *Iowa* was assigned to patrol the North Atlantic, based out of Casco Bay in Portland, Maine. Portland had a naturally deep port and was very large, allowing many large American warships to berth there at the same time. It was a perfect spot for a battleship the size of the *Iowa*.

Jim and the *Iowa* got back underway, heading for Argentia, Newfoundland. The *Iowa* was sent there to counter the threat of the German battleship *Tirpitz*, which was reportedly operating in Norwegian waters. The North Atlantic was cold, raw and damp, quite a change from the hot, tropical weather Jim was used to in the Pacific.

In addition, the Atlantic hurricane season was quite active beginning in August 1943. No sooner had the third hurricane dissipated when the fourth began forming. This new tropical storm was on the cusp of hurricane intensity when identified about 630 miles southeast of Bermuda on September 1. The system steadily strengthened as it moved erratically, attaining peak winds of 120 mph on September 4. It passed within 120 miles of Bermuda, delivering a period of strong tropical storm-force winds to the island. The hurricane's path directed north and then northeast. By that time, it turned into a Category 3 hurricane, barreling up the East Coast toward Newfoundland. It brushed Nova Scotia before moving ashore on the southern coastline of Newfoundland.

As luck would have it, the *Iowa* rode straight into the hurricane. Riding out any hurricane aboard a ship, no matter how big that ship is, is a very scary thing. You may recall that a ship either pitches or rolls or both. A battleship, like a carrier, only pitches as it plows throw the ocean. That means the ship moves up and down as it moves forward. Jim described the hurricane as one of the scariest things he had ever been through. And that was saying a lot. The bow rose and dove through the waves as the *Iowa* plowed through the hurricane. The waves crashed over the deck of the ship time and time again. As he stood watch on the bridge, Jim saw waves crash over the top of the mast in front of him.

No one was allowed on deck. Period. The sea was so rough anyone on deck would surely have been washed overboard. The wind was blowing at more than 100 mph. The rain was coming down in sheets and blowing sideways. It was difficult to even see what was going on outside the bridge. For Jim, this display of the awesome strength and power of nature was just as frightening as any battle he had gone through in the Pacific. He knew that if they had to abandon ship, the crew would not likely survive in this weather. He looked off to the starboard side and there was a little destroyer escort (DE) there. The waves were so big that the ship would completely vanish from his eyesight into the trough between waves, and then – ZOOM – she would pop up again into view. It seemed to Jim that the waves were 50 feet high or taller. The destroyer escort, like a destroyer, both pitches and rolls. This means they were going up and down and side to side, all through 40- to 50-foot waves. The *Iowa* was hit so hard during the storm that she lost two planes that were either blown off deck or washed off into the ocean.

Jim knew that if his battleship was getting hit this hard, then the men on that little escort must have really been battered around. The little DE kept repeatedly flashing signals to the *Iowa*, "slow down, slow down." But the *Iowa* kept pushing straight into the storm. They were trying to outrun it and get to safe harbor at Argentia.

Eventually, the *Iowa* arrived safely in Newfoundland and got into port to wait out the rest of the hurricane. As they arrived, two tugboats were tied to the bow and two were tied to the stern. The tugs remained under power and kept the *Iowa* steadied during the remainder of the storm to prevent the big ship from blowing aground. "It was quite a storm and quite a drill," Jim said. It was the only hurricane he was ever in at sea and he was glad it was the last.

The crew didn't go ashore their first few days in Newfoundland as everyone was ordered to stay aboard ship. Sailors assigned to the Navy base in Newfoundland hated it there. The weather was cold, damp, and raw. As the weather turned colder, they had to continually scrape ice off the decks of the ships and would be exposed to the elements for long periods. They couldn't seem to escape the weather. First it got in their bones. They never felt like they could warm up. Then it got in their heads. They would do almost anything to get members of the *Iowa* crew to swap duty with them. The sailors came to the *Iowa* and literally offered money to the sailors aboard to take their place. Some even dropped to their knees, begging and praying to switch places. Jim had never seen anything like it. Forget the proper procedure for transfer, they were desperate to get rid of that cold, damp, miserable duty in Newfoundland. They would board any ship, take any detail, go anywhere they could just to get away. Jim wasn't interested. After nearly three years in the Pacific, Jim didn't like the cold weather. He remembered when he was in New York in February 1943 and saw sailors coming in from the North Atlantic with icicles hanging from their beards, mustaches and eyebrows. No thanks.

Luckily for Jim, after only a couple of weeks, the *Iowa* headed back to Casco Bay in Portland. They continued to go in and out of the harbor and take short cruises in the North Atlantic looking for submarines and blockade runners. Navigators had to be very careful coming or going out of Casco Bay as there was a large, submerged rock ledge in the middle of the entrance channel and extra care was needed to make sure not to get hung up on it. Once a ship passed the ledge, it would need to take a turn to port and head into the harbor. Unfortunately, on one occasion, the assistant navigator on the *Iowa* plotted a turn a little too early. The *Iowa* hit the ledge on the port side, tearing a gash in its side and putting a hole in one of the fuel tanks, which resulted in fuel oil spilling into the water. They had to proceed back into the harbor and anchor and the damage eventually got repaired.

The Navy didn't find the whole incident amusing. According to Jim, the investigation found fault with the assistant navigator. As a result, he took the brunt of the blame for running aground on the ledge because he was the one that plotted the course. As a consequence, he was transferred to "less than desirable" duty in Guantanamo Bay, Cuba. According to Jim, at that time, Guantanamo Bay was one of the worst assignments a Navy officer could go to. It was a lesson that Jim would not forget. A short time after the mishap, the Navy had the rock ledge blasted and removed so it would no longer be a navigational hazard for incoming or outgoing ships.

On September 23, 1943, while in Casco Bay after their return from Newfoundland, Jim received quite a surprise. His studying had paid off. He was notified that he had been accepted into the Officers Candidate School Program (OCS). Out of the entire Atlantic fleet, 50 sailors had been selected and he was one of them. Jim found out he was accepted from his buddies, Mo Shifley and Louie Shapiro, as they were the first to find out. They rushed down to his bunk and let him know and told him to pack his gear. He was getting on another ship within four to six hours. Jim gave them a long goodbye and his friends talked while Jim packed. While on the *Iowa*, Jim and Mo once tried to teach Louie how to dance. He danced himself into a corner and couldn't get out. Every time they got together, they would tell the story of trying to teach Louie how to dance and they would laugh until they had tears in their eyes. They were good guys and they had become great friends. They stayed the best of friends for the rest of their lives.

The next thing Jim knew, he was aboard the USS *Prairie*
heading for Bainbridge, Maryland, where all candidates were sent
until assignments were to be posted in approximately three weeks.
During that time, it was a lot of rest and relaxation. They had no duty
assignment, except waiting for the posting telling them where they
would attend officer training. Jim requested MIT or Cornell. He got
neither. Instead, he was assigned to the Harvard College V-12
Officers Training Program. He was not disappointed. As Jim always
said with a wink and a grin, it was his tough luck to get assigned to
go to Harvard. Jim had spent nearly three years in the Navy and was
eligible to wear eight battle-stars on his uniform. He had paid his dues.
Now, he was heading home to Massachusetts to go back to school at
Harvard for a two-year program. Still, he had doubts about his
qualifications. In high school, Jim was an OK student, receiving
mostly B grades. During his senior year, Jim took college-level
courses and struggled. He was barely able to maintain a C average
that year, so he stayed on for a post-graduate year to bring his grades
up. Again, while these were all college courses he was taking, he did
better the second time around. However, he was more than a little
nervous about going back to school after being away from it for
several years – especially at an institution like Harvard. He knew he
would be competing against some pretty smart guys. Unbeknownst to
Jim, as it turned out, he was in the top 10 percent of the applicants of
enlisted men from the Fleet.

An odd thing happens when an enlisted man is accepted into
Officers Candidate School – he gives up his current rating and starts
all over. It didn't matter that Jim had been in all these battles. It didn't
matter that he was a survivor of the *Northampton*. It didn't matter that
he had probably seen more action than most of the other sailors in the
program. Jim was back to being an apprentice seaman.

All the OCS candidates had to find their own way to their
assigned schools. It was October 1943, so Jim jumped a train in
Maryland and headed to Cambridge. He was assigned to D company
at the Eliot House. By the end of the first week, each candidate had
his photo taken. If he succeeded in the program, it would be his
graduation picture in the yearbook. Jim was told that about one

quarter of his class would fail the program. But he had something the other candidates didn't have---three years of grit.

Every morning at 6:00 a.m. – in rain, sleet, snow or sunshine – candidates had to run an approximately two-plus mile circuit from their dorm room to the Anderson Bridge over the Charles River, around the Weeks Bridge and back to their dorm. They had to shower, change, have breakfast, and get to class by 8:00 a.m. They had a full class schedule of English, history, engineering, chemistry, physics, and physical education. In physical education, they practiced boxing, wrestling, judo, swimming, and calisthenics. They had Navy courses as well. At night Jim studied until lights out. He didn't have a lot of time to himself.

For relaxation, Jim liked to go to the lounge in one of the other residence halls, the Kirkland House. There was a piano there and a fella that liked to play it most nights after dinner. Jim made it a habit to go and listen to him. The piano player's name was Jack Lemmon

III. The future celebrated actor also was part of the V-12 program. Jack was about three years younger than Jim and also was from Massachusetts, born in the town of Newton. He had come from a slightly different background than Jim had, attending the prestigious Phillips Academy before being accepted at Harvard. It was at Harvard that Jack found his love for theater. He later served as an ensign aboard an aircraft carrier, before returning to Harvard to finish his studies.

Others in the program included Robert F. Kennedy, also a Massachusetts native and brother of John F. Kennedy Jr., as well as John D. Rockefeller III. When fellow students wanted to be a wise guy, they would ask Rockefeller if he would loan them a buck or two. It was no wonder Jim was a little apprehensive about his competition. For Jim, the experience was mentally strenuous and challenging. While it wasn't easy for him, he held his own. Despite the academic challenges he faced, he was really enjoying his stay at Harvard. He especially enjoyed the athletic programs, which gave him a chance to release some stress, get some exercise and remain in shape. Most of all, he liked that he wasn't getting shot at or torpedoed.

He was exposed to all sorts of new "interesting" experiences. As an example, a religion professor at Harvard lived on Jim's floor in the Eliot House. Although he could not recall the professor's name, Jim described him was a particularly odd fellow. Many said he was one of the smartest guys in the world. Occasionally, the professor would have his door open. As Jim and other students went past his room, the professor would be lying on his couch, buck naked, listening to classical music and reading. He was oblivious to his public exposure. Jim couldn't figure out how such a smart guy could be so odd.

On one occasion, as Jim was making his way through Harvard Square to his eight-o'clock class, a bus driver coming through Harvard Square with a packed bus had a heart attack and lost control of the vehicle. He struck two young girls and pinned them between the bus and a building, killing them both. The bus driver died as well. Jim, having witnessed the tragedy, immediately threw up his breakfast. He quickly regained his composure and determined there was nothing he could do to render assistance to anyone involved. Now running behind, he rushed off to class, trying to put the awful event behind him.

Jim got quite a surprise one day in December 1943 when his dad came to Cambridge to visit. It wasn't often that his father could get away. Accompanying his dad was Jim's brother, Lionel, who was on leave after the loss of his newborn girl. Since Lionel was the first to join the Navy in 1938, while Jim was still in high school, they hadn't seen each other in nearly five years. They had a wonderful heartfelt meeting, which was particularly emotional in light of the loss of their brother, Bob. They spent several hours together before Jim had to shove off to go back to classes. They gave each other a very warm goodbye as they weren't sure when they would see each other again. A week later, Jim tried to get a Saturday "day pass" to visit his brother while he was still home. Unfortunately, Jim had a low grade in one of his classes and was not permitted to leave the grounds. Nonetheless, Lionel's visit had given Jim's spirits quite a boost, so, as always, he made the best of it.

1944 More Loss, Hard Decisions, Bud Turcotte Enlists

It wasn't long before Lionel was back in Dutch Guiana. In light of everything going on, he was especially anxious to get mail from home. He received his first letter from his mother on February 6, 1944 and responded immediately. He was worried that he had not heard from her for some time:

Dear Mom,

I got your first letter today since I got back from leave. Gee, you certainly had me worried for a while. I couldn't dope out what was wrong. Now that I know I feel OK. You see Mom, unless you send them air mail it takes months for the mail to us. I'll bet Dot [his sister] felt bad about not mailing that letter but you tell her not to worry about that as we all do it now and then. It's swell to know Jim is doing well in school. Boy, if he keeps that up he'll make us all feel like a bunch of chumps, won't he.

Incidentally, does Jim know about the accident that happened to Vinnie [An old friend Vincent Raymond] on the West Coast? Gee I really felt bad about that as I was with him one night while I was home, you know. I'll bet it was pretty tough on his folks, huh Mom? People say "Well, that's war" but to me, even though I'm right in the middle myself it means a lot more than it used to. It can really hurt now.

What is Dick's wife like, Mom? You know, I don't know what my new aunt looks like either.

I can just imagine how tall Dot is getting as she wasn't exactly standing still while I was home. She is going to take after Rob and Jim, Mom, and be a long drawn out string bean, for a while anyway. How's Bud, by the way? Has he started to fill out any at all? It's kinda hard for me to believe that before very long he'll be in the service too. Boy I really am getting to be an old man, aren't I. Just think – 25 in just four more months. How about that, Mom?

Poor Mary is right. She certainly does have a tough time whether it is with her boyfriends or anything else. One thing I'm happy about though is that she is doing so well at the hospital. How does she look, Mom? Not too tired and drawn, is she? I hope her vacation did her some good.

I'm still waiting for a letter from Dad too, so you had better tell him to get hot or I'll take a round out of someone by initials Oswald [His father's middle name]. I hope everything is good with him at the airport.

We're being kept as busy as a bunch of bees here now and for the past few weeks. It doesn't give me as much time to myself as I had previously but I like it better that way then I don't have to moon around wondering what to do. Makes the time go by much faster too.

It's time for me to hit the road to dreamland, Mom, so I'll leave you now so you write to me when you can, huh? I'll always answer right away. Take care of yourself and the kids and say hello to everyone for me.

Love to all,

Lionel #1

P.S. Please note the new address

In a letter written over two days, February 10th and 11th, 1944, his mother writes Lionel:

Lowell Mass
Feb. 10, 1944

Dear Lionel,

I will send all my letters Air Mail hereafter so that you will get them more often.

You should have been here tonight. Dot was modeling Mary's evening gowns. She had on one of Mary's blue ones and it looked swell on her only she did not quite fill it out in places so Sis took her into the bed room and put in a couple of fake ones and you should have seen the look on Dot's face. She was showing Em in the front hall and they fell out. We all laughed so hard that I was almost sick and Dot was shocked to death.

They are singing a very new song "By the Light of the silvery Moon." Bing is singing it with Dot + Bud trying to help him.

I have not heard any more from that J.P. Morris yet. Maybe he will come up over the weekend. Jim hopes to be here when he does come.

Can you imagine Dot's going to her first dance tomorrow night? Is she a young lady or is she? It won't be long before she will be wanting to have her a boyfriend. It does not seem possible that my baby is getting that old.

Jim knew about Vinny Raymond and he and Gigs who was home on a 15 day furlough went to the funeral. His folks felt pretty bad as he was the only boy and their baby. He had two older sisters.

Pa is doing pretty good out at the airport. He does not go to school anymore as he has to teach three nights a week so he cannot go to school anymore.

I will finish this tomorrow some time as the kids want to put the light out and listen to the music. I will say goodnight and see you tomorrow.

Feb. 11

Here I am again and boy since I last night wrote to you there has been about six to eight inches of snow. It has snowed all day and it is still going strong.

Dot has gone to her first dance even the storm would not stop her. She told me she had to write a letter to someone in the service so she wrote a letter to you. I don't know when you will get it as the teacher has to read and check it before they can send it to you.

Bud got a letter from Paul Gigs and he is in England. Mary's Donald is in England. I don't know what they are going to do, but they sure are getting ready for something. Big Gigs was home and just went back Wednesday. He says he does not expect to stay in the camp long when he gets back. You know what that means.

Now that I have your letter all written I find that Sis and Mary have (2) used all my envelopes. I will have to wait until I go to the store tomorrow.

Would you like to come for dinner we are having a Chine roast, green beans, carrots, potatoes, tomatoes, bread, butter and lemon meringue pie. Not bad what?

Notice the capital B on the butter. I have been lucky, the last for months. I have a chicken that I am going to hide just in case that fellow J.P. Morris comes then I will not get caught with my cupboard bare.

I will close now as I have quite a cold and I am going to look at my bottle and then go to bed and see if it will be gone in the morning.

Write when you can and I will send mine airmail hereafter.

> *Love from all.*
> *Ma*

Herman and Helen heard from one of Bob's shipmates, J.P. Morris, in February. He claimed to have information on Bob and wanted to meet with them and give them details "as one of the few understanding the situation." Bob's mother held out hope that Morris would be able to shed some light on the case and give her a reason that, against all odds, Bob was still alive. Nothing ever came of the J.P. Morris situation. Although probably well-intentioned, it simply perpetuated his mother's grief and prevented her from healing and moving on with her life.

Lionel wrote a letter dated February 12 and postmarked February 14, 1944:

Dear Mom,

It sure was good to hear from you again. You just go ahead and write when you can, Mom. I know how hard it is to keep the house going and keep the letters going too. But you're doing swell mom, so I wouldn't worry about it.

I'd like more than anything I know to be there when Rob's friend gets to tell what happened to him.

Whatever you do Mom be sure that you write to me as soon as you find out what the details of the case may be.

I'm going to write to him Mom as soon as I can find time as I'd like to get the dope straight. You see as one sailor to another he can probably tell me something that he can't to you. At least I'm going to find out any way.

By the way, Mom, when you see Helen say hello to her for me and tell her I was asking about her. I kinda thought she was a pretty darn nice kid when she and Bob and Claire and I used to go out together the few chances that we did get. Have you seen her since she got the news about Rob's accident? I remember she took it pretty bad and was wondering how she was now.

How is Dad making out at the airport? Is he still kicking aircraft engines and their ignition systems around, Mom? Tell him I hope to give him a run for his money some one of these days. I haven't heard from him since I got back mom, so kinda drop a hint- here and there- will you as I would sure like to hear from him.

"Claire was talking to me about how well Mary and Sis are making out at the hospital. It sure is swell. How's Bud and Dot?"

"I'm going to leave now Mom, as I have to arise early tomorrow. You'll hear more from me very soon though."

Love to everyone.

Lionel #1

On the afternoon of February 17, 1944, the odds caught up with Lionel. The pilot, Lieutenant (jg) Malcolm E. Nafe was making a test flight in an aircraft that had been experiencing maintenance difficulties. Lionel Turcotte was the engineering chief. In addition to Lionel, the other crew members were listed as William Scholfield, Roland Cardone, and Harvey Caldwell. The plane was a Ventura PV-1 Bomber, Baker-10, Bureau No. 33351. Shortly after leaving Zandry Field, Dutch Guiana, Lt. Nafe radioed that he was coming in for an immediate landing. One minute later, the plane reported it was experiencing a small fire and was landing immediately. A few seconds later a message was received which was unintelligible. Then, at 3:03 p.m., the aircraft went out of control and crashed into the jungle in a wooded area along the edge of a small creek about three miles from the landing field. Lionel's luck had run out.

A rescue party was immediately dispatched to the crash but there was difficulty in getting there due to the density of the jungle in the vicinity. One of the search parties, consisting of 8 Navy and 10 Army personnel, recovered the remains of the five crew members and their personal affects. Upon setting a course back to Zendry Field, but being unable to beat their way out of the jungle before darkness, spent an uncomfortable night in the jungle. Rather than take the chance of becoming separated in the complete blackness encountered, they decided to camp until daylight when they all returned to base safely except for minor scratches sustained from the heavy brush.

Lionel's death was due to multiple and extreme injuries. Naval records reflect that he suffered a compound-complex fracture of the right femur, right tibia and fibula, with almost complete severance of the right leg. He also had a compound-complex fracture of the left leg and a compound-complex fracture of the lower one-third of the right humerus, as well as a crushed right chest and a fractured skull.

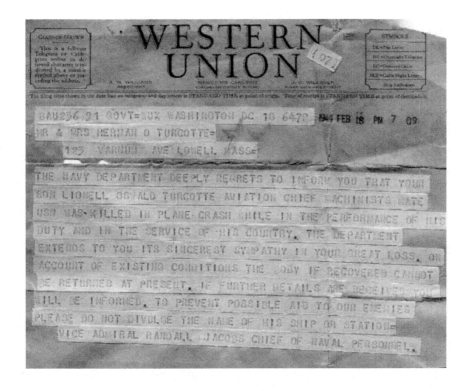

The Navy send a telegram to both his wife and his parents, notifying them of his death: "The Navy Department deeply regrets to inform you that your son Lionel Oswald Turcotte Aviation Chief Machinist Mate USN was killed in a plane crash while in the performance of his duty and service to his country…"

There are no words that can convey the loss that both Lionel's mom and Claire felt. Helen was notified of her oldest son's death after having just lost both her granddaughter and her son Bob. Poor Claire had lost both her daughter and now her husband in a span of two months. Unimaginable.

Lionel's remains were recovered, but they could not be returned to Lowell at that time. As a result, he was given a full military funeral in Dutch Guiana with Dutch sailors acting as pallbearers. Lionel was interned locally in the U.S. Army Cemetery, Camp Paramaribo, Dutch Guiana, South America, Grave No. 24. This was not a permanent cemetery. It was determined that, after the war, Lionel's remains would be repatriated back to Lowell.

Military funeral for Lionel in Dutch Guiana [Suriname] in 1944. His coffin is being carried by Dutch sailors. Photo sent to Lionel's parents by one of his shipmates in attendance.

Sometime later, Lionel's remains were removed to Grave 252, Row 5, Plot B, U.S. Military Cemetery, Fort Buchanan, Puerto Rico. This also was not a permanent cemetery, and no permanent cemetery was going to be established there. It would be some time before Lionel could be returned to his family. He died doing what he loved, flying. And he did it fighting for his country. War is hell, for all.

The responsibility fell to Lt. (jg) J.H. Scully to author the letter to Lionel's wife, Claire. It was dated February 20, 1944:

Dear Mrs. Turcotte,

It is with extreme regret that I have to inform you of the death of your husband, Lionel Oswald Turcotte, Aviation Chief machinist. He lost his life in a routine flight in line of duty on Thursday February 17, 1944. He died instantly and I am sure you will find some comfort in the knowledge that he suffered no pain.

I hope, too, that you will find comfort in the fact that he was given a Christian burial and full military funeral attended by his former shipmates.

We all liked and respected Lionel and there is no enlisted man or officer here who does not feel his passing as a keen personal loss.

All of us here extend to you our deepest sympathy and pray that God may comfort and guide you in this lonesome hour.

I can, if you desire, write you later at more length answering any questions you may care to ask within limits of security. I shall consider it a privilege to be of further service to you.

Sincerely,

J.H. Scully,

Lt.(jg)A-V(s) USNR

After she was notified of Lionel's death, Claire wrote to one of Lionel's shipmates, Ray "Shorty" Bayson. She had a lot of questions about how Lionel had died. He wrote her back in a letter dated February 24, 1944:

Dear Mrs. Turcotte,

I had intended writing you before but we were not permitted to write before now. Even now I cannot answer all of the questions you asked in your letter which I received today.

Certainly I do not mind you addressing me as 'Shorty." After all "Turc" has told me about you. I feel that I know you as a friend.

I will try and answer what I can. The cause of the accident is at present unknown and perhaps will never be known. "Turc" had the utmost faith in both the plane and the pilot. In a later letter I will give you all the facts. "Turcs" body was recovered and he was given a military funeral with his comrades. His personal possessions are on their way to you. There was no insurance policy among his possessions but he had $10,000 government insurance and you will receive the proceeds from the government even if you do not have the policy.

Now Claire, if I may call you that, I want you to know that this has been a real loss to me and to the other chiefs. I looked on "Turc" as a younger brother and may I sincerely say that I have suffered as much as if he were a brother. He was a fine, clean boy and why he had to be taken with his whole life ahead of him is hard to understand. God's ways may seem strange at times but he must have had a reason.

The only comfort we can take is the fact that his memory shall live after him. He was kind, thoughtful and generous and when the great scorekeeper writes the score, He will truly write "Here is a man who played the game cleanly and squarely."

Oh! I could go on for reams about it. All I can say is he was a wonderful friend.

Now as for you young lady- let me say I feel deeply your great loss. But Lionel did not die in vain. You have suffered a great loss-greater than any- But remember what a fine boy you were married to, how much you suffered and enjoyed together. If I know "Turc" and if I know you, he would want you to keep your chin up, be brave, Remember him for the fine upstanding youth he was- and how much others thought of him and loved him. Try and be brave the way "Turc" would want you to be brave.

I appreciate the honor you did me in writing to me. And I want you to feel that I am your friend as I was "Turc's". If there is anything I can do I want you to call on me and I shall feel honored.

Please express my sincere deep regret to his parents. And if you feel you would care to write anytime may I assure you I will answer and assist in any way I can.
Sincerely,

Ray Bayson

Lionel's father also had questions as well. On February 28, 1944, he reached out to one of Lionel's shipmates, Herman (H.C.) "Pop" Riley, inquiring about any information that he might be able to share regarding Lionel's death. In a letter dated March 3, 1944, Riley responded with:

Dear Mr. Turcotte,

I received your letter of Feb.28 today and I am taking this early opportunity to answer it.

If Lionel was helped by association with me I certainly feel honored. He was a fine clean boy and I miss him more than words can tell.

I appreciate your feelings but let me say that Lionel died in the line of duty.

Lionel's body was recovered and now rests in the military reservation. He died instantly and his body was not marred in any way. I understand that after the war the Navy Department will send his body home. His personal effects have been sent to his wife.

As far as we know the cause of the accident has not been determined and probably never will. Lionel had the utmost confidence in the plane and the pilot-He was flying as Chief Mechanic. They had a small fire aboard and were trying to get back to the field- The plane landed in a river in the jungle but the bodies were thrown clear.

My understanding is that a letter from the skipper has gone either to you or Lionel's wife.

If there is anything further I can do please advise me. Lionel's tools were not sent due to an error. Will you advise me what you want done with them.

I certainly appreciate your kind words and the confidence you place in me.

Believe me to be,

Sincerely yours,

H.C. "Pop" Riley

Herman C. Riley

On February 19, 1944, Jim's dad drove to Harvard. He didn't get out of his car and had Jim get in. His father was very sorrowful and emotional. He told Jim that Lionel had been killed in an airplane crash in the South American jungles aboard a Ventura Bomber. Jim was crushed. He had always looked up to his brother Lionel. Nonetheless, he was so grateful that he had been able to see Lionel in December. Now Jim was the only one left of "The Three Turks."

Obviously, this time in Jim's life was not without challenge. He went through a very tragic and emotional eight months. First, his brother Bob was declared missing in action in June 1943, then the death of Lionel's daughter, Ann, and now Lionel's death in a plane crash. All this happened while he was trying to adjust to college. At times, everything made it hard for him to study or concentrate. It took all his grit and determination to push through the pain and doubt. Jim did his best to stay on track with his studies, despite these losses. He also tried to go home to Lowell on as many weekends as he could to visit his family. He still had his youngest brother Bud at home, as well as his three sisters. But they all could clearly feel the difference in the house given the loss of the two oldest brothers. Jim could sense that his mother and father took it very hard. They all tried their best to keep up their own spirits and those of their parents.

In October 1944, Jim completed the lifesaving and teaching programs. As a result, he was asked to assist in teaching swimming to the other candidates. To Jim, there were a surprising number of sailors who didn't know how to swim or were afraid to jump off the high diving board. The high diving board exercise simulated jumping off the side of a ship. Because of his experience aboard the *Northampton*, he was able to relate how important it was for them to become proficient in swimming, as it could actually save their lives. There were a few sailors that took several days of coaxing to finally get them to jump. But with some encouragement, they all got through it.

Jim's roommate in the Eliot house was a fellow named W.E. Werner, who everyone called Gunner. Although the Eliot House was located inside of Harvard's Gate, it just so happened that their room had a private entrance on the first floor of the building which was physically located *outside* the gate to Harvard. In effect at the time for all cadets was a curfew of 7:00 p.m. during weeknights with lights out at 10:00 p.m. If a cadet attempted to come in through the gate after curfew, they would get a demerit, or worse. Because of Jim and Gunner's strategic location, one could enter through their window and go out through the dorm into the main hallway of the Eliot house without being seen. Jim and Gunner would conveniently leave the window unlocked at night. As a result, they would often have guys coming through their window at two in the morning to avoid getting caught. Jim often said that, after taps, his room was like Grand Central Station. On one occasion, when they went to breakfast, some jokester put a drawing on the blackboard in the cafeteria of a couple of sailors coming through the window. Everyone had a good laugh and knew exactly whose room they were referring to.

Jim was promoted to company commander of Company H at Harvard and, as a result, was transferred to Kirkland House. This time his room was on the top floor facing the front of the building – no more late-night guests. He was in charge of the 50 to 60 sailors assigned to Company H and would muster them each morning at 6:00 a.m. for the bridge run. He also made sure they got to breakfast, squared away their gear and made it to class by 8:00 a.m.

Gunner and Jim had similar experiences prior to attending Harvard. Gunner had a lot of overseas duty. Like Jim, he struggled with studying. There were times when Gunner would throw his books against the wall and sneak out for a beer. Even though he had been through the stress of sea battles, the academic pressure got to him. During his last semester at Harvard, Gunner quit, one of the 25 percent that typically didn't make it through the program.

Finally, in May 1944, although nowhere near the top of his class, Jim successfully completed his studies at Harvard and graduated from the V-12 program. Grit.

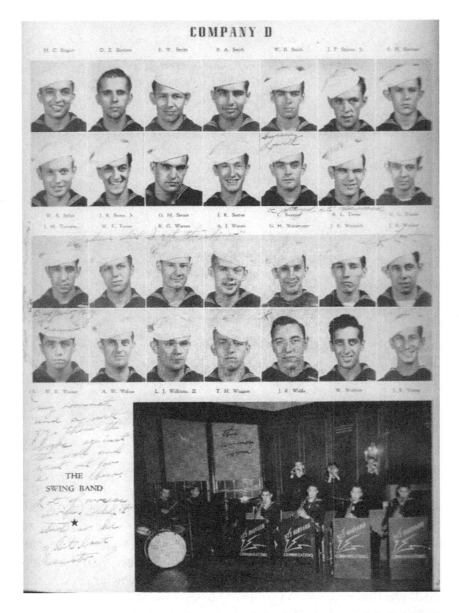

Harvard Graduation Yearbook: Jim is in third row from the top and far left. While he didn't graduate from the program, W.E. "Gunner" Werner is directly below him.

Walter "Bud" Turcotte

Walter, known to all as Bud or Buddy, was the youngest of the Turcotte boys, born on October 6, 1926, and younger than Lionel by a full seven years. Growing up, Bud looked up – figuratively and literally – to his older brothers. He really wasn't allowed to hang around with them because he was so much younger than they were, so he watched them from the sidelines. Still, he was always in their shadows. Bud was only 11 years old when Lionel went into the Navy, and 14 when Jim joined.

After his brother Jim left for the service, Buddy was home with two older sisters and one younger one. Between his father working and teaching and all his brothers in the Navy, for much of the time, Bud was the only male in an all-female house. Before he was a teenager, he had seen his brothers come and go from the house in their Navy uniforms. He had just turned 15 when the war broke out. He heard about his brother's adventures and read their letters home. He knew all three had gone clear across the country to California and two had traveled to Hawaii. Bud idolized them all.

Kneeling, Bud, left, and Dorothy. Standing, left to right, Lionel, Maude, Mother Helen, Mary and Bob.

In the late spring of 1944, Bud graduated from Lowell High School. Just around that time, the Navy officially notified Herman and Helen that their son Robert was finally declared dead. Bob was posthumously awarded the American Defense Service Medal, the World War II Victory Medal, A Fleet Service clasp, The American Campaign Medal, the European-African Middle East Campaign Medal and a Good Conduct Medal.

Since no remains were recovered, the Navy presumed drowning as the cause of death. The only arrangements to be made with the Navy were the return of his personal effects. For a second time, they were dealing with Bob's loss after also recently losing Lionel.

NMB-Form N 2 DK
(1945)
5735-2

CERTIFICATE OF DEATH

From: Bureau of Medicine & Surgery, Washington, D. C.

To: *Bureau of Medicine and Surgery, Navy Department, Washington, D. C.*
(See Circular Letter R-6, Appendix D, Manual of the Medical Department, for instructions)

1. Name TURCOTTE, Robert Thomas 201 69 95 Rank or rate ACMM(AA) USN

2. Born: Place Massachusetts Date 1 December 1920

3. Nationality White - U.S. Religion Catholic
   (White—U. S., Colored, Samoan, etc.) (Denomination)

4. Eyes Brown Hair Dk. Brown Complexion Ruddy Height 69 Weight 128

5. Marks, scars, etc. (noted in health record)

FINGERPRINT

State which finger
(Right index preferred)

6. Relation, name and address of next of kin or friend Parents: Mr. & Mrs. Herman Oswald Turcotte,
113 Varnum Avenue, Lowell, Mass.

7. Original admission: Place USS CINCINNATI Date Presumptive 5 June 1944
   (Ship or station to which attached when first admitted to sick list)

8. Died: Place At sea, Atlantic Area Date 6-5-1944 Hour

9. Cause of death { Principal DROWNING 2521 Key Letter I B
                  { Contributory

10. Death is not the result of own misconduct and is in the line of duty.
    (Is or is not) (Is or is not)

11. Disposition of remains Not recovered.

CASUALTY
SECTION
JUL 7 1944

12. Summary of facts relative to the death: This man was officially reported to be MISSING as of 4 June 1945, when the plane which he was aboard was lost in mid-Atlantic. In compliance with Section 5 of Public Law 490, as amended, all available information relative to his disappearance has been reviewed and the Secretary of the Navy has made a finding of presumptive death. The date of death for administrative purposes within the naval service was determined to be 5 June 1944.

EDW. H. HOGAN.

The war was still on and at a critical stage. The tide was turning in both Europe and the Pacific. It came as really no surprise that Bud wanted to enlist in the Navy, just like his three older brothers.

The problem was that, at 17 years old, he was still under-age and needed his parent's consent. Nonetheless, Bud wanted to do his part. Hell, every man did. Every family did. In addition to his three brothers having enlisted, two of his three sisters were Navy nurses as well. However, to enlist early, he needed a parent's signature on the application. That was not going to be easy and he knew it. He, too, had experienced the loss of his brothers and saw what it did to his parents and his siblings. However, he was bound and determined to carry on the Turcotte legacy in the Navy. He went to his parents and told them he wanted to join up.

Bud and his sister Mary.

It's a guarantee there were a lot of sleepless nights in the Turcotte house. Helen was now a two-time Gold Star Mother, having lost two boys in the service of their country, the second one only three months earlier. She had nearly lost Jim when his ship went down in the Pacific. To top it all off, she had lost her newborn granddaughter only six months earlier. As one can imagine, these were very difficult, emotional times. All of this was weighing on Herman's, and especially Helen's, minds. You can be sure there was a lot of discussion about Bud's enlistment. One thing for certain, for Helen, there was no way in hell she was going to lose a third son. To say the least, Bud didn't have the best timing with his request.

Helen was a regular attendee to mass at St. Rita's Church. She prayed morning and night for her sons in the service and about Bud's request. She asked God to give her guidance and strength. In the end, after much prayer, discussion, and soul-searching, on May 19, 1944, Herman and Bud went to the recruiting station and Herman signed the enlistment application approving his son Walter's admission into the U.S. Navy for a two-year enlistment.

263

NAVPERS — NRB FORM 24A   NAVPERS—NRB—43417—20 Jan 44—150M, 2-9-10-11
THIS APPLICATION MUST BE MADE OUT IN APPLICANT'S OWN HANDWRITING

APPLICATION FOR ENLISTMENT
NAVAL RESERVE CLASS V.

579-54-24   6 QA

5th Congressional District, County of Middlesex State of Mass.

Having been informed that any false statements made by me would bar me from enlisting, I certify that the following statements are correct: LOWELL, MASS.

Last school grade completed: 12th
Reason for enlistment: duty to country   MAY 19 1944   6/16
Language qualifications: none
What is your trade? none   I desire to enlist for 2 years

Name in full: Walter Herman Turcotte

Date of birth: October 6, 1926 Place of birth: Lowell, Mass

What is your race? White If you were born in foreign territory, how did you acquire citizenship?
                                        Are you now a U.S. citizen? Yes
When did you acquire citizenship? Birth
Have you anyone solely or partially dependent upon you for support? No
Are you married? No Have you ever been married? No
Status: (Married) (Divorced) (Legally separated) (Widowered)
Local Board # Address:
Address when registered   Selective Service Classification

Home Address: 113 Varnum Ave. Lowell, Mass

Where was your father born? Lowell, Mass. Where was your mother born? Dracut, Mass.
Is your father living? Yes Is your mother living? Yes

Are your parents divorced? No Separated? No Have you a stepfather? No stepmother? No

Name and relationship of next of kin or legal guardian: Herman Oswald Turcotte

Father   Home address of next of kin or legal guardian:
113 Varnum Ave Lowell Middlesex Mass

Have you ever been arrested or in the custody of police? No If so, for what?

Have you ever been in a reform school, jail, or penitentiary, or have you ever been convicted of any crime? No

Have you previously applied for enlistment in any branch of the armed services? No
Have you ever served in the U.S. Navy No Marine Corps. No Army No or Coast Guard? No
If so, how long? What is the date of your last discharge?
Character of discharge No Are you now or have you ever been a member of the National Guard, Naval Militia, or Marine Corps Reserve, or Civilian Conservation Corps? No
If so, what company or unit?

Sighted discharge (USMC) (CCC) (ARMY) (C.G.) (N.G.) Recruiter's Signature

(Applicant sign full name here)X Walter Herman Turcotte

Consent Fingerprints
Birth verification Proof of divorce
Custody Citizenship
Guardianship Mother's Name
Father's name

REMARKS:

No rel. reg.

GCT (63)

He was enlisted in Naval Reserve class V-6 as an apprentice seaman. On the application, in response to the question, "Reason for Enlistment," he wrote: "duty to country." He had lost two older brothers in the war but still felt, more than ever, it was his duty to serve.

Bud's recruitment physical showed that he was 5' 8" tall and weighed 118 pounds. He had brown hair, brown eyes and a medium complexion, as well as a variety of scars and marks on his knees, back and buttocks, the latter details signs of an active childhood. The scar on his butt was from sliding down a snowy hill using an old car hood as a sled. The hood hit a rock and stopped abruptly. Bud didn't and he cut himself, but good. He couldn't sit comfortably for more than a week.

Bud was called to active duty three days after he enlisted in the Reserves and sent to the U.S. Navy Training Center in Sampson, N.Y., for ten weeks of Navy Basic Training (i.e., Boot Camp). His training included physical fitness, swimming, and basic seamanship. Because the center was hundreds of miles from the nearest saltwater, it had replicas of ships' bridges on dry land which were used for training. Bud qualified in swimming 50 yards, received Gas Mask Instruction, and completed a course on Elementary Fire Fighting.

Fire suppression exercise UNTC Sampson, summer 1944.

In mid-July, Bud wrote home a quick series of letters:

July 12, 1944

Dear Mom and Dad,

How is the weather back there in Lowell [illegible]. Speaking of weather, we have a heck of a thunderstorm every day and our company always seems to get caught in them.

Right this minute I am waiting and listening to see if the mail man calls my mail off.

By the way Ma, I haven't received any mail from home for over 2 weeks. I got one from Jim about 2 days ago and one from Gram + Granpa.

(same letter continued: July 14, 1944 8:11 p.m.)

Hi Mom, well I was out to lunch for a few days. I was sort of sick since Wednesday night. I had a slight fever but I didn't go to the dispensary.

By the way ma, How's about sending some candy or fudge, or something. Every fellow has received packages from home and when they do I feel pretty low down inside.

By the way ma, I have a guardian up here. His name is Donald Halselman. He is a graduate of several colleges and he is only 25 years old. Whenever someone starts a fight, he grabs me and pulls me away.

We've been restricted all week and it's a good thing I was sick or I would have marched every night.

Well ma, here comes the chief to check and see if I'm all right. So long for now.

Your #4 son

Love,

Bud

P.S. *Don't forget the candy ma, I'll pay you when I come home. You can't buy it up here.*

July 15, 1944

Dear Ma,

Well, today is Saturday and we just finished our inspection and guess what, ma. Our inspection was excellent. This afternoon we have our regimental review and due to the inspection, we are serious company in the <u>rooster</u> competition. If we win the rooster flag that means weekend liberty in the city of Geneva. That is an hour ride on motor launch.

Now we know why we were restricted for the week. Not because there was something wrong but to prepare for today.

It will be swell if we could win. That means that our company will be rooster, color and honor company all rolled into one.

Well, lets dodge the subject. How is Dotty getting along these days. Still full of pep and trotting off to the movies as usual I suppose.

By the way, I bought something for Dot and I might send it home, then again, I might bring it home myself.

So Kenny Wright's mother said that he would be home the 22nd. Well ma, don't worry, I'll be coming home the same time he will. Well ma, I have to close now. So long for a while.

Love,
Bud

P.S. Don't forget to send my ring and some candy.

July 15, 1944

Dear Mom,

I got some good news ma. We are now a rooster company. That is the best there is. Boy did that feel great. We were congratulated by the commanding officer of the base and all our instructors who in the beginning said we were no good.

We were competing with companies that have been here for 8 weeks. We were the youngest company in the competition. Well, that's all for now.

Love,
Bud

P.S. Don't forget to tell Jim

On August 23, 1944, Bud's rating was advanced to seaman second class [Sea.2c]. From there, things moved fast for him. It seemed like every time he turned around, he was getting transferred. On September 7, 1944, Bud was transferred to Camp Macdonough, Plattsburgh, N.Y., for temporary training duty. After completion of

268

his training at Camp Macdonough, his service rating advanced from
seaman second class to seaman first class [Sea1c], to become
effective on November 1, 1944. On December 1, 1944, he was
ordered transferred to U.S. Receiving Station, Pier #92, New York,
N.Y. Bud was in New York for only a short period of time, but still
made time to visit his folks in Lowell.

Jim and Bud in Lowell in 1944.

On December 20, he was ordered to U.S. Naval CASA Fort
Ord in California. He reported six days later and was then moved over
to The Presidio. The two bases were separated by only eight miles.
California in December sure beat New York in December. The
Presidio had beautiful views of Monterey Bay. Bud was trained in one
of the most beautiful bases in the country. Lucky him. After only a
short time, the Navy informed him that once he completed his
instruction he was heading overseas.

1945 Second Thoughts, Okinawa and the War Ends

Bud was now about to be shipped out, likely headed to the Pacific. In the last year alone, a number of battles in the Pacific had been all over the newspapers, including at Saipan, Leyte Gulf, Philippine Sea, and Iwo Jima. Helen's worst fears were being realized. At this point, Bud's parents seriously questioned whether they had made the right choice allowing Bud to enlist. After countless discussions, prayers and sleepless nights, Herman wrote a letter in February to Edith Nourse Rogers, Representative for the 5th District, Massachusetts, in the U.S. Congress. Rogers was from Lowell and was the first woman elected to Congress from Massachusetts. In her 35 years in the House of Representatives she was a powerful voice for veterans and sponsored important legislation, including the Servicemen's Readjustment Act of 1944, commonly known as the G.I. Bill.

Politics was a big part of her family. In 1912, her husband was elected as a Republican to the 63rd Congress of the United States as the Representative from the 5th District of Massachusetts. During World War I, Edith Nourse Rogers was known as a "Gray Lady" with the American Red Cross in France and with the Walter Reed Army Medical Center in Washington, D.C. These two positions were the start of what became a lifelong commitment to veterans. These experiences served her well when her husband died on March 28, 1925, in the middle of his seventh term. Spurred by encouragement from the Republican Party and the American Legion, she ran in a special election for her husband's vacant seat. She won with a landslide 72 percent of the vote.

In his letter to Representative Rogers, Herman explained that two of his other sons who were in the Navy had been killed. He briefly explained to the congresswoman the details of each of their deaths. Herman asked that his son Walter be assigned to the new college program which was replacing the V-12 OCS program. He wanted to honor his son's desire to be in the Navy but at the same time ensure he was safe. There is no indication that Bud was aware of his parent's efforts to prevent him from going into action. If he had, there is no doubt he would not have been in favor of it. He had signed up as a matter of personal pride, duty, and honor to his country. He was not going to take the easy way out.

Representative Rogers wrote a letter, dated February 27, 1945, to Rear Admiral Randall Jacobs, Chief of Personnel for the Navy Department. She explained the plight of the Turcotte's and requested that Walter be assigned to the new college program:

> *My Dear Admiral Jacobs:*
>
> *I am sending to you herewith a letter from Mr. Herman O. Turcotte, 113 Varnum Avenue, Lowell, Massachusetts.*
>
> *You will note from his letter that two of his sons who were in the navy [sic] have been lost:*
>
> *Robert T. Turcotte, A.C.M.M. lost on patrol flight from the U.S.S. Cincinnati in June 1943.*
>
> *Lionel Turcotte, A.C.M.M. His bomber crashed while on a mission in south [sic] America in February 1944.*
>
> *The father of these two men asks that a third son, Walter H. Turcotte S.1/c U.S. N., C.A.S.A., Co. C, Div. 1, Presidio of Monterey, Monterey, California, be assigned to the new college program to replace the present V12 program.*
>
> *I shall deeply appreciate your kind assistance in the matter. Please advise me of your action.*
>
> *Edith Nourse Rogers*

(Mrs. John Jacob Rogers)

By that time in the war, both Representative Rogers and Rear Admiral Jacobs had received countless requests for special treatment for both soldiers and sailors alike. On March 2, 1945, Rear Admiral Jacobs dutifully had one of his officers reply to "Mrs. Rogers:"

Dear Mrs. Rogers:

This is in reply to your letter of 27 February 1945 enclosing a letter from Mr. Herman O. Turcotte requesting his son Walter Herman Turcotte, Seaman First Class, be assigned to the Naval Reserve Officer's Training Corps.

Candidates for this training are not chosen by the Bureau of Naval Personnel. A small V-12 class for enlisted men has been authorized for 1 July 1945 and men who are on duty within the continental limits of the United States may, if in all ways qualified, apply for this training via their commanding officer during the first week of April. These men will ultimately be transferred to NROTC.

Complete information is available on all navy [sic] ships and stations and Turcotte may obtain information concerning his eligibility from his Personnel Officer.

By direction of the Chief of Naval Personnel,

Sincerely Yours,

C.K. Duncan

Commander, USN

Director, Officer Procurement

The answer was no. No one was going to pull any strings. Herman and Helen's #4 son, Bud, would have to suffer the fates of luck like everyone else.

On March 8, 1945, Bud was transferred to "TADCEN, Shoemaker California and further via Pre-embarkment Center, Treasure Island, California, then to report for duty." TADCEN was the Naval Training and Distribution Center. TACDEN, Shoemaker was the Grand Central Station of the 11th Naval District. For the men fresh from training and headed for duty overseas, it would be their last contact with the mainland for a while.

Walter "Bud" Turcotte

On March 14, 1945, Bud was ordered to report aboard the USS *Sea Flasher* for transportation on March 19, on a trip with a destination of Okinawa, Ryukyu Islands, Japan. He was assigned duty in the Civil Affairs Team, a multi-service team which included Navy, Army and Marine personnel.

The Battle of Okinawa was the last major battle of World War II, and one of the bloodiest. On April 1, 1945, Easter Sunday, the Navy's Fifth Fleet and more than 180,000 U.S. Army and U.S. Marine Corps troops descended on the Pacific Island of Okinawa for a final push toward Japan. The invasion was part of Operation Iceberg, a complex plan to invade and occupy the Ryukyu Islands, including Okinawa. The Ryukyu Islands are south and west of mainland Japan.

Upon graduation at Harvard, Jim was transferred to Fort Schuyler in New York for Midshipman's School. In 1941, several new Naval Reserve Midshipmen's Schools were established, primarily on college campuses around the country. Between 1940 and 1945, their junior officer candidates, many alumni of the Navy's V-12 training program, completed an indoctrination course as apprentice seaman where instruction was provided in ordnance and gunnery, seamanship, navigation, and engineering. Graduates were awarded an ensign's commission and placed in active status. One such program was at Fort Schuyler. Jim was assigned to Platoon 232. Two of the other men assigned to the platoon were John Abdun-Nur and Joe Grilli. The three hit it off well together.

Platoon 232 Fort Schuyler: John Abdun-Nur, front row, center, and Jim, second row, last on the right.

To Jim, the program was challenging but uneventful as it was a lot of marching and military drilling, the last attempt for the military to round you out as a Naval officer. One of the things that Jim did enjoy was training on a Navy Yard patrol boat, known as a YP. YPs were used to teach familiarization with watercraft, basic damage control, docking, and underway instruction of basic to advanced seamanship and navigation.

Yard patrol craft provided realistic, at-sea training in navigation and seamanship for midshipmen. If you were going to crash a ship in the U.S. Navy, it was best to do it on a YP rather than a battleship, cruiser, or destroyer. Jim had a lot of bumpy efforts docking a YP, but enjoyed the training and, in the end, really got the hang of it. Near the end of the program, he and his group were fitted for officer's uniforms that were ordered from Saks Fifth Avenue in New York.

When Jim received his uniform and tried it on, he couldn't help but feel proud of his achievement. He had fought in numerous sea battles, rode out a hurricane, lost two brothers and went from being an apprentice seaman (twice) to a U.S. Naval officer.

On July 3, 1945, Jim was commissioned as an ensign at St. John the Divine Church in New York City. The successful candidates pinned each other's ensign shoulder-board epaulets. That night they went out to celebrate in the city. More than two years of studying and training had finally come to an end. Upon graduation each of the graduates received their orders to report to various ships and assignments.

Jim's graduation photo, Midshipman's School.

The Commander
of
U.S. Naval Reserve Officer Training Center
New York
and
The Commanding Officer
U.S. Naval Reserve Midshipmen's School
Fort Schuyler
request the honor of your presence at
The Graduation Exercises
of the
Second Class of Reserve Midshipmen
and their commissioning as
Ensigns in the United States Naval Reserve
11 o'clock
Tuesday, July Third
Nineteen Hundred Forty-five
The Cathedral of St. John the Divine
Amsterdam Avenue at 112th Street

GUESTS ARE REQUESTED TO BE IN THEIR SEATS BY 10.40 A.M.
PRESENTATION OF THIS CARD IS REQUIRED FOR ADMISSION.
ENTER NORTH OR SOUTH DOOR

The Class of Reserve Midshipmen

of the

U.S. Naval Reserve Midshipmen's School

at Fort Schuyler

announce their exercises for

commissioning as

Ensigns

United States Naval Reserve

Cathedral of St. John the Divine

New York City

Tuesday, July third

nineteen hundred forty-five

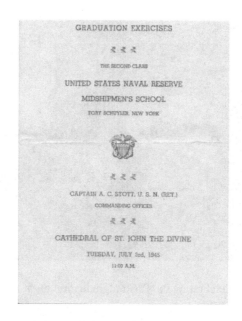

Fort Schuyler graduation book, July 1945.

Celebrating in NYC on graduation night.

Despite his previous war experiences, Jim was anxious to get back aboard ship. He quickly found himself on a train with a couple of other graduates heading to California – none other than his old pals, John Abdun-Nur and Joe Grilli. The trip took three days to get to San Francisco. They had been friendly throughout their time at Fort Schuyler, but after three days on a train together they really got to know each other. It was a relaxing trip with a lot of laughs. The three made their way to Tarzana, California, to John Abdun-Nur's family home. The Abdun-Nur's put them up for a few days. John's father was a physician and was well known in the Tarzana community. They had a beautiful home. The Uruguayan Consul was one of their next-door neighbors. The first night Jim was there, Dr. Abdun-Nur made the three ensigns mint juleps to celebrate. Jim always joked that it was the best mint julep he ever had, adding that it was also the only mint julep he ever had. The Abdun-Nur's were wonderful hosts. They treated their guests like family. Like all parents, they loved having their son and his friends home for a visit, even if it was for only a couple of days. The boys ate to their heart's content. John showed his buddies around Tarzana and San Francisco, including all the hotspots and highlights. They had a wonderful time. After two days and two nights, the officers thanked Dr. Abdun-Nur and his wife for their hospitality and said their good-byes.

After their stay with the Abdun-Nur's they headed into San Francisco. They were going to celebrate one last time before heading out to separate assignments. They splurged and spent the night in the Sir Francis Drake Hotel on Powell Street. Since his father was well-connected, John Abdun-Nur knew a lot people in the area. He took Jim and Joe to Charlie Low's Forbidden City, a very popular supper club in San Francisco. It was a classic 1940's club with a "cigarette girl" and a photographer. It was always crowded, and it was very difficult to get a reservation. John knew Charlie Low's daughter, so she got them in, and everything was on the house. They had a few drinks, a little something to eat and plenty of laughs. At some point during the night, they all switched hats and had their picture taken. Each of the young ensigns got a copy of the photo, a keepsake that they each kept forever.[15]

Photo holder from Charlie Low's, San Francisco, July 1945.

---

[15] When researching this book in 2019, I crossed paths with John Abdun-Nur's grandson, John Abdun-Nur Durrett, who forwarded me a copy of his grandfather's photo album of their last night in San Francisco, with the same photo taken at Charlie Low's, as well as photos at the house in Tarzana.

From left, Joe Grilli, Jim Turcotte and John Abdun-Nur
at Charlie Low's San Francisco.

John Abdun-Nur's photo album with various photos taken in California.

The next morning, they said their goodbyes. Each headed out to a different ship, heading in a different direction. They didn't see one other for the rest of the war. After the war was over, Joe Grilli went on to become a jeweler in Chicago and John Abdun-Nur followed in his dad's footsteps and became a very successful doctor in Tarzana.

Okinawa's dense foliage, hills and trees made it the perfect location for the Japan's last stand to protect their homeland. Both sides knew if Okinawa fell, so would Japan itself. The Americans knew securing Okinawa's airbases was critical to launching a successful Japanese invasion. On April 1, the Fifth Fleet and more than 180,000 U.S. Army and U.S. marine Corps troops descended on Okinawa for the final push. The fleet launched the largest bombardment ever to soften Japanese defenses, to support the American troop landing. As dawn arrived, morale among American troops was low. Soldiers and Army commanders alike expected the beach landings to take heavy casualties, worse than D-Day. Many felt like they were going into Okinawa facing a firing squad. But the Fifth Fleet's offensive onslaught was almost unnecessary and landing troops could have literally swum to shore. Surprisingly, the expected mass of awaiting Japanese troops wasn't present. Wave after wave of troops, tanks, ammunition, and supplies went ashore, almost effortlessly, within hours. The troops quickly secured both the Kadena and the Yontan airfields.

As they moved inland, American troops wondered when they would finally encounter enemy resistance. What they didn't know was the Japanese Imperial Army had the Americans just where they wanted them. Some 130,000 Japanese soldiers were there to defend Okinawa. Japanese troops had been instructed not to initially fire on the American landing forces but instead wait for them, especially in Shuri, a rugged area of southern Okinawa where Imperial commanders had set up a triangle of defensive positions, known as the Shuri Defense Line.

The Maeda Escarpment, also known as Hacksaw Ridge, was located atop a 400-foot vertical cliff. The American attack on the ridge began on April 26. It was a brutal battle for both sides. To defend the escarpment, Japanese troops hunkered down in a network of caves and dugouts. They were determined to hold the ridge at all costs. The Okinawa campaign was brutal and bloody. The Japanese fought such that they decimated some American platoons until just a few Americans remained.

Much of the fighting by the regular American forces was hand-to-hand and particularly ruthless. All Americans who fought in the Battle of Okinawa were heroic, but one soldier stood out, Corporal Desmond T. Doss. He was an army medic, a Seventh Day-Adventist and conscientious objector, who refused to raise a gun to the enemy. He single-handedly saved more than 70 American lives. For his actions, he was the first conscientious objector to win the Congressional Medal of Honor. His heroics were later recognized in the movie "Hacksaw Ridge."

This is what Bud Turcotte walked into. He reported to Okinawa on May 3, 1945, when the battle was already in full swing. Bud was sent to the northern part of Okinawa with Civil Affairs Unit D-1. These Civil Affairs teams were integrated with Army, Navy, and Marine personnel. Their job was to secure, care for and feed the civilian Okinawan population that had been driven from their homes by the Japanese. This was not going to be an easy task. There were hundreds of thousands of civilians who had literally been living underground. They had been sent by the Japanese into the hills with 30 days of food. By the time the teams found them they had suffered weeks of near continuous bombardment and isolation. Many were suffering symptoms of "shell shock" and malnutrition. Nearly all had lice and fleas.

Before ordering the Okinawans out, the Japanese Army had told them if they were captured by the Americans their children and the elderly would be sent to San Francisco, where they would be ground up and turned into dog meat. The Okinawans believed the propaganda and also feared that the Americans would kill the male population and turn their woman over to their soldiers. As a result, some Okinawans, particularly the older inhabitants, were panic-stricken when taken into American custody. To complicate matters for the Civil Affairs Units, the Japanese, just prior to retreating, released a large colony of lepers to wander the island. Medical staff had to identify those inflicted with the disease and take measures to quarantine them from the regular population. As of that time, a widespread treatment for leprosy had not been developed and distributed.

For the safety of the Americans as well as the Okinawans, intelligence officers within the units would interview the Okinawans to make sure that there were no Japanese infiltrators or hostiles. Ultimately, the locals would realize the Americans Civil Affairs Units would treat them well. It was very soon apparent that the behavior of the Okinawans would pose no problems. This was, in part, because only the less aggressive elements of the populace remained as the Japanese Army had conscripted almost all males between the ages of 15 and 45.[16]

---

[16] All of the photos of Okinawa were taken by Bud Turcotte.

Bud and the others wasted no time putting their skills to work. They built hospitals, battalion aid stations and medical-aid units to treat wounded Americans, the civilian Okinawan population and even some of the wounded Japanese soldiers.

The Civil Affairs Units also were tasked Okinawans. Before it was a popular phrase, these units wanted to "win the hearts and minds" of the Okinawans. They wanted to show them that they would be treated fairly and with dignity, not in the way the Japanese had treated them.

    Within 25 days of the invasion, the Civil Affairs Teams had more than 150,000 Okinawans under their direct control. The American military government supplied the necessities of existence – food, water, clothing, shelter, medical care, and sanitation. Local food stores, sufficient to take care of civilian needs for two to four weeks, were discovered. As it was near harvest time, additional food quantities were available from the fields. Growing crops were harvested on a communal basis under American direction. Horses, cows, pigs, goats and poultry, running wild after eluding the invading troops, were rounded up and turned over to the civilian camps. Initially, the Okinawans were held in stockades, but after only a short period, tent encampments were established.

Bud spent a great deal of time in the countryside with the Okinawan civilian population. They would go out as a team, usually five or six guys as a time, to the villages to see what they could do for them. He felt good about the work they were doing with the civilians.

Despite the good work that the Civil Affairs Teams were doing and the relationships they were building, the war was raging across the island. The teams had to keep their eyes peeled, looking for any Japanese soldiers or other hostiles.

It was nearing the end of the war and the Japanese military was getting desperate. Most Japanese troops believed that the Americans forces would take no prisoners and they'd be killed on the spot if captured. As a result, countless took their own lives. To encourage their surrender, Lt. General Buckner initiated propaganda warfare and dropped millions of leaflets declaring the war was all but lost for Japan. About 7,000 Japanese soldiers surrendered, but many others chose death by suicide. Some jumped from high hills, others blew themselves up with grenades. Still others continued the fight singlehandedly.

On Okinawa, death and the risk of death was all around Bud. On one occasion, his team was returning from a village back to camp. They were hiking along a road which had a ditch on both sides. Behind the ditch, only a few feet away, was a thick web of jungle landscape. It was getting very late in the day.

As the sun began to set behind the wall of thick jungle growth, deep shadows were cast along the road, encompassing the ditch all the way to the brush line. Bud was concerned that someone could easily crawl out of the cover of the jungle and into the ditch to lie in wait. He had played plenty of "Cowboys and Indians" with his brothers out at Mud Pond and knew this was a perfect spot and the conditions were right for an ambush attack. All his instincts told him to be extra cautious. As a result, he kept a close eye on the ditch on the side of the road. As they proceeded along their trek, Bud noticed the slightest movement just off to the right, barely above the top of the ditch. It could have easily been dismissed as an insignificant change in shadow.

Instead, Bud's training kicked in. He thought the shadow resembled the shape of a Japanese helmet. In fact, a Japanese soldier was hiding, waiting to ambush the group, and had slowly raised his head up to see where Bud's group was. Bud instinctively raised his rifle and pointed it in that direction. As Bud readied himself, the soldier popped up from the ditch with his rifle at the ready. Before the Japanese soldier could get off a shot, Bud fired his rifle multiple times, striking the soldier and knocking him back into the ditch. Bud's team immediately ducked for cover. They were concerned that the soldier was not alone and there may be other Japanese in the immediate area. They quickly scanned the area for other hostiles, finding none. They carefully approached the soldier to make sure he was not playing possum and confirmed he was dead. The soldier was wearing a Japanese flag around his waist. Bud removed the flag and stuffed it in his gear. It had bullet holes in it, as well as the soldier's blood on it. Another one of the team took the soldiers' weapon. Bud's heart was racing from all that adrenaline. They didn't have time to reflect on what happened. The sound of the gunfire was sure to draw the attention of any enemy in the area, so they hightailed it back to camp.

Flag removed from Japanese soldier, Okinawa 1945.

When you are 18 and "in the moment," you don't think about how close you came to death. But, in the quiet of the night, it creeps into your thoughts and dreams. You can't help but think about it. You had to take someone's life. You justify it because it was war. You rationalize it. It was self-defense. It was him or me. That's what happens in war. As they say, war is hell.

Not long afterward, on June 22, when faced with the reality that further fighting was futile, Japanese General Ushijima and his Chief of Staff, General Cho, committed ritual suicide, effectively ending the Battle of Okinawa. Bud carried the images and memories of Okinawa with him for the rest of his life, as did every other soldier or sailor on the island. Bud also had some happy memories of the good they did for the Okinawan people, especially the children.

Back in San Francisco, Jim boarded a transport and was on his way to pick up his new ship, the *USS New Orleans*. He would have to make a few stops along the way. First stop was Okinawa, Japan. While on Okinawa he lived in a temporary military tent camp. In the camp, they were living in tents and eating Army C-Rations, which meant canned breakfast, canned lunch, and canned dinner. He had flashbacks of the survivor's camp in New Caledonia. The camp was located near the remains of Shuri Castle, the summer palace of Emperor Hirohito, located just above the city of Naha, Okinawa. Naha is in the southern part of Okinawa. Jim was given an escort up to Shuri Castle, which had recently been the sight of pitched battles. There were still dead Japanese soldiers that had not yet been cleared from the site. At Shuri Castle, there were a pair of brass cups that were presented to the emperor by the youth of Naha in May,1936. The cups were from the Okinawa District Junior High School Oratory Contest Winner. Jim pried the brass inscriptive plates off the cups and kept them as souvenirs. He also went through "Tank Valley," the site of recent tank battles between the Americans and the Japanese. There were still remnants of destroyed tanks from both sides there.

So, as luck would have it, just a short time after the battle ended, Bud was on one end of Okinawa and his brother Jim was on the other end. They were likely within 50 miles of each other. Even though they were on the same island, halfway around the world, Jim and Bud never made contact with each other. Another opportunity lost.

Although the hostilities had ended some months earlier and the Japanese had surrendered, Bud was still on Okinawa in October 1945. On October 4, a typhoon was spotted developing in the Caroline Islands and tracked as it moved on a predictable course to the northwest. Although expected to pass into the East China Sea north of Formosa on October 8, the storm unexpectedly veered north toward Okinawa. That evening the storm slowed down and, just as it approached Okinawa, began to greatly increase in intensity. It was named Typhoon Louise. The sudden shift of the storm caught many ships and small craft in the constricted waters of Nakagusuku Wan (Buckner Bay) by surprise and they were unable to escape to sea. On October 9, when Louise passed over the island, winds of 92 miles per hour and 30- to 35-foot waves battered the ships and craft in the bay and tore into the Quonset huts and buildings ashore. A total of 12 ships and craft were sunk, 222 were grounded and 32 were severely damaged. Personnel casualties included 36 killed, 47 missing, and 100 seriously injured. Almost all food, medical supplies and other stores were destroyed, more than 80 percent of housing and buildings knocked down, and all the military installations on the island were temporarily out of action. More than 60 planes were damaged as well, though most were repairable. Although new supplies had been brought to the island by this time and emergency mess halls and sleeping quarters built for all hands, the scale of the damage was still very large. If the war had not ended on September 2, this damage, especially the grounding and damage to 107 amphibious craft (including the wrecking of four tank landing ships, two medium landing ships, a gunboat, and two infantry landing craft) would likely have seriously impacted the planned invasion of Japan (Operation Olympic).

Conditions on shore were no better. Twenty hours of torrential rain soaked everything and made quagmires of roads. The hurricane winds destroyed from 50 and 95 percent of all tent camps and flooded the remainder. Because of the strength of the winds, some of these Quonsets were lifted and thrown hundreds of feet; others were torn apart, galvanized iron sheets ripped off, wallboards shredded, and curved supports torn apart. Damage to Quonset huts ran from 40 percent to 99 percent of the destruction. Driven from their housing, officers and men alike were compelled to take shelter in caves, old tombs, trenches, and ditches in the open fields. Some even took refuge behind heavy road-building machinery, to avoid the wind-swept tents, planks and sections of galvanized roofing flying through the air.

At the Naval air bases, planes of all types were damaged, some of which had been tossed about unmercifully. Installations suffered far more severely. The seas churned under many of the concrete ramps and broke them up into large and small pieces of rubble. All repair installations were either swept away or severely damaged. At Yonobaru, all of the 40-foot by 100-foot buildings were demolished. Communication and meteorological services were blown out at most bases on the island.

Food stocks were left for only ten days. Medical facilities were so badly damaged that an immediate request had to be made for a hospital ship to support the shore activities on the island.

As a result of the experience in an earlier Pacific typhoon in September, extra stocks of food and tents were to be stored on Okinawa. These were already in route on October 9 when Louise hit. As a result, in less than a week after the storm, repair work began rapidly ashore on the island and supplies were arriving and were fairly well replenished. Emergency mess halls and sleeping quarters had been erected for all hands and 7,500 men had been processed for return to the United States. Timing was everything. Without the existing order for supplies, things would have been drastically different.

Bud wrote his father on October 25, 1945:

Hi Dad,

I received your letter about an hour ago. Just before I went to chow to be exact. I sure was glad to hear from you. So you heard about our little typhoon out here. Well it was a pip I can assure you of that. But there is no reason for any worrying dad. I'm fit as a fiddle and dying to get home.

Dad you mentioned to me about Jimmie being here on September 29th. Well I haven't seen him as yet. I guess he's about gone by now. When he landed here it must have been south somewhere. Because that where the all came in and it's also on the other side (Pacific) of the island. Maybe I'll see him yet: And then again he may have written a note to me. (I hope)

Well dad the fellows and in this tent got ourselves a little mascot this morning. He's a little orphan that was sent to us from the sea-bees. He speaks better english [sic] than we do. He is 5 years old and as cute as can be. We'll keep him here until the last of us leave the island.

Speaking of leaving, eleven more of the boys left for home about 30 minutes ago. Well, that's it dad, So until I hear from you again

Love

Bud

The "orphan" Bud referred to, was a dog. Initially, it had been taken care of by the Seabees on Okinawa. When they were ordered off the island, they left the dog with the Civil Affairs Team.

On November 12, 1945, Walter Turcotte was discharged from the United States Naval Reserves as a seaman first class for the purpose of enlisting in the regular Navy. He had served one year, four months and twenty-six days in the Naval Reserves. As a result of his service on Okinawa, he was authorized to wear one bronze star on his Asiatic-Pacific Campaign Ribbon. His reenlistment physical indicated that he was 5' 9 ½" and weighed 135 pounds. Bud had grown an inch and a half and put on 17 pounds while serving. He enlisted for a two-year hitch beginning November 13, 1945.

From Okinawa, Jim had to grab another two ships to get to the *New Orleans*. The first took him to Korea. The second, a transport, took him to the *New Orleans*. To board the transport, Jim had to climb up a cargo net hung over the side of the ship, with all his gear slung over his shoulder. Both vessels were moving up and down with the sea. In order to make the transfer, his timing had to be just right. Jim thought for sure he was going in the drink. The last time he had to climb a cargo net was when the *Northampton* sank and he was rescued by the USS *Fletcher*. Luckily, this time he wasn't being pulled out of the water covered in oil (and he was now an officer). He made it aboard safe and sound. The *New Orleans* was a heavy cruiser and had been in the Battle of Tassafaronga, along with the *Northampton*, which Jim had been on at the time. It was in that battle that the *New Orleans* had 150 feet of her bow blown off by a torpedo (see photo).

The *New Orleans* had been hit by a single torpedo which exploded her forward magazines. The extensive damage was to everything forward of Turret No. 2. Eleven days later, the ship sailed to Sydney, Australia, arriving on December 24. There, repairs were made, including the installation of a temporary stub bow. On March 7, 1943, she left Sydney for the Puget Sound Naval Yard, sailing backward the entire voyage. At Puget Sound a new bow was fitted and attached. For guns, they harvested the USS *Minneapolis'* No. 2 turret. All the battle damage was repaired, and the *New Orleans* was overhauled to almost new condition. She continued her life at sea with the back portion (aft) riveted and the front portion (bow) welded.

Jim's stateroom was in the new bow they had welded on. According to him, the new bow shook, vibrated, and made terrible noises in heavy weather. He constantly feared it was just going to fall right off the ship and take him with it. He rarely had a restful night's sleep.

Jim was assigned as junior division officer to the Sixth Division aboard the *New Orleans*, leading roughly 100 men. His group oversaw everything associated with the after guns and after deck.

Very shortly after Jim boarded the *New Orleans*, the ship joined up with the Pacific Fleet and headed for China. They went to the city of Qinhuangdao (pronounced "Chin Wang Tao"), the spot where the Great Wall meets the sea. The National Chinese Army oversaw that city, under the authority of General Chiang Kai-shek, who was very friendly to the Americans. They remained at this port for some time and, while there, the *New Orleans* provided medical assistance to residents in the city. They were waiting to find out if they were going to assist in any invasion of Japan, should that occur, and were ordered seaward in case an invasion came to fruition. Little did they know that, at the time, bombers were in route with the first of the two atomic bombs to be dropped on Japan. It was at this time that the USS *Indianapolis*, after dropping off the two atomic bombs, was sunk and many hundreds of men were lost. The first atom bomb was dropped on Hiroshima on August 6, 1945, and the second on Nagasaki three days later. On August 15, 1945, the Japanese surrendered unconditionally, effectively ending World War II.

The *New Orleans* sailed on August 28 with a cruiser-destroyer force to ports of China and Korea. The Japanese officially surrendered on the USS *Missouri* on September 2, 1945. The war was over. She covered the internment of Japanese ships at Tsingtoa, the evacuation of liberated allied prisoners of war, and the landing of troops in Korea and China. The *New Orleans* was ordered to go into Sasebo, Japan, to unarm the Japanese.[17] All Japanese weapons were seized and stored aboard in the ship's armory. More returning troops came aboard at Sasebo. Later, in October 1945, each officer of the *New Orleans*, including Jim, was given a Japanese Arisaka bolt-action rifle with a bayonet as a souvenir. The bolt was fixed shut so it could not be used. Jim kept it throughout his life, stored in a closet and rarely took it out.[18] Many soldiers and sailors received guns and other weaponry as mementos after the surrender of Japan. The *Northampton* sailed on November 17 from the mouth of the Peking River carrying veterans homeward bound.

---

[17] Sasebo is a city in the Nagasaki Prefecture, only 57 miles from the City of Nagasaki where the bomb was dropped. Jim always wondered about any radiation exposure he might have received.
17 After his passing the gun was handed down to his son, who will eventually hand it down to his son.

U.S.S. NEW ORLEANS

From: Commanding Officer.
To: Ensign James H. TURCOTTE, (D)L, USNR, (455066).

Subject: Japanese Rifle, authority for possession of.

Reference: (a) CTF 71 dispatch 281137 of October 1945.

  1. You are hereby presented with a Japanese rifle as a memento of your service aboard this vessel in North China and Korean waters after the cessation of hostilities with the Japanese Empire.

  2. You are given this rifle with the understanding that you are to remove it from the ship when transferred for duty, or, at the first available opportunity after this vessel reaches a port in the United States.

  3. This letter and reference (a) authorizes you to have this rifle in your possession.

           C.T. STRAUB
           By direction.

Rifle No.

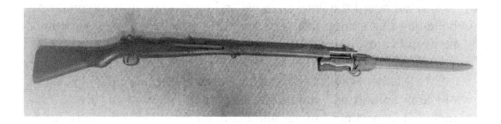

Japanese Arisaka rifle given to Jim 1945.

  Hallelujah! Jim and the crew of the *New Orleans* were headed back to the States. All the soldiers were disembarked at San Francisco on December 8 and the *New Orleans* steamed to Hawaii. When he arrived in Pearl Harbor, Jim made a point of going to the Officer's

Club. This was the first time he was back at Pearl since becoming an officer and he was going to take full advantage of it. And that he did. He drank and toasted with men who, for the most part, understood what he had been through. Ironically, most of the officers in the club were not in the service in 1941. Most had been officers for only a couple of years. Many others had discharged from the service back to their civilian lives. Amazingly, at 23 years old, Jim was a grizzled old veteran, having been in the Navy since before the war started. He had been involved in many of the major naval events of the Pacific during World War II. For the first time in nearly four years, he wasn't at war and no one was shooting at him. He and his fellow crewmembers weren't dodging torpedoes or Kamikazes. Directly or indirectly, he had been dealing with death since December of 1941. He had lived through so much in such a short period of time. For Jim, it was enough for 100 lifetimes. It was an indescribable relief. The drinks flowed and celebration continued until the early morning hours.

After he had recovered from his night out, Jim, like many of his fellow sailors, had to decide what he was going to do at this point. He had several options – he could leave the service, stay aboard the *New Orleans* or seek duty on another ship. Many ships were preparing to perform "Magic Carpet" duty, sailing around the world picking up soldiers and sailors and bringing them back to the States. Jim decided to stay on board the *New Orleans* and participate in these pick-ups, believing that sailing the open sea during peacetime was something he would enjoy.

Many of the Navy's ships ordered "offset firing" to get rid of old ammunition and munitions now that the war was over. This included disposing of mines and depth charges. Unfortunately, some of this ordinance did not explode and was left drifting around the oceans.

One afternoon, Jim was sunning himself on the fantail (the farthest you can go on the back of a ship). The officer of the deck suddenly came over the loudspeaker with, "Standby for collision with a mine!" The ship veered sharply to starboard. Jim looked left and saw a large anti-ship mine that was going to hit the *New Orleans* not far from where he was. "Oh shit," he thought, as the mine hit at the port quarter (right rear) of the ship and, amazingly, bounced off and didn't detonate. Jim gave a huge sigh in relief, thinking it truly would have been a shame to have survived all those war battles and then get blown up while just getting a tan. The captain ordered the ship to a full stop so that a group of Marines could go to the port quarter and fire at the mine to blow it up. The captain didn't want the mine drifting around the ocean until it hit another ship. The Marines obliged and made short order of the hazard. Never a dull moment, and Jim's luck hadn't run out.

The *New Orleans* made various stops throughout the Asia-Pacific region, including at the Philippines, picking up U.S. personnel. After a few weeks, they headed back to Honolulu to drop off their guests. When they arrived in Hawaii, Jim received new orders. He was going to New York and was joining the crew of the USS *Missouri*, also known as "Big Mo." He didn't waste a moment getting there and headed cross-country as fast as he could to celebrate the Christmas of 1945 in Lowell before reporting to the *Missouri*.

On December 8, 1945, Bud received his orders to report to the Commanding Officer in Boston for leave and a new assignment. As for leave, he was to receive five days rehabilitation leave, 30 days reenlistment leave, and five days travel time. Hot dog! Both Jim and Bud were going to be home for Christmas and New Year's. Their mom and dad were thrilled. The war was over, and their two surviving sons would be home for the holidays, even if it was for just a few weeks. Helen cooked and the boys ate. They spent time with their mom and dad and sisters. They hit all the hot spots, visited neighbors, and attended mass at St. Rita's. After the new year, Jim and Bud had to report for their new assignments.

Left to right: Jim, Herman and Bud at home for the holidays in 1945.

1946-1947 Two Turks Cruise to Turkey

Jim, a young ensign aboard the USS *Missouri* in 1946.

After the new year, Jim and Bud had to report for their new assignments. On January 20, 1946, Jim boarded the USS *Missouri*. It was his third battleship assignment, this time on a ship generally the same size and class as the USS *Iowa*. The Missouri was the symbol of American military dominance. It was on this very ship, only a few months earlier, that the Japanese formally surrendered to the United States. They installed a brass plaque on the spot where the ceremony took place. It was forever to be known as "the Surrender Deck."

Plaque on the Surrender Deck of the USS *Missouri*.

Initially, Jim was assigned to the Signalman's Division. It wasn't long before a position opened for an assistant navigator. Despite having had a difficult time in the navigation class at Fort Schuyler and not receiving a high grade, Jim actually enjoyed navigation and decided to apply. Of the five officers that applied, three were Naval Academy officers. After an intensive application and interview process, Jim was selected as the new assistant navigator aboard the *Missouri*.

Jim as the new assistant navigator for the USS *Missouri*.

Bud was given orders to report no later than February 12, 1946, to Port Hueneme, California, for intake. The Port of Hueneme is the only deep-water harbor between Los Angeles and the San

Francisco Bay area and is located in Ventura County on the Santa Barbara Channel. Once again, Bud was able to enjoy the California sunshine until he received his new assignment, which came just over a month later.

On March 18, 1946, Bud was transferred back to the East Coast to the Brooklyn Navy Yard for further transfer to the USS *Providence* (CL-82). For the first time, he was getting sea duty. Before that could happen, however, fate was once again going to intervene in the Turcotte boys' lives. Would it be for the good this time? It depends on your point of view. Bud's order stated, "To USS *Missouri* for further transfer to the USS *Providence*." In order to get to the *Providence*, Bud was ordered to ship out with the *Missouri*, his brother Jim's ship. The Navy was going to take the *Missouri*, and thus the Turcotte brothers, on a "Mediterranean Victory Cruise." The ship was going to numerous countries around the Mediterranean Sea to the welcome and thanks of their hosts. It would be during this cruise that Bud was to pick up the *Providence*.

The *Missouri* was a huge battleship. Its nickname was "Big Mo" or "Mighty Mo." It had a complement of more than 2,700 officers and enlisted men. In addition to his other duties aboard ship, Ensign Turcotte, as a junior officer, was assigned to supervise a group of sailors while aboard ship. Every day the officers would muster their men and go over any activities and assignments for the day. What were the chances? Of all the units and all the officers on the *Missouri*, Bud was assigned to his brother Jim's unit. Whether this was done intentionally, no one knows. For Jim, however, it posed a problem. He had to keep discipline and order amongst his men. To show his brother any preferential treatment, or even appear to do so, would sow dissension amongst the ranks.

For Bud, his older brother would, once again, just like when they were kids, be telling him what to do. Except now it would be as his Navy superior. This time, if he didn't follow his brother's orders, he could be disciplined by the U.S. Navy! Perhaps Bud saw this as an opportunity. Maybe he felt he should get preferential treatment. After all, it was his older brother, and he was only aboard the *Missouri* for a short time.

As described by Jim, on one occasion, Bud didn't feel like getting out of bed and reporting on deck for muster. Jim sent one of the crew down to his bunk to get him. But Bud refused to get out of the rack. Annoyed, Jim went down personally and told Bud to get up on deck. Bud said, "No."

"What do you mean, no?" Jim responded, now greatly irritated. "No" Bud repeated. Jim was now seeing red. He now ordered his brother to get up on deck or he was going to write him up. Bud responded with a mischievous grin, adding, "You'd better not or I'll tell Ma!" Jim did not find this amusing. Bud found it hilarious. Jim dragged Bud out of his bunk and up deck side. Not surprisingly, Bud did not remain in his brother's unit.

During this Mediterranean cruise they visited all the area countries that participated in World War II. Each officer from the *Missouri* was assigned to take a dignitary from each capital or city they visited and entertain them. There were meetings, parties, dinners and celebrations galore.

When in England, Jim was assigned to the head of the Royal Air Force. He asked Jim to take him to the highest point on the ship so he could look down on The Surrender Deck. Jim took him up to the Admiral's Deck and had him sit in the Admiral's chair. He pointed out the surrender plaque to the British officer. The officer, in turn, pointed out all the "Brits" coming aboard ship to look at the surrender plaque. He knew them all and made interesting, funny, and sometimes not so complimentary comments about each one. He had Jim in stitches.

Photo # 80-G-365725 Card game in Flag Cabin on USS Missouri, April 1946

Left to right, Alexander W. Weddell, U.S. ambassador to Turkey; Admiral H. Kent Hewitt, commander, U.S. Naval Forces Europe; Captain Roscoe H. Hillenkoetter, the *Missouri*'s commanding officer; and Turkish Minister of Protocol M. Kadri Rizan.

When the *Missouri* arrived in Gibraltar on March 31, 1946, she became flagship for Admiral Henry Kent Hewitt, Commander, U.S. Naval Forces Europe, and commander of the 12th fleet. The *Missouri* was to escort the admiral to Turkey, as well as bring the remains of the late Turkish ambassador to the United States, Mehmet Munir Ertegun, home for burial. The admiral would be the official representative of the United States at the funeral. When Jim and members of the *Missouri* passed through the Strait of Gibraltar for the first time, they became members of the Order of the Rock. This was yet another of the many unofficial maritime recognitions Jim acquired.

To get to Turkey, the ship had to navigate up the Dardanelles, one of the world's narrowest straits used for international navigation. The Dardanelles connects the Sea of Marmara with the Aegean and Mediterranean seas, while also allowing passage to the Black Sea by extension via the Bosporus, which forms part of the continental boundary between Europe and Asia.

Jim demonstrating his prowess in the use of the sextant for his duties as assistant navigator.

As the assistant navigator, Jim took the *Missouri* up the Dardanelles and back down again. Throughout the trip, he always remembered that poor assistant navigator aboard the *Iowa* that ran aground in Casco Bay, Maine, and vowed that would not happen to him and the *Missouri*. In 1946, the Navy was not the high-tech enterprise it is today. There was no GPS, Loran, or other computerized navigational instruments. There was no pinpoint precision. They plotted their course and position by means of celestial navigation. They navigated much like sailors 200 to 300 years earlier, using a sextant and star sights. Jim felt a great deal of pressure. He had a great many dignitaries aboard. If he screwed this up, he knew he would finish out his career in the worst assignment imaginable. He sweated it all the way up the Dardanelles. Luck was looking down on Jim. No problems encountered.

The USS *Providence* was a relatively new light cruiser, commissioned just a year earlier on May 15, 1945. The ship was 610 feet long, had a complement of 1,225 officers and enlisted men and could reach speeds of just over 32 knots. Departing Boston in November 1945, the *Providence* headed for the Mediterranean, making its first cruise one intended to expand American prestige through naval visits that would last until 1947. The *Providence* and *Missouri* would meet up in Turkey. The *Missouri* anchored in the waters just off Istanbul. On April 5, when first arriving in Istanbul with the *Missouri,* Bud said goodbye to Jim, made sure there were no hard feelings and effectuated his transfer to the *Providence* for duty.

The *Providence* stayed in Istanbul until April 9. From there, with Bud aboard, the *Providence* journeyed to Alexandria, Egypt, where, in May, she ran aground. The incident didn't cause any serious damage, except to the service record of the ship's navigator.

The USS *Missouri*, USS *Power* and Turkish Battlecruiser *Yavuz*,
Istanbul, April 5, 1946.

The *Missouri* was to be in Turkey from April 5-9 and members of her crew were to participate in Ambassador Ertegun's funeral ceremonies. Upon their arrival on the 5th, the first order of business was arranging for the transfer of Ambassador Ertegun's remains to shore. This was quickly accomplished and most successfully carried out about noon of the same day. With the *Missouri*'s crew at quarters, the Marine guard at "Present," and the band playing the Turkish national anthem, the casket was slowly lowered into one of the *Missouri*'s boats, where it was received by the chief petty officer body bearers.

Photo # 80-G-376893 USS Missouri saluting. April 1946

As the boat left the side, an ambassador's salute was fired with the Turkish flag at the fore. Passing honors were rendered by all the men-of-war as the boat proceeded slowly to the landing. "Passing Honors" are those honors other than gun salutes, usually all personnel standing at attention and giving a hand salute, rendered on occasions when ships or embarked officers or officials pass or are passed within 600 yards for ships. At the landing, the casket was solemnly turned over to Turkish hands and placed on the traditional artillery caisson. The funeral procession through the streets of Istanbul was preceded by a military escort composed of Turkish army and naval units, and detachments of U.S. Marines and bluejackets, (i.e. enlisted sailors below the rank of chief petty officer from the ships present). Then came the caisson with the body bearers, officers of the various Turkish services as honorary pallbearers, and on the flanks in single file, an honor guard of Turkish soldiers with rifles carried at the reverse. Following all, also on foot, were the official mourners, among whom Ambassador Weddell, Admiral James, and Admiral Hewitt were included.

The *Missouri*'s presence in Turkey served another purpose – to emphasize to the Soviet Union and other nations the United States' concern about political instability in the region.

Photo # 80-G-702555 Funeral procession of Turkish Ambassador to U.S., 1946

As part of the itinerary, the Turkish government held a formal reception in honor the officers of the *Missouri* and the USS *Power*, held at the Dolmabahce Palace, a large structure overlooking the Sea of Bosporus. It was once the residence of the sultans and as such it was quite opulent. The building's ceiling and all the chairs had gold leaf on them. More than fourteen metric tons of gold was used to gild the ceilings. The ornate, yet eclectic palace was decorated in a mixture of Baroque, Rococo, and Neoclassical styles and had the world's largest Bohemian crystal chandelier in the Ceremonial Hall. All the American officers were dressed in their dress white uniforms. The event was attended by Admiral Hewitt, Captain Hillenkoetter, as well as many Turkish dignitaries. The highlight of the evening was the remarkable exhibition of traditional Turkish dances in costume. Each officer received a color-printed paperback book about Turkey and two packs of commemorative cigarettes with the Turkish and American flags on them, as well as an image of the *Missouri*. It surely was a night to remember.

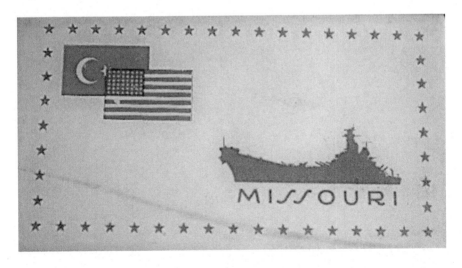

The outside of the box of commemorative cigarettes.

312

Inside the box of commemorative cigarettes.

Cover of commemorative book, a gift from the Turkish government.

Drinks were served at the event and a lot of toasts made. Jim had never been a seasoned drinker. It didn't take much, and it didn't take long before Jim and his wingman, another junior officer, decided to ditch the reception and take a joy ride for some sightseeing. The trouble was there wasn't any transportation for them, except for the U.S. Navy jeep parked out front. The standard American jeep of WWII, either a Ford or Willys, did not have a keyed ignition switch. The ignition was activated by a simple lever-action switch. In other words, any fool could steal a jeep. It appeared that Jim wasn't just any damn fool. First, this jeep had a chain running from the steering wheel to a grommet on the floor. Due to the chain, the driver could only take a quarter turn at a time, either right or left. Second, this was the admiral's jeep, and no one was guarding it.

That didn't stop Jim from "borrowing" it. The streets were very narrow with high walls on either side. As described by Jim, there were shops on street level with apartments riding up four or five stories. As they drove around the area, they got pretty good at negotiating the narrow streets with only quarter turns. That is until they came to a dead end.

They were stuck. It was hard to back up so they tried to turn around. They had to make about 25 quarter turns, forwards and backwards, in order to get the jeep turned around. As they were executing this not so graceful maneuver, they could see Turks looking down from open windows high above them, smoking cigarettes. In the dark, they could barely make out the figure of a person, but they could see the glow of the cigarette. One can only imagine what the Turks were thinking about these two young U.S. Naval officers. In any event, they made their way back to the reception, having sobered up quite a bit by then. When they arrived back at the gala, the Admiral was standing with two Navy Shore Patrol waiting for them. To say the least, the admiral was not happy. The only things that saved Jim was some fast talking and the ribbons and stars on his uniform. The admiral asked Jim what his current position was, where he was serving and where he had earned his stars and ribbons. After Jim explained that he was the assistant navigator aboard the admiral's flagship and a little about the battles he had been in, the admiral recognized that Jim had seen quite a bit of action. Admiral Hewitt was satisfied with a good chewing out and dressing down of this junior officer. Jim wasn't even confined to quarters. The next morning when he woke up, he shook his aching head in disbelief. Jim was very grateful that the Admiral had been so understanding. Jim thanked his lucky stars . . . mainly, his eight battle stars. By traveling back through the Dardanelles, Jim and the rest of the *Missouri*'s crew could claim they were members of the Flying Carpetiers. Like similar recognitions, when a sailor traverses the Dardanelles, he becomes a Flying Carpetier. As the *Missouri* went back down the Dardanelles, Jim was on the bridge navigating. The uniform of the day for the officers was a Turkish fez and tie. The captain was towed around the ship on a Turkish rug by the senior marine officer to review his entire crew on the main deck. The captain sat cross-legged with his arms crossed and folded on his chest. He was playing the part of Aladdin on his flying carpet. The captain wore a wide grin the entire time. The crew was thoroughly entertained. It must have been quite a sight to see.

Photo # 80-G-702531 Adm. Hewitt with Greek Archbishop on USS Missouri, 1946

The *Missouri* then visited Piraeus, Greece, from April 10-14. Archbishop Damaskinos, regent of Greece, boarded the *Missouri* and was greeted by all the officers. April 11 was proclaimed U.S. Navy Day in Piraeus, with a parade and a luncheon by the city fathers. At the luncheon, the Missouri was entertained by a chorus of charming young ladies in native costume.

On April 13, a ball was held for the officers of the *Missouri* and the *Power* at the Grand Bretagne Hotel in Athens. Originally scheduled for April 11, it was rescheduled due to the funeral in Turkey.

U. S. S. MISSOURI

FLAG SHIP

Admiral Henry K. Hewitt USN
Commander Twelfth Fleet

Captain Roscoe H. Hillenkoetter USN
Commander U. S. S. Missouri

ATHENS GREECE   10-14 APRIL 1946

The United States Naval Attache
and
Assistant Naval Attaches
request the pleasure of your company
at a ball to be held at
The Grande Bretagne Hotel
April 14, 1946 at 9.30 p. m.
in honor of the officers of the
USS MISSOURI and USS POWER

Please present card at entrance.

Constitution Square

The next stop on the tour was Italy and Vatican City. While in Italy, Jim was assigned to entertain the U.S. ambassador to Italy, and had dinner at the ambassador's residence, which was an Italian admiral's home. Jim described how the grand foyer had intricate inlaid images of sea creatures in the flooring. The ambassador provided Jim with a military driver and a Rolls-Royce limousine to get him to and from the ship. He also took Jim on a personal tour of the area. While in Italy, many of the crew of the *Missouri* went to Vatican City. They toured St. Peter's Basilica and viewed the Sistine Chapel. A large delegation of officers and enlisted men had a private reception with Pope Pius XII at the Vatican in a large audience room just off the Pope's private chambers. They all received rosaries or medallions, which had been especially blessed for them. It was a great occasion for those who were present.

Crew of the *Missouri* with Pope Pius XII at the Vatican.
Note the ship's chaplain kissing the ring of the Pope.

It turned out that Jim and Bud were both in Naples, Italy, in mid-April. While there, they attempted to visit each other. Jim went to the *Providence* but Bud was off sightseeing. On his return, Bud went to the *Missouri*, but Jim was in Naples. Unfortunately, they were never able to connect. They wrote each other as they continued to tour the Mediterranean. Jim found out that the *Providence* went to Alexandria in May, where she ran aground.

In late April, at another diplomatic function which Jim believed was in Algiers, Algeria, he and his wingman ran into Admiral Hewitt again. When the Admiral arrived and spied Jim from across room, he gestured to Jim with just his index finger that he wished him to approach. Behind the admiral were two shore patrol (SPs). Noticing this, Jim thought for sure the admiral had changed his mind and he was in big trouble for the jeep excursion. The admiral did tell Jim that the two gentlemen were going to keep an eye on him and his partner in crime. He mentioned there was a stable of Arabian white stallions out back and he didn't want Jim getting drunk and deciding to go for a "pony ride." Jim grinned from ear to ear, saluted sharply and said, "Yes sir, Admiral," then dismissed himself. Jim said the admiral grinned just as broadly. There were no further troubles.

The *Missouri*, after visiting ports in England, Gibraltar, Greece, Turkey, Italy, Morocco, and elsewhere, returned to the United States in early May, having successfully reestablished the Navy's presence in what soon became the "Cold War" home waters of the Sixth Fleet.

On May 10, 1946, Jim sent home two letters simultaneously that he had written to his parents. The first was initially dated April 27, but was not finished and mailed for nearly two weeks:

April 27, 1946

At Sea enroute Tangiers

Dear Mom and Dad,

So far we have had a wonderful cruise full of interesting sights and plenty of fancy-pant balls, dances, and cocktail parties. It's one cruise which I'll never forget because it has been such an active one.

Bud boarded the Providence in Istanbul around April 6 and his ship joined us again in Naples, Italy last week; but we were unable to see each other. I visited his ship and he came over to mine on different days and so we missed seeing each other as one of us was always away in town. I imagine he will see plenty in the next few months as his ship sailed out of Naples one day after mine and it is headed to Beirut, Syria and then Alexandria & Cairo, Egypt. We spent three days in Algiers after Naples and are now headed for a three day visit to Tangiers, two more days in Gibraltar and then U.S.A. for one day as I understand it. We've been told that our ship has been ordered to Cuba again on May 9, for more gunnery; so you see I'll probably be at sea until my last day in the service.

(have to eat lunch)

I just discovered another letter that I was writing to you April 27, so I will finish them both now.

I received no word from Bud since he left the MO. I'm waiting for his Division address so that my letters to him won't get lost. For the last week in the Mediterranean I received a lot of mail sent to me last October while I was off the China coast. My mail is still catching up to me.

Today we received a card which makes us members of the Flying Carpetiers for traveling through the Dardanelles. I have three titles you might say- "Shellback", "Golden Dragon", and now "Flying Carpetier".

It's now 2230 and I have to "hit it" at 0430, so I think I will turn in. Will finish this letter tomorrow.

Such a short time! It seemed that I just got to sleep and the quartermaster called me to take the morning star sights. It is now 0630 and I've been up in the chart house trying to figure out our position since 0445. My fix wasn't good because the stars were few and too high. The navigator had trouble also; but he used his fix as best he could which brings us about 1770 miles from Norfolk, VA. at 0800 o'clock this morning. I'm even getting to sound like a navigator.

One thing I found of interest in Europe and North Africa was watches. I never saw so many in all my life, all sizes and shapes, and all prices. In Rome I bought a chronograph for *three cartons of cigarettes ($1.65) and it can do everything except boil an egg.*

Upon arriving in Norfolk, approximately 700 men are leaving the ship to be discharged. How the ship will get underway again is beyond me; unless we get replacements in 24 hours after arrival.

You are certainly keeping mighty busy working and fixing the car, plane and house. I'll have to wait until I come a civilian before I inherit some of that vim and vigor, Dad.

I'm still wondering about school. Maybe I should do more than wonder, but when you are so far from the States it's pretty difficult to do more than to keep thinking about what I plan to do when I get out. But it's serious thinking- believe me. The schools are so crowded that it's hard to get a break in many of the larger ones. My marks at Harvard aren't anything to brag about truthfully when talking about a big-name college accepting my application. But I'll get into school in time I'm sure.

With summer coming on, Dot must be getting anxious for her summer vacation. You'll have your hands full again, Mom, when you have both Dot and I running around wondering what to do.

I must close but I'll be always thinking of all of you.

Love to all,

Jim

May 1946

At Sea

Dear Mom and Dad,

The weather was rough for about three days, but today it had become very calm.

I won't be able to mail this letter until I arrive in the States but I want to make sure you get one while I am there. Our stay in the U.S.A. will be about 24 hours which isn't much. An active ship isn't it? We are due on maneuvers around May 14.

You will be surprised to know, Dad, after remembering how much trouble I had with Navigation, that I am the new assistant navigator on the Missouri. A Commander Mann is my boss, the navigator, and I like the work very much. It is quite an experience being assistant navigator on this big ship after only navigating small YPs at middy school. We the navigators usually rise at 0430-0530 in the morn to take morning sights and, brother, it's certainly early. Of course I used to stand night watch during nights at sea before, but now I rise early every morning to get a fix.

I received the pictures of the plane, Dad, and I'll take them home with me. I just discovered that part of this letter written on 4 May has been mailed with a letter written April 27. You'll have to figure it out I'm afraid.

When we left the Med. area we took aboard two ambassadors, a bunch of civilian business men and we always carried a bunch of newsreel and correspondents. This looks like a civilian passenger liner now with all those people aboard. We even have two or three women aboard living in the Cap't's Cabin. (My writing gets worse every day)

The other night while miles out to sea, we were singing around the piano in the wardroom and one civilian came over to sing with us. He was really "tanked". He must have a barrel in his room. He was from Texas so we made him sing a western song for us. We died laughing.

If I get the chance I'll call you from Norfolk. If I don't get the chance to call, I'll write and until I see you, I'll write you another letter.

Here's hoping we navigators don't run her aground before we get in and until I see you again-the best of everything.

Your son,
Jim

On June 5, 1946, Bud wrote his dad:

Tangiers

Spanish Morocco

Dear Dad,

To begin with dad I want to say I'm sorry for not writing sooner. There was really no excuse for it. I guess I was just darn forgetful. I realize I should have written a long time ago.

Say, I'm sure sorry Jim didn't get a chance to get home when he did. By the time you get this letter he'll be back there. That is according to your letter you said he would be back by the first and here it is the fifth already. Incidentally dad I received your letter dated the nineteenth just this afternoon. I [sic] sure was great hearing from you. You see we've been traveling quite a bit and haven't been getting our mail.

As for my getting back to the states, well dad we expect to get in Boston around the first or tenth of July somewhere. Keep your eyes and ears open about the ship. That is if I am not transferred from the ship before we get back. There's talk of transferring men to Commanders in the other ward. Comdr. of Navy in Europe. That to Admiral Hewitt's crew. You remember he's the Admiral that was on Jim's ship over here?

Things are going along swell over here, but we don't have much time for anything over here. We don't even get sufficient amount of sleep. We're lucky if we get five hours a day. You see we're short of radio men, here on the ship. And we have to stand two watches a day. One on eight hours and then off five and then on for five. It's kind of rugged but I get used to it.

As for radio, I think it's pretty good. I'm the break-down man. Every message that goes out and comes in I de-code it, one way or the other. If it comes in I decode it so it can be read and if it goes out, I put it into code. So you see I know quite a bit about what goes on even before it occurs but they've made me take an oath of secrecy. I feel pretty important. I'm the only enlisted man with to [sic] ensigns helping me out, that is when they're not on liberty. At present I'm on watch but there is no traffic coming in as yet. A few minutes ago I was breaking down on radio. Watch. And I will be again in a minute. The operator just yelled there was another one coming in. I've got at least five minutes yet though.

About the railroad strike I understand it ended a while back. I'm glad of that.

By the way dad, keep that jalopy running. I'm coming home you know. And I hope.

Well dad, it's time to get back to work. So until later I'll say so long.

Love

Bud

P.S. I'm awfully sorry I didn't write before dad. I'll try not to have it happen again.

He wrote his mom and dad again on June 9. This time he types the letter:

At Sea

Dear Mom & Dad

Well folks here I am again. This time we are on our way to Algiers for a five day visit. After that we are going to Gibraltar for a couple of days then we go to the States. We are supposed to start back on the sixteenth of the month.

I'm sorry to say that we are not going to stop off in Boston for our dry-dock period. We are scheduled to go right into Phila PA. for the three months. Although I am hoping to get a leave out of this cruise. (I hope) You see most of the present radio gang getting discharged when we get back to the States. That will only leave three of us left here in the shack. So we do stand a good chance of getting at least ten days anyway. I guess I just wished too hard for Boston. Now I'll never get a chance to get back there again. When I get back to the States I'll give you people a call, just as soon as I am able to get off this confounded ship.

Most of the boys are pretty happy about the whole thing at the present time. Well I guess these guys rate it. After all I was only thinking of myself again. Well at least I'll be able to get home on a weekend. Say, Dad, How about getting the plane out and coming down and getting me? By that way I'll be able to save some time. I could take the train back to Philly. How about it Pop??????? Gee Wizz, that will give you a chance to get some cross-country time. What do you say?????????? O.K. Good

I know one thing though, I'm not going to like staying down there for three solid months. If it was Boston I could get home every night. But here I'll have to wait for the weeks end and that's going to cost quite a bit of money, which at the present time I haven't got.

I'm just as flat as a pan-cake. And that's just putting it mildly. If I'm lucky I'll be able to pick up my travel allowance from Calif. To Lowell, Mass. As yet I haven't been able to get it. I'll just about haunt these paymasters here until I get it. Other-wise I'll have to wait a spell before I can get home.

While I was over here I spent a considerable amount of money. By that I mean a considerable amount of what little I do get over here.

By the way Mom. I got those souveniers [sic] I told you I would pick up while I was over here. I got something in about every port we pulled into. With the exception of a couple of them When I ran out of funds. I've got quite a few of them just the same. And if I do say so myself, most of them are pretty nice. I did how-ever pick up quite a few knives from these desert countries out here. I still don't know why I picked them up but never-the-less they're down in my locker now.

326

Well Folks I don't really know just what to say so I'd better sign off for now. I really get griped over getting so near to home and not being able to get there. Maybe some day I'll get the breaks. Well anyway folks I'll give you a call on the phone as soon as I can get off this rattle-trap. O.K.? O [sic] until then I'll say so long for now. Give my regards and love to the kids.

Love from your son,

Bud

Love to all

Photo of knives acquired by Bud during the Mediterranean tour.

Leaving the Mediterranean on June 16, the *Providence* arrived at Philadelphia on June 25. Bud was excited. He was back in the States and he was given leave from July 1-17. He took a couple of days and visited all the tourist attractions in Philly. Then he jumped on a train and headed to Lowell. Bud had just toured many beautiful and exotic countries in the Mediterranean, but he couldn't wait to get home to Lowell. He spent his leave visiting friends and neighbors. He visited the old haunts. He loved being back in Lowell. It was home. It was the place he felt most comfortable.

Around the same time, Jim and the *Missouri* crossed the Atlantic Ocean and headed back to Casco Bay, Maine, thereby completing its cruise. He remained in Portland, Maine, until July 23, when, without much fanfare, he was discharged from active duty in the Navy, completing his World War II service. While he headed back to Lowell, he remained in the Reserves. Like so many other discharged soldiers, he was looking to go back to school through the G.I. Bill and then search for employment opportunities.

When he initially got home, he was a little restless, bouncing around through several part-time jobs, including installing new systems for Shell Oil and burglar alarms for ADT. Eventually, Jim went to study at the New England Aircraft School. When he completed his studies there, Jim decided that he wanted to finish his college degree, so he applied for admission to Boston University and was accepted. He was given credit for his time at Harvard, attended two years and graduated with a degree in engineering. He thereafter worked for Pratt & Whitney Aircraft, headquartered in East Hartford, Connecticut, in the company's experimental engine testing department. The job required him to move to South Bend, Indiana, where he developed his lifelong love of Notre Dame football. It also gave him the opportunity to occasionally visit Chicago and his old pal, Joe Grilli. Jim was adjusting to civilian life and getting into a routine. But Jim had not seen the last of active duty.

Meanwhile, Bud had yet to complete his service. After drydocking for three months, Bud and the *Providence* headed to the Delaware Bay area. Following departure from the Delaware Capes in October 1946, the *Providence* shipped out to Guantanamo, Cuba, and the Caribbean for training exercises, before returning to Norfolk, Virginia. On February 3, 1947, the *Providence* headed back to the Mediterranean for additional exercises and various port visits.

On April 1, while in Italy, Bud sent a picture postcard to his sister Mary and her husband, Gerry O'Connell:

328

Hi Kid,

Just another stop in my so-called travels. Not bad here. How are things with you two. Be home soon I hope. How about hearing from you. So long for now.
    Love

                           Bud

    To his parents he sent a postcard from the area of Genoa, Italy:

Hello Mom and Dad,

Arrived here three days ago. Haven't gone ashore yet. Leaving tomorrow for Naples. Heading for Turkey soon. Expect to be in Boston around 24 of May. See you then.

                           All my Love
                           Bud

The *Providence* went back to Turkey and then returned to Italy. On May 14, Bud sent another picture postcard to his parents, this time from Naples:

Hello folks;

Well here I am back here again. Still the same old place. No changes hardly at all. This is a castle that is still standing. As yet I haven't really seen the inside. Just saw it from the outside. Give you more dope in letter that follows. Thanks for sending Pete's address.

Love from your son,
Bud

Napoli - Maschio Angioino
Angioino Castle

The *Providence* stayed in the Mediterranean and traveled to Greece, before heading back to the States. Bud arrived in Boston later in May. According to Navy records, on June 15 he had served for three years. As far as can be determined, The *Providence* and Bud remained in Boston until September 1947, when he was ordered to Naval Training Station (NTS) Newport for discharge. He reported to Newport on September 19. Walter Herman "Bud" Turcotte was about to turn 21 years of age. Given credit for accumulated leave time, on September 30 he was given an honorable discharge for his service to his country. He had served three years, three months and two days. He was the last of the four brothers to go into the service and the second to make it home alive.

Walter "Bud" Turcotte

1951-52 Jim Turcotte is Recalled

After the war, Jim had remained in the Naval Reserve. For one weekend a month and two weeks during the summer, he attended classes and training. He was recalled during the Korean Conflict in April 1951 as a lieutenant (jg) and assigned to another heavy cruiser, the USS *Des Moines*. Part of the Sixth Fleet, the *Des Moines* was 716 feet long, weighed some 17,000 tons and could travel at 33 knots.

The USS *Des Moines,* September 8, 1952.

The Navy's last all-gun heavy cruisers were the *Des Moines* class built by Bethlehem Steel Company Fore River in Quincy, Massachusetts. The Navy used the *Baltimore* class of heavy cruisers as the blueprint, making the *Des Moines*, built in 1948, larger and upgrading her with a newly developed, semiautomatic, eight-inch gun. The ship was home to 1,500 officers and men who enjoyed some of the conveniences of the larger battleships, including a crew's lounge, library, retail store, dental and medical spaces, post office, barber shop, a gedunk stand with a soda fountain, and a laundry. The *Des Moines* also published its own bi-monthly newspaper and, as on all ships, movies were shown nightly.

Officers of the *Des Moines*. Jim Front row, center, just to the right of the captain.

The ship was nicknamed "Daisy Mae" from a crew contest to name her in the ship's onboard newspaper. The name was picked from the popular 1950s "Li'l Abner" cartoon strip. The busty, blonde bombshell's character won the contest and the name stuck. Her ship class was completed too late for service in World War II, but the class was employed extensively as fleet flagships during their active careers. Instead of the old, catapulted float planes, the *Des Moines* operated utility helicopters on the stern with a hangar plus an elevator. Her weapons were the massive, main, eight-inch/55-caliber guns in three triple turrets that had a muzzle velocity of 2,800 feet per second and a range of 30,100 yards. Each shell weighed 260 pounds. Armor-piercing shells weighed in at 335 pounds. Each 451-ton turret had a crew of 45 men and the guns had a rate-of-fire of 10 rounds per minute. The ammo resembled a five-inch shell in that the projectile was encased in a brass cartridge. Not having the silk powder bag as the propellant increased the rate of fire and the safety for the crew.

On July 2,1951, the wardroom officers presented Jim with a small silver plate as a token of their appreciation for his service aboard the *Des Moines*. A welcoming gift, of sorts.

Jim was assigned to the Seventh Division as gunnery officer. His varied experience aboard the *Northampton* and the *Missouri* made this a perfect assignment for him. Responsibilities for his division included storekeeper duties, gunnery duties, maneuvering of the ship, and assorted other general seamanship responsibilities. Name a deck division duty and the Seventh Division had it.

On September 1,1951, the *Des Moines* received orders that it was being sent to the Mediterranean as part of the Sixth Fleet Cruise.

SEVENTH Division

IN PEACETIME, the primary function of the Seventh Division is to shoot holes in target sleeves; in wartime it's modified to the extent that the sleeve is replaced by an enemy plane. This function is fulfilled through clever manipulation of the starboard 3-inch battery. The ability to operate, maintain, and repair these radically new pieces of sea-going artillery was developed only after many months of operational practice and concerned study with the cooperation of all personnel. The mount captains, controlmen, and loading crews of each mount are justly proud of the efficiency with which the function of their battery has been effected. Each man is certain that pilots of an enemy nation will have made their last mistake if they decide to attack the starboard side of the DES MOINES.

Whether the man be seaman, or gunner's mate, he is a necessary part of the 3"/50 battery. Hours of drill and training, instructing, and maintenance of the machinery are a few of their duties which make them better equipped to handle war or peacetime emergencies. Being on exposed stations, they must also constantly be alert and proficient in the duties of a lookout.

The secondary, and less violent divisional function is carrying out general seamanship duties and shipboard maintenance of compartment spaces. Whether it be handling lines, rigging booms, or accommodation ladders, cleaning or painting the ship, or maneuvering a ship's boat, the deck hands can be counted on to work with skill and enthusiasm at their tasks.

Replenishment and provisioning provide a few of the other seamanship responsibilities of this division. Name a deck division duty and the Seventh has it.

FRONT ROW: R. E. Beard, SN; F. F. Tetsel, SA; D. M. Lindsay, GM3; R. L. Boss, SA. . . . SECOND ROW: K. D. Adkins, SN; J. J. Healy, SN; G. L. Jadoin, SA; T. M. Osborne, SA; R. E. Tomsu, SA; J. E. Oden, BM3; P. S. McLoughlin, SA. . . . THIRD ROW: W. E. Giroux, SA; E. M. Hammond, GM1; A. N. Henry, SA; C. R. Rich, SN; J. H. Turcotte, LT (j.g.); R. Borkowski, SA; R. C. Kerr, SN; S. A. Bovi, SN; G. E. Foreacre, SN. . . . FOURTH ROW: E. L. Gurgonious, SN; D. I. Egler, SA; F. L. Waite, SA; L. G. Nabrega, SA; A. J. Hinson, SN; M. R. Shapiro, SN; G. C. McAfee, SN; T. F. Lerton, SN; R. T. Kollfels, SA; J. J. Conlay, SA.

Holystoning.

Scrub down.

PORTS OF CALL

DEPARTED NORFOLK	3 September 1951
GIBRALTAR	19 September — 21 September
LISBON, PORTUGAL	22 September — 26 September
AUGUSTA BAY, SICILY	1 October — 6 October
NAPLES, ITALY	8 October — 16 October
VILLEFRANCHE, FRANCE	21 October — 2 November
ATHENS, GREECE	9 November — 14 November
SUDA BAY, CRETE	15 November — 16 November
ISTANBUL, TURKEY	20 November — 27 November
BIZERTE, TUNISIA	3 December — 7 December
VALLETTA, MALTA	11 December — 14 December
AUGUSTA BAY, SICILY	14 December — 15 December
REJECKA, YUGOSLAVIA	17 December — 21 December
VILLEFRANCHE, FRANCE	23 December — 3 January
BARCELONA, SPAIN	9 January — 15 January
GIBRALTAR	21 January — 25 January
ARRIVED NORFOLK	4 February

Most likely to the delight of his parents and family, he never saw action during this second-tour of duty. Instead, Jim revisited some of the ports from his tour with the *Missouri*, but there were other new ports of call and adventures as well. He was really looking forward to this cruise. He was going back to sea and had been away from it for a few years, but it was like going back home. As a bonus, he would be in the Mediterranean for nearly five months. The *Des Moines* departed Norfolk on September 3, arriving in Gibraltar on September 19. They then stopped in Lisbon, Portugal on the 22nd and Sicily on October 1. The ship spent a week in Sicily and another week in Naples, Italy. On October 16, the *Des Moines* departed Naples with the Supreme Commander of NATO, General Dwight D. Eisenhower, and Admiral Carney aboard. They remained on board until October 18, when they departed for Nice, France, by helicopter.

From 1951 to 1953, Admiral Carney served as commander-in-chief of the NATO's Allied Forces of Southern Europe, where he was responsible for the fleets of five countries and the armed forces of Italy, Greece, and Turkey. On May 13, 1953, now President Eisenhower selected Carney as the next chief of Naval Operations.

The *Des Moines* then went to Nice, stopped in Athens, Greece, Suda Bay, Crete, and then cruised back to Athens. On November 20, it arrived in Turkey. Jim spent Thanksgiving in Istanbul, this time without any incidents.

From Turkey the ship headed to Bizert, Tunisia. After four days there, it departed for Malta, where they received Gerald Creasy, the Governor of Malta aboard for an official visit.

Gerald Creasy, Governor of Malta, 1951.

From Malta, they cruised to Sicily and on to Rijeka, Yugoslavia. After four days, they headed back to France, arriving on December 23. Jim spent Christmas and New Year's in Villefranche, France, a city on the French Riviera located near the French-Italian border next to the Principality of Monaco. On January 3, 1952, the *Des Moines* departed France and headed to Barcelona, Spain. After nearly a week there, they headed back to Gibraltar for their final stop of the cruise and departed Gibraltar on January 25. In all, they visited 11 different countries and 14 different ports on a cruise that lasted five months.

They arrived back in "Shit City" (as Jim lovingly referred to Norfolk) on February 4. Located in southeast Virginia, Norfolk was home to the biggest Navy base in the world. Amongst Navy personnel, it was also the worst Navy base in the world in terms of quality of life. Residents complained that the base housing was trashy, there was too much crime, and the traffic was bad. You needed to use the highway to get anywhere and everywhere. The overall area was called Hampton Roads, which encompassed the entirety of the surrounding metropolitan region in southeastern Virginia and northeastern North Carolina. Some people also disliked how "Navy" the area was, suggesting that there was no way to escape because everywhere you looked it was military. Adding insult to injury, the entire city is below sea level, so when it rains the whole city floods.

Jim remained aboard the *Des Moines,* in Norfolk, until September 15, 1952 when he was discharged from active duty, this time for good. No one could have anticipated the future of the four Turcotte boys on July 20, 1938 when Lionel enlisted in the U.S. Navy. The world was a much bigger place then, and these four men went on to see a large part of it, often under the worst of circumstances. For Lionel and Bob, their time in the Navy was where they, as Lincoln said in his Gettysburg address, "gave the last full measure of devotion." So many American men, from an incredible diversity of backgrounds, rural farms, small towns, big cities, rich and poor, young and not so young, gave that same measure of devotion. Would these four brothers from Lowell have joined up if they had the slightest inkling of their future? It is impossible to say. But, given their character and spirit, it is more than likely they would have done little different if they had known ahead of time that war was in their future. The Turcotte brothers, like so many others, were ready to step up for their country and take those huge risks we have asked, throughout our history, of our men and women in the armed services of the United States of America. What makes them do it? Pride? The love of adventure? A sense of duty? Family tradition? There are probably too many reasons to list them all. And while these young men of WWII gave so much, so did their families, friends, and loved ones who were left at home clutching worn photographs, folded letters, post cards and precious, often painful, memories, trying to make some sense of the loss.

When Jim walked away from Norfolk that September day, he was not greeted by parades in the streets. There were no blowing of trumpets heralding his achievements. His name wasn't lit up on any marquees. He just went home. He went to start a new future, a new chapter in his life. These experiences built his character the same way that fire tests gold and makes it purer. Likewise, these four brothers, part of something bigger than themselves, helped save the world, helped build the character of their nation by the giving of their blood, sweat and tears.

Epilogue

The Navy had Lionel's remains returned home to Lowell for a final resting in May 1948. It was very emotional for the whole Turcotte family as it dredged up old feelings of loss. As with Bob years before, it was like losing Lionel all over again. As his widow, Claire had Lionel buried in St. Patrick's Cemetery in Lowell, alongside his daughter, Carol Ann. The following articles ran in the *Lowell Sun* onApril 29 and May 4, 1948, respectively:

Body of Local War Hero Due Here Tomorrow

Lionel O. Turcotte Killed in Pacific Plane Crash, 1944

LOWELL—The body of Chief Machinist Mate Lionel O. Turcotte, U. S. Navy veteran, killed in a plane crash off Surnan, Dutch Guinea, Feb. 17, 1944, will arrive here tomorrow at 6.22 p. m.

Born in Lowell, the son of Herman O. and Helen G. (Willett) Turcotte, 113 Varnum avenue, he was a graduate of the Pawtucket school, Bartlett junior high and Lowell high school, class of 1936.

He was the second of two sons killed in the service. His brother, Robert T. Turcotte, was killed in a plane crash in a flight from the deck of the USS Cincinnati, a cruiser, June 5, 1943. In addition to his parents, he is survived by his wife, Mrs. Clare (Brennan) (Turcotte) Monro; three sisters, Mrs. James Lyman, Jr., Mrs. Gerard O'Connell of Jamaica Plain and Dorothy I. Turcotte; two brothers, James H. Turcotte and Walter Turcotte; his paternal grandparents, Mr. and Mrs. Oswald A. Turcotte; several uncles, aunts, nieces and nephews.

Prior to his enlistment in the Navy he had been a member of the Headquarters company of the 182nd Infantry, Massachusetts National Guard.

Full Military Honors for L. O. Turcotte

LOWELL—With full military honors the funeral of Chief Machinist Mate Lionel O. Turcotte of 113 Varnum avenue was held yesterday.

The cortege, preceded by a flower car, left the Savage Memorial home, 390 Pawtucket street, for St. Rita's church where at 10 o'clock a solemn funeral mass was celebrated by Rev. John E. Murphy, assisted by Rev. Jeremiah J. Collins of St. Michael's church as deacon, and Rev. John J. Fallon as subdeacon. Frederick Turcotte, a nephew, was one of the altar boys. The choir, under the direction of Mrs. J. Clifford Goodwin, the organist, sang Terry's requiem mass. The solos were sustained by Mrs. Warren P. Riordan, Mrs. John A. Clement, Mrs. Robert McLaughlin and Raymond Bissallion.

Present at the mass the following delegations, representing St. Rita's Holy Name society were John Ginivan, Christopher Downing, James Commerford, Alfred Cooney, Thomas Brosnan, Michael Larkin, John Walsh and John McManmon; the Lowell post 87, American Legion, who also acted as the firing squad, consisted of J. William Buckley, John E. Avila, Rudolph J. Emond, Peter J. Robinson, George M. McDonough, Walter J. Lyons, Warren Wilson and John Grenier, bugler; the American Gold Star Mothers were represented by Mrs. Sylvia Nadeau, Mrs. Laura Gilbert, Mrs. Elizabeth Shenley, Mrs. Theresa Donaghue and Mrs. Josephine Keefe. Also present were Raymond Webb and Joseph Duffy. At the close of the mass the national anthem was played.

The bearers were M-Sgt. Henry F. Baker, M-Sgt. George D. Hogan, M-Sgt. Earl H. Wescom, F-Sgt. Robert B. Jones, S-Sgt. Charles E. Martin and S-Sgt. James E. Everett, all members of the U. S. Army.

At the grave the committal prayers were read by Rev. Fr. Fallon and the flag that draped the casket was presented to the father by Chief Machinist Mate George Charrette, who acted as the escort. A volley was fired over the grave and taps was sounded. Arrangements were in charge of Peter H. Savage Son.

Lionel would always be remembered for the fact that he died doing what he loved, flying. And he did it fighting for his country.

Like many women of her generation, Claire was tough as nails. She picked herself up and dusted herself off and got on with living. She enlisted in the United States Navy to become a Navy nurse. On August 17, 1944, she reported as an Apprentice Seaman to "Wave" bootcamp at the Naval Training School in Bronx, N. Y.

By the time his remains were returned home, Claire had become Claire Munro. While working as a nurse in Lowell, she met John R. Munro, who went by "Jack." Jack was a Navy man as well and a Pearl Harbor survivor. At the time of the Japanese attack, Jack had been aboard a ship in the harbor. Claire and Jack married in 1945 in Lowell. Everyone was happy for her, as she had experienced so much loss in such a short period of time.

Initially, Claire and Jack made a home in Lowell. In 1969, Claire attended her 30th high school reunion for Lowell High School's Class of 1939. Claire and Jack moved to Arizona, where his brother lived. Jack and Claire adopted two children, Linda and Robbie. Linda rode horses and Robbie rode dirt bikes. Jack and his brother worked in the aerospace industry. His work caused them to move to

California, where he also was very involved in the Pearl Harbor Survivor's group. Jack and Claire often traveled to their reunions.

Claire and Jack Munro, circa 1945.

In 1991, Jack passed away. As a true seaman, he was cremated and buried at sea. Claire moved in with her daughter, Linda. She was a doting grandmother. The whole family moved back to Arizona, where Claire died on March 1, 2007. By all accounts, Claire led a happy and fulfilled life.

Claire and Jack Munro, circa 1990.

After the war, the East Coast Memorial was erected at Battery Park in New York City "…in proud and grateful remembrance of her sons who gave their lives in her service and who sleep in the American coastal waters of the Atlantic Ocean." Robert (Bob) Turcotte is listed there as missing in action or at sea.

TUCKER CLIFFORD ...
TUCKER EARL M · · STEWARD'S MATE 1C · · · U S N R · · · NEW JERSEY
TULL RICHARD M · · SEAMAN 2C · · USNR · · · U S N · MASS
TURCOTTE ROBERT T · AVN CHIEF MACHINIST'S MATE · U S N · CONNECTICUT
TURDIN ALEXANDER M · WATER TENDER 2C · U S N · NEW JERSEY
TURNER ALFRED J JR · SHIP'S COOK 3C · U S N R · ARKANSAS
TURNER BILLIE GENE · MESS ATTENDANT 2C · U S N · ILLINOIS

His pilot, Sidney Goodman, also is listed on the East Coast Memorial.

345

Through the G.I. Bill, Walter "Bud" Turcotte attended Boston University and then also went on to study at the New England Aircraft School, where his father was an instructor. Bud married Ann Bakey, who was also from Lowell. They had two children, Brian and Patricia (Patti). Ann passed away on September 18, 1976. Bud was a senior draftsman at the Middlesex County Registry of Deeds in Lowell, retiring in 1990. He also was an accomplished amateur artist. Walter "Bud" Turcotte passed away on December 22, 1997. For his service to his country, Bud was awarded:

The World War Two Medal

The American Area Campaign Medal

The Asiatic-Pacific Area Campaign Medal and Ribbon with a star for the Battle of Okinawa

The Good Conduct Medal

After his second stint in the Navy, Jim returned to work at Pratt & Whitney Aircraft in East Hartford, Connecticut. Jim married Doris Matthews, also from Lowell, and they raised five children – Hugh ("Bud"), Thomas, Mary, James, and Marsha. Jim remained in the Reserves until he formally retired from the Navy in 1983, following 43 years of service. He received the following awards and recognitions for his years of U.S. Navy service:

Asiatic-Pacific Campaign Medal with 1 silver star and 3 bronze stars

American Defense SVC Medal with Fleet clasp

Navy Occupation SVC Medal with Europe and Asia Clasp

American Campaign Medal

China Service Medal

World War II Victory Medal

National Defense Service Medal

Good Conduct Medal

American Defense Ribbon (1 star)

Asiatic Pacific Ribbon (8 stars)

World War II Victory Ribbon

American Theatre Ribbon

Honorable Service Lapel Button

Connecticut Wartime Veterans Service Medal

Jim's military career set a fine example for his children and grandchildren. His son Hugh enlisted in the U.S. Navy and served one tour. After college, Hugh joined the U.S. Army. He was a career officer, retiring as a major. Hugh's daughter, Diana, also served in the U.S. Army. One of Jim's grandsons and namesakes, Jimmy, currently is a first lieutenant in the United States Army National Guard in Connecticut.

Jim always enjoyed the routine and rhythm of Navy life and the camaraderie of his fellow servicemen, whether they were enlisted men or officers. Jim never met a serviceman he didn't like. When we were kids traveling on vacation in our station wagon, if Jim saw a serviceman on the highway hitchhiking, he always pulled over and gave him a ride. "Move over kids, get in the back and give this serviceman your seat," he'd say. He always asked the serviceman where he was headed (usually they were on leave) and where he served. Because he had been both an enlisted man and an officer, he could talk to any member of the service and could relate to their situation. Jim had been in their shoes.

Using their military travel benefits, Jim and Doris traveled extensively. On a Space-A military flight many years later, when Jim was in his eighties, he struck up a conversation with a gentleman slightly older than he. It turned out the seatmate was a retired rear admiral who had been a lieutenant commander in the Navy aboard the USS *Honolulu* during WWII, the ship directly in front of the *Northampton* during the Battle of Tassafaronga. The pair spent the next four hours telling each other stories not only about that night in 1942 but also about other events throughout their respective Naval careers. Neither one had had a better flight in their life. They were just as excited telling their stories as when they were 21-year-old kids, maybe more. When the flight was over, they shook hands and gave each other a very uncustomary hug. Jim stepped back and saluted his new friend. The admiral returned the salute.

Jim was very proud of his family's service to our country and the sacrifices the Turcotte family made. He passed away on January 2, 2014, at nearly 92 years of age, of natural causes.

The City of Lowell remembered the sacrifices the Turcottes made during the war. Lowell and the American Legion invited Helen Turcotte to be the guest of honor, along with some disabled vets, at a dinner and parade on August 24, 1946. On November 17, 1947, the city named the intersection of Varnum Avenue and Pawtucket Boulevard "Turcotte Square" in honor of Lionel Turcotte and Robert Turcotte, who lost their lives in the service of our country. To this day a sign with a gold star marks that location, near where they grew up, as a tribute to their sacrifice.

Herman continued with his teaching, eventually becoming dean of the Boston Diesel Engineering School. The school was later acquired by Boston University and thereafter Herman was made an associate professor of Aeronautical and Electrical Engineering, teaching at B.U. until his retirement in 1962. The following year, Herman and Helen planned to sell the family home in Lowell and moved to Florida. They dreamed of buying a house and a small boat with the idea that they would live out their lives in the relative comfort of retirement.

Helen Turcotte, the family's matriarch, was never able to enjoy that dream of a Florida retirement. She never moved to warmer climates. Her health began to fail shortly after Herman's retirement. However, despite her declining health, Helen continued to be active in the Gold Star Mothers until her illness prevented her from doing so. Even then, she continued to pay her membership dues to the Lowell Chapter of the Gold Star Mothers until her passing.

Helen Turcotte, last row, second from left.

Helen at a Gold Star Mother's event, front row, second from right.

Perhaps no one in the Turcotte family, who survived the war, suffered more than Helen. She had lost her two oldest sons in the cause of freedom and lived with the pain of that loss for another 22 years. After her sons' deaths, she remained a devoted mother, faithful wife, loving grandmother, and great grandmother. However, she was never the same. There was always a subtle sadness about her. It is clear that the loss of her two sons aged her beyond her years.

Helen passed away on December 13, 1966, St. Joseph's Hospital, Dracut, MA at the age of 69. Herman died just over a year later on January 3, 1968 at the age of 68.

Everyone in Lowell knew and respected the sacrifice the Turcotte family had made for the war effort. In July 1944, St. Rita's Church posted a tribute to the Turcottes in the parish bulletin:

A well-known family in the Parish, and one that might be considered to have been hit hardest by the war, are the Turcottes. This Varnum Avenue family has lost one son, Lionel, who was killed in a plane crash. Another son, Robert, is still listed as missing in action. Jimmy, the youngest of the three has seen plenty of action. . .A fourth son, Walter has just entered the navy [sic] and is in boot camp. Maude, a graduate nurse as of this month, is planning on being a Navy nurse some day, and Mary is a cadet nurse, now in training at St. Joseph's. With just Dorothy, the youngest child at home, Mr. & Mrs. Turcotte can certainly be said to have given more than their share in this war, and we all admire their trust in God, and their resignation to His Will in a time of such trial.

352

References

Cover Photo (Courtesy of Patricia Cossette)

p.1 Photo of Helen Turcotte at Goldstar Mother's Dinner November 12, 1957 (Turcotte Family Collection)

p.2 Photo of Installation of Officers Gold Star Mothers Ticket (Turcotte Family Collection)

p.3 Photo of Helen Turcotte with Jacqueline Kennedy Luncheon 1958 (Turcotte Family Collection)

p. 4 *Lowell, Massachusetts,* Retrieved from https://en.wikipedia.org/wiki/History_of_Lowell,_Massachusetts, Accessed June 9, 2019

p.4 *Saint Jean-Baptiste Day,* Retrieved from https://en.wikipedia.org/wiki/Saint-Jean-Baptiste_Day, Accessed June 9, 2019

p.4 *St. Jean-Baptiste celebrations*, Retrieved from https://www.thecanadianencyclopedia.ca/en/article/st-jean-baptiste-celebrations-emc, Accessed June 10, 2019

p.4 *Le Comite´ Franco-Américain de Lowell*, Newspapers, Retrieved from https://francolowellma.wordpress.com/newspapers/, Accessed June 9, 2019

p.7 Herman and Helen Turcotte's wedding photo (Turcotte Family Collection)

p.7 Photo of Lionel Turcotte Age 2 (Turcotte Family Collection)

p.8 Photo of Mary, Maude, Jim, Robert, and Lionel Turcotte as children (Turcotte Family Collection)

p.9 Two photos of Herman at Turcotte's Shell Station, Lowell, MA (Turcotte Family Collection)

p.12 Turcotte children at Lake Althea (Mud Pond) (Turcotte Family Collection)

p.12 Children with Helen in Lake Althea (Turcotte Family Collection)

p.13 Herman, Helen and Lionel at Lake Althea (Mud Pond) (Turcotte Family Collection)

p.15 Photo of Herman Turcotte building plane at his home garage (Turcotte Family Collection) p.16 Photo of plane built at Herman Turcotte's garage without the wings

p.16 Photo of Herman Turcotte's plane on frozen Merrimack River (Turcotte Family Collection)

p.18 Lionel Turcotte in National Guard (Turcotte Family Collection)

p.19 Lionel Turcotte's discharge from National Guard (Turcotte Family Collection)

p.21 Lionel Turcotte's bootcamp unit photo (Turcotte Family Collection)

p.21 *Naval Air Station Pensacola,* Retrieved from https://en.wikipedia.org/wiki/Naval_Air_Station_Pensacola, Accessed June 14, 2019

p.23 Photo of Lionel Turcotte in blue Navy Uniform (Turcotte Family Collection)

p.24 Photo of Robert Turcotte in Newport, bootcamp (Turcotte Family Collection)

p.25 *The Lowell Sun,* January 11, 1940, Navy Notes, p. 15

p.25 *Byron McCandless,* Retrieved from https://en.wikipedia.org/wiki/Byron_McCandless, Accessed July 5, 2019

p.25-26 *USS Cincinnati (CL-6),* Retrieved from https://en.wikipedia.org/wiki/USS_Cincinnati_(CL-6), Accessed June 25, 2019

p.25-26 *USS Cincinnati CL-6,* Retrieved from http://www.historyofwar.org/articles/weapons_USS_Cincinnati_CL6.html, Accessed June 25, 2019

p.25 Photo of USS *Cincinnati,* late 1930's (U.S. Naval History and Heritage Command Photograph #NH67531)

p.26 Photo of Float plane from USS *Cincinnati,* City of Vancouver Archives, James Crookall fonds, photo # AM640-S1-CVA260-687), Retrieved from https://searcharchives.vancouver.ca/biplanes-on-the-deck-of-u-s-ship-cincinnati, Accessed on June 25, 2019

p. 27 *Information Bulletin,* July 1942, Number 304, Bureau of Naval Personnel World War II Command File, Operational Archives Branch, Naval Historical Center, Washington, DC, Retrieved from Naval History and Heritage Command, The Sullivan Brothers: U.S. Navy Policy Regarding Family Members Serving Together at Sea https://www.history.navy.mil/browse-by-topic/disasters-and-phenomena/the-sullivan-brothers-and-the-assignment-of-family-members/sullivan-brothers-family-members.html, Accessed July 25, 2019 p.30 Photo of Lionel Turcotte with his squadron, NAS Pensacola (Turcotte Family Collection)

p.30-31 *Petty officer,* Retrieved from https://en.wikipedia.org/wiki/Petty_officer, Accessed July 18, 2019

p.30-31 *Petty officer third class,* Retrieved from https://en.wikipedia.org/wiki/Petty_officer_third_class, Accessed July 18, 2019

p.30-31 *Aviation machinist mate,* Retrieved from https://en.wikipedia.org/wiki/Aviation_machinist%27s_mate, Accessed July 18, 2019

p.31 Robert and Lionel Turcotte on front steps of house (Turcotte Family Collection)

p.34 Map of Oahu and Pearl Harbor, U.S. Navy, Department of Navy Bureau of Docks and Yards, *Building the Navy's Bases in World War II Vol. II Part III History of the Bureau of Yards and Docks and the Civil Engineer Corps 1940-1946,* (1947), 123, Retrieved from https://www.history.navy.mil/research/library/online-reading-room/title-list-alphabetically/b/building-the-navys-bases/building-the-navys-bases-vol-2.html, Accessed September 18, 2019

p.35 *U.S. Navy Squadron Designations and Abbreviations,* Appendix 4, Retrieved from https://www.history/navy/mil/content/dam/nhhc/research /histories/naval-aviation/dictionary-of-american-naval-aviation-squadrons-volume-1/pdf/Appendx4.pdf, Accessed July 12, 2019

p.37 Robert Turcotte's Golden Dragon Certificate (Turcotte Family Collection)

p.38 Robert Turcotte's Post card from Guam (Turcotte Family Collection)

p.39 Jim Turcotte in white Navy uniform (Turcotte Family Collection)

p.42 Jim Turcotte's graduation photo from Newport, bootcamp (Turcotte Family Collection)

p.42 Jim Turcotte's unit photo Newport, R.I. 1940 (Turcotte Family Collection)

p.43 Photo of USS *Constellation* (Naval History and Heritage Command #NH 5360)

p.43 *USS Constellation,* Retrieved from https://en.wikipedia.org/wiki/USS_Constellation_(1854), Accessed September 20, 2019

p.44-45 *USS King, (DD-242),* Retrieved from https://en.wikipedia.org/wiki/USS_King_(DD-242), Accessed September 19, 2019

p.45 Photo of USS *King* (Naval History and Heritage Command NH73278)

355

p. 44-5 Answers, https://www.answers.com/Q/Why_are_destroyers_called_tin_cans, Accessed July 6, 2019

p.50- *Line crossing ceremony*, Retrieved from https://en.wikipedia.org/wiki/Line-crossing_ceremony, Accessed September 24, 2019

p.4 Abdulhafedh, A. *The Panama Canal: A Man-Made Engineering Marvel* (March 2017) International Journal of Social Science and Humanities Research, Volume 5, Issue 1 Retrieved from https://www.researchgate.net/publication/337499463_The_Panama_Canal_A_Manmade_Engineering_Marvel, Accessed October 29, 2019

p.52 *NAS Jacksonville, Florida*, Retrieved from www.scharch.org/Ed_Scharch/08-nas-jax-oper.htm, Accessed August 16, 2019

p.52-53 *Britannica*, Aviation, Retrieved from https://www.britannica.com/technolgy/avaiation, Accessed August 16, 2019

p.52 *Link Trainer*, Retrieved from https://en.wikipedia.org/wiki/link_trainer, Accessed August 16, 2019

p.53 Image of Lionel's Institute of Instrument and Radio Beam Flying Certificate, NAS Jacksonville (Turcotte Family Collection)

p.54 *Neutrality Patrol, The Objective*, Retrieved from www.sixtant.net/2011/artigos.php?cat=the-neutrality-patrol&sub=neutrality-patrol-&tag=1)-the objective, Accessed September 23, 2019

p.54 *Line crossing ceremony*, Retrieved from https://en.wikipedia.org/wiki/Line-crossing_ceremony, Accessed September 24, 2019

p.54 *Line crossing ceremony*, Retrieved from https://military.wikia.org/wiki/Line-crossing_ceremony, accessed September 24, 2019

p.57 Team Mighty, *The Meanings Behind 19 Classic Sailor Tattoos*, July 15, 2016) Retrieved from https://www.military.com/undertheradar/2016/07/here-are-the-meanings-behind-19-classic-sailor-tattoos, Accessed September 24, 2019

p.60 *Ratings*, Retrieved from https://bluejacket.com/usn_ratings.html, Accessed July 6, 2019

p.60 Photo of Jim Turcotte "in jail" San Francisco, 1941 (Turcotte Family Collection)

p.61 *USS Northampton (CA-26)*, Retrieved from https://en.wikipedia.org/wiki/USS_Northampton_(CA-26), Accessed July 9, 2019 p.61 Rickard, J. USS *Northampton CA-26,* (March 10, 2014) Retrieved from http://www.historyofwar.org/articles/weapons_USS_Northampton_CA26.html, accessed July 9, 2019

p.61 Photo of USS *Northampton* (Naval History and Heritage Command NH -67844)

p.62 *Storekeeper,* Retrieved from https://en.wikipedia.org/wiki/Storekeeper, July 18, 2019

p.63 Photo of Jim Turcotte and another sailor on a bicycle built for two, San Francisco, 1941 (Turcotte Family Collection)

p.64 Image of Lionel Turcotte's telegram to Herman for Father's Day, 1941 (Turcotte Family Collection)

p.65 *Neutrality patrol,* Retrieved from https://en.wikipedia.org/wiki/Neutrality_Patrol, Accessed September 23, 2019

p. 65 Polmar, N. *Historic Aircraft,* Naval History Magazine, Volume 21 Number 6, (December 2007). Retrieved from https://www.usni.org/magazines/naval-history-magazine/2007/december/historic-aircraftwwiibrazil.com/, Accessed September 27, 2019

p.65 Photo of USS *Cincinnati* July 8, 1942 (Naval History and Heritage Command #19-N-32590)

p. 65 *USS Cincinnati (CL-6),* Retrieved from https://en.wikipedia.org/wiki/USS_Cincinnati_(CL-6), Accessed June 25, 2019

p.66 Photo of Robert Turcotte in white Navy Uniform (Turcotte Family Collection)

p.67 Photo of Jim Turcotte on Waikiki Beach, 1941 (Turcotte Family Collection)

p. 67 *Royal Hawaiian,* Retrieved from https://www.royal-hawaiian.com/history-overview/, Accessed June 5, 2020

p. 67 *Royal Hawaiian Hotel,* Retrieved from https://en.wikipedia.org/wiki/Royal_Hawaiian_Hotel, Accessed June 5, 2020

p.68 Zimmerman, D. J. *Insulting the Flying Tigers* (March 30, 2012). Retrieved from https://www.defensemedianetwork.com/stories/insulting-the-flying-tigers/, Accessed June 14, 2019

p. 68 *American Volunteer Group,* Retrieved from https://en.wikipedia.org/wiki/American_Volunteer_Group, Accessed June 14, 2019

p. 68 *Flying Tigers,* Retrieved from https://en.wikipedia.org/wiki/Flying_Tigers, accessed June 14, 2019

p. 70 *US Warships At Brisbane* (1941, August 6) Barrier Miner, Ed. Broken Hill, Retrieved from https://trove.nla.gov.au/newspaper/article/48393284, Accessed October 8, 2019

p. 70 Taplett, R.D. *So This is War: A Young Marine Officer's Account of Pearl Harbor and the Pacific Conflict* (August 3, 2020) Retrieved from https://www.historynet.com/so-this-is-war-a-young-marine-officers-account-of-peral-harbor-and-the-pacific-conflict.htm, Accessed October 8, 2019

p.71 Photo of USS *Northampton* Brisbane Australia, August 5, 1941 (Naval History and Heritage Command #NH94596)

p.72 Map of world showing Equator and 180th Meridian (Created by Matthew I. N. Turcotte)

p.73 Image of Jim Turcotte's Certificate (Turcotte Family Collection)

p. 73-7 *Domain of the Golden Dragon,* Retrieved from https://en.wikipedia.org/wiki/Domain_of_the_Golden_Dragon, Accessed September 24, 2019

p.73 *Line crossing ceremony,* Retrieved from https://en.wikipedia.org/wiki/Line-crossing_ceremony, accessed September 24, 2019

p.74 Photo of Jim Turcotte on Waikiki Beach, 1941 (Turcotte Family Collection)

p.74-75 *Esther Williams,* Retrieved from https://en.wikipedia.org/wiki/Esther_Williams, Accessed October 5, 2019

p. 74-75 *Esther Williams,* Retrieved from https://www.sunsigns.org/famousbirthdays/d/profile/esther-williams/, Accessed October 5, 2019

p.75 Giberson, A. (1983, September 23) *"The Fighting Nora". Gosport* Vol. XLII No. 38 p. 10

p. 75 Naval History and Heritage Command, Today in Naval History, December 5 Retrieved from https://www.history.navy.mil/content/history/nhhc/today-in-history/december-5.html, Accessed on October 4, 2019

p. 7 Kaushik, N. (2012, March 12). Difference Between General Quarters and Battle Stations, Retrieved from /www.differencebetween.net/technology/protocols-formats/difference-between-general-quarters-and-battle-stations/, Accessed on October 6, 2019

p. 76 General Quarters, Retrieved from https://en.wikipedia.org/wiki/General_quarters, Accessed on October 6, 2019

358

p.77 Diagram of Ship (Created by Matthew I. N. Turcotte)

p.77 CXAM Radar, Retrieved from https://en.wikipedia.org/wiki/CXAM_radar, Accessed on October 6, 2019

p.78 Image of JR Talker (Modified image from Naval History and Heritage Command #NH 96783)

p.79-81 Giberson, A. (1983, September 23) *"The Fighting Nora"*. Gosport Vol. XLII No. 38 p. 10

p.79 Photo of SOC Seagulls from USS *Northampton* flying over Hawaii early 1941, GOSPORT Vol. XLII No. 38, September 23, 1983 p. 11 (Permission to publish courtesy of Edward J. Omelina)

p.80 Photo of USS *Northampton* arriving Pearl Harbor December 8, 1941 (Naval History and Heritage Command #NH 80-G-32548)

p. 81 *USS Enterprise CV-6*, Retrieved from https://en.wikipedia.org/wiki/USS_Enterprise_%28CV-6%29, Accessed June 29, 2019

p. 82 *Naval Air Station Squantum*, Retrieved from https://en.wikipedia.org/wiki/Naval_Air_Station_Squantum, Accessed June 30, 2019

p.83 Photo of Claire Brennan (Turcotte Family Collection)

p. 83 *The Lowell Sun, September 20, 1938, p. 9, Sports*

p. 84 *Quonset Point Air National Guard Station*, Retrieved from https://en.wikipedia.org/wiki/Quonset_Point_Air_National_Guard_Station, Accessed June 30, 2019

p. 84 fn. 5 *Quonset hut*, Retrieved from http://en.wikipedia.org/wiki/Quonet_hut, accessed June 30, 2019

p.85 Photo of Bob and Herman Turcotte in Lowell, Massachusetts (Turcotte Family Collection)

p 85-93 U.S. Navy, Office of Naval Intelligence, Naval History and Heritage Command, *World War II 75th Anniversary Commemorative Series Combat Narratives Early Raids in the Pacific Ocean; February 1 to March 10, 1942 Marshall and Gilbert Islands, Rabaul, Wake and Marcus, Lae and Salamaua*, 1-34, Retrieved from http://www.history.navy.mil/content/dam/nhhc/browse-by-topic/war%20and%20Conflict/WWII/Early-Raids-170407.pdf, Accessed June 8, 2019 p.91 Photo of USS *Northampton* port guns during attack of Wotje (Naval History and Heritage Command #NH50943)

p.93 Photo of USS *Northampton* firing eight-inch guns in attack on Wotje (Naval History and Heritage Command #NH50942)

p.94 Arial photo of Wotje Atoll seen burning (Naval History and Heritage Command #NH97593)

p. 94 *Clean sweep (naval)*, Retrieved from https://en.wikipedia.org/wiki/Clean_sweep_(naval), Accessed June 10, 2019

p.96 Image of a Bell P-39, Bell Airacobra, Ashman, L.M. Cpl. U.S National Archives Photo Collection, Retrieved from https://catalog.archives.gov/id/74237205.Accessed June 16, 2019

p.95-109 U.S. Navy, Office of Naval Intelligence, Naval History and Heritage Command *World War II 75th Anniversary Commemorative Series Combat Narratives Early Raids in the Pacific Ocean; February 1 to March 10, 1942 Marshall and Gilbert Islands, Rabaul, Wake and Marcus, Lae and Salamaua* (2017), 40-51, Retrieved from http://www.history.navy.mil/content/dam/nhhc/browse-by-topic/war%20and%20Conflict/WWII/Early-Raids-170407.pdf, Accessed June 8, 2019

p.98 Map of Wake Island U.S. Navy, Office of Naval Intelligence, Naval History and Heritage Command (p. 51) *World War II 75th Anniversary Commemorative Series Combat Narratives (2017) Early Raids in the Pacific February 1 to March 10, 1942, Marshall and Gilbert Islands, Rabaul, Wake and Marcus, Lae and Salamaua,*(2017), 51, Retrieved from http://www.history.navy.mil/content/dam/nhhc/browse-by-topic/war%20and%20Conflict/WWII/Early-Raids-170407.pdf, Accessed June 8, 2019

p.101 Photo of deck of USS *Enterprise* with USS *Northampton* visible astern. (Naval History and Heritage Command #80-G-66038)

p.102 Map of Wake Island bombardment by USS *Salt Lake City* and USS *Northampton* U.S. Navy, Office of Naval Intelligence, Naval History and Heritage Command, *World War II 75th Anniversary Commemorative Series Combat Narratives, Early Raids in the pacific February 1 to March 10, 1942, Marshall and Gilbert Islands, Rabaul, Wake and Marcus, Lae and Salamaua* (2017), 54 http://www.history.navy.mil/content/dam/nhhc/browse-by-topic/war%20and%20Conflict/WWII/Early-Raids-170407.pdf, accessed June 8, 2019

p.105 Photo of USS *Northampton* being attacked by Japanese fighters, Wake Island (Naval History and heritage Command #NH50942)

p.109-110 U.S. Navy, Office of Naval Intelligence, Naval History and Heritage Command *World War II 75th Anniversary Commemorative Series Combat Narratives (2017) Early Raids in the Pacific Ocean; February 1 to March 10, 1942, Marshall and Gilbert Islands, Rabaul, Wake and Marcus, Lae and Salamau* (2017), 51-56 Retrieved from http://www.history.navy.mil/content/dam/nhhc/browse-by-topic/war%20and%20Conflict/WWII/Early-Raids-170407.pdf, Accessed June 8, 2019

p. 109-110 *USS Northampton CA-26,* Retrieved from www.historyofwar.org/articles/weapons_USS_Northampton_CA26.html, Accessed July 9, 2019

p.109-110 *USS Northampton CA-26,* Retrieved from www.ibiblio.org/hyperwar/OnlineLibrary/photos/sh-usn/usnsh-n/ca26.htm, Accessed July 10, 2019

p.110 Map of Marcus Island, U.S. Navy, Office of Naval Intelligence, Naval History and Heritage Command, *World War II Commemorative Series Combat Narratives, Early Raids in the pacific February 1 to March 10 1942, Marshall and Gilbert Islands, Rabaul, Wake and Marcus, Lae and Salamaua* (2017), 51 Retrieved from http://www.history.navy.mil/content/dam/nhhc/browse-by-topic/war%20and%20Conflict/WWII/Early-Raids-170407.pdf, Accessed June 8, 2019

p.11 Image of Herman Turcotte's Electrical Test Bench (Turcotte Family Collection)

p.115-121 U.S. Navy, Office of Naval Intelligence, Naval History and Heritage Command, *Doolittle Raid 18 April 1942* Retrieved from https://www.history.navy.mil/browse-by-topic/wars-conflicts-and-operations/world-war-ii/1942/halsey-doolittle-raid.html, Accessed September 20, 2019

p.115-121 Hickman, K. *World War II: Doolittle Raid* (July 3, 2019) Retrieved from https://www.thoughtco.com/world-war-ii-doolittle-raid-2360534, Accessed October 3, 2019

p.118 Photo of Mitchell B-25 take-off from USS *Hornet*, Doolittle's Raiders taken from deck of the *Hornet* (Naval History and Heritage Command 80-G-41196)

p.119 fn. 7 U.S. Navy, *Action Report: USS Hornet (CV-6) from Captain Marc A. Mitscher to Admiral Chester A. Nimitz,* (April 28, 1942) Retrieved from www.ibiblio.org/hyperwar/USN/ships/logs/CV/cv8-Tokyo.html, Accessed November 7, 2019

p.121 Photo of USS *Northampton* refueling at sea, April 1942 (Naval History and Heritage Command #NH97808)

p.121 U.S. Navy, Office of Naval Intelligence Naval History and Heritage Command, *Coral Sea,* Retrieved from https://www.history.navy.mil/research/histories/ship-histories/danfs/c/coral-sea.html, Accessed July,19, 2019

p.122 *Degaussing,* Retrieved from https://en.wikipedia.org/wiki/Degaussing, Accessed July 22, 2019 p.122-123 *Molokai Leper Colony Kalaupaupa Hawaii*, Retrieved from https://wanderlustcrew.com/molokai-leper-colony-kalaupapa-hawaii/, Accessed July 22, 2019

p.122-123 *Molokai,* Retrieved from https://en.wikipedia.org/wiki/Molokai, Accessed July 22, 2019

p.123-131 U.S. Navy, Office of Naval Intelligence, Naval History and Heritage Command, *World War II 75th Anniversary Commemorative Series Combat Narratives, Battle of Midway June 3-6, 1942* (2017) Forward, Retrieved from www.history.navy.mil/content/dam/nhhc/browse-by-topic/war%20and%20Conflict/WWII/midway-170519.pdf, Accessed July 11, 2019

p.123-132 U.S. Navy, Office of Naval Intelligence Naval History and Heritage Command, *World War II 75th Anniversary Commemorative Series Combat Narratives, Battle of Midway June 3-6, 1942* (2017),4-22, Retrieved from www.history.navy.mil/content/dam/nhhc/browse-by-topic/war%20and%20Conflict/WWII/midway-170519.pdf, Accessed July 11, 2019

p.127 Photo of USS *Yorktown* deck after being bombed, Battle of Midway (Naval History and Heritage Command #80-G-312021).

p.129 *Gedunk Bar,* Retrieved from https://en.wikipedia.org/wiki/Gedunk_bar, Accessed November 13, 2019

p.130 Photo of USS *Yorktown* burning, Battle of Midway (Naval History and Heritage Command #NHF-00401)

p.132 Children in History, *World War II Pacific Island Territories: New Caledonia*, (May 22, 2008) Retrieved from https://www.histclo.com/essay/war/ww2/cou/island/pac/w2pi-nc.html, Accessed October 28, 2019

p.132 *Espiritu Santo,* Retrieved from http://en.wikipedia/wiki/Espiritu_Santo, accessed October 28, 2019

p.132 *Distance from New Caledonia to Espiritu Santo,* Retrieved from http://www.bing.com/search?q=Distance+from+New+Caledonia+to+Espiritu+Santo&cvid=4c89904b170641b5a374f6fd0279d23f&pglt=43&FORM=ANNTA1&PC=U531, Accessed June 7, 2020

p.132 *Rabaul Jewel of the Pacific,* Retrieved from https://sites.google.com/site/simpsonhafen/home/japan-s-invasion, Accessed October 28, 2019

p. 131-132 U.S. Navy, History and Heritage Command, *Battle of Savo Island 9 August 1942*, -Retrieved from https://www.history.navy.mil/browse-by-topic/wars-conflicts-and-operations/world-war-ii/1942/guadalcanal/battle-of-savo-island.html, accessed July 24, 2019

p. 131-132 U.S. Navy, Office of Naval Intelligence, Naval History and Heritage Command, *World War II 75th Anniversary Commemorative Series Combat Narratives, Battles of Savo Island 9 August 1942 and the Eastern Solomons 23-25 August 1942* (2017) Retrieved from https://www.history.navy.mil/content/dam/nhhc/browse-by-topic/war%20and%20Conflict/WWII-Pacific-Battles/Savo%20Web.pdf, Accessed July 24, 2019

p.134 *USS Wasp (CV-7)*, Retrieved from https://en.wikipedia.org/wiki/USS_Wasp_(CV-7), Accessed July 25, 2019

p.135 *USS O'Brien (DD-415),* Retrieved from https://en.wikipedia.org/wiki/USS_O%27Brien_(DD-415) Accessed July 25, 2019

p.134-136 U.S. Navy, History and Heritage Command, *Wasp (CV-7) 1940-1942*, Retrieved from https://www.history.navy.mil/browse-by-topic/ships/modern-ships/uss-wasp.htm, Accessed July 25, 2019

p.136 Photo of *USS Wasp* sinking (Naval History and Heritage Command #80-G-391481)

p.137-138 *USS O'Brien (DD-415,* Retrieved from https://en.wikipedia.org/wiki/USS_O%27Brien_(DD-415) Accessed July 25, 2019

p. Giberson, A. (1983, September 23) *Gosport* Vol. XLII No. 38, p. 11

p.138 *USS Northampton (CA-26)*, Retrieved from https://en.wikipedia.org/wiki/USS_Northampton_(CA-26), Accessed July 9, 2019

p.138-141 Hornfischer, J.D., *Neptune's Inferno: The U.S. Navy at Guadalcanal*, Chapter 22 *Strike Strike-Repeat Strike,* (Bantam, March 6, 2012) Retrieved from https://erenow.net/ww/neptunes-inferno-the-u-s-navy-at-guadalcanal/, accessed August 7, 2019

p.138-141 Frank, R.B., *Guadalcanal, The definitive Account of the Landmark Battle* (Penguin, 1990), 333-346

p.138-141 Id at p. 351

p.138-141 Id. at p. 388-389

p.138-141 *Admiral Halsey,* Retrieved from https://usselmore.com/war_effort/admirals/halsey/halsey.html, Accessed August 11, 2019

p.14-151 U.S. Navy, Office of Naval Intelligence, Naval History and Heritage Command, *World War II 75th Anniversary Commemorative Series Combat*

*Narratives, The Battles of Cape Esperance 11 October 1942 and Santa Cruz
Islands 26 October 1942* (2017), 25-26 Retrieved from
https://www.history.navy.mil/browse-by-topic/wars-conflicts-and-
operations/world-war-ii/1942/guadalcanal/battle-of-santa-cruz-islands.html,
Accessed August 18, 2019

p.142 Photo of Japanese bombers attacking USS *Hornet*, October 26, 1942 (Naval History
and Heritage Command#80-G-33947)

p.14 Photo of Damage to stack of USS *Hornet* after plane attack, October 26, 1942 (Naval
History and Heritage Command #80-G40300)

p.146 Photo of USS *Hornet* under tow by USS *Northampton* (Naval History and Heritage
Command #80-G-33897)

p.150 *SS President Coolidge,* Retrieved from
https://en.wikipedia.org/wiki/SS_President_Coolidge, Accessed June 16, 2020

p.150 *USS President Coolidge,* Retrieved from
https://southpacificwwiimuseum.com/historical-gallery-coolidge-sinking/, Accessed June
16, 2020

p.150 *Captain Elwood Joseph Euart,* Retrieved from
https://southpacificwwiimuseum.com/euart/, Accessed June 16, 2020

p.150 *Lost at sea, WWII veteran finally comes home to R.I.,* Retrieved from
https://thericatholic.com/stories/lost-at-sea-wwii-veteran-finally-comes-home-to-ri,8380,
Accessed on June 16, 2019

p.151-156 *Atlantic Blockade Runners,* Retrieved from
researcheratlarge.com/Atlantic/Blockade Runners/Summary/, Accessed September 27,
2019

p.152-156 Naval History and Heritage Command, Today in Naval History, November 21,
Retrieved from https://www.history.navy.mil/today-in-history/november-21.html, Accessed
September 27, 2019

p.151-156 *The Anneliese-Essberger,* Retrieved from
sixtant.net/2011/artigos.php?cat=commander-south-atlantic-force&sub=usafsa-(38-pages--
14-images)&tag=15)the-anneliese-essberger, Accessed September 28, 2019

p.153 Modified map of Atlantic Ocean Neutrality Zone, Retrieved from
researcheratlarge.com/Atlantic/Blockade Runners/Summary/ (Declassified October 27,
2011)

364

p.154 fn 10 *United States Naval Administration in World War II, Commander South Atlantic Force, Narrative Outline,* Retrieved from www.ibiblio.org/hyperwar/USN/Admin-Hist/146-SoLant-Narrative.html, Accessed on September 28, 2019

p.156 *Naval Battle of Guadalcanal,* Retrieved from http://en.wikipedia.org/wiki/Naval_Battle_of_Guadalcanal, Accessed September 12, 2019

p.158-170 U.S. Navy, Office of Naval Intelligence, Naval History and Heritage Command, *World War II 75th Anniversary Commemorative Series Combat Narratives, Battle of Tassafaronga 30 November 1942 Japanese Evacuation of Guadalcanal 29 January-8 February 1943* (2017) Retrieved from http://www.history.navy.mil/content/dam/nhhc/browse-by-topic/war%20and%20Conflict/WWII/Tassa%20Evac%20Final.pdf, Accessed September 11, 2019

p. 158-170 U.S. Navy Department Bureau of Ships, *USS Northampton (CA-26) Loss in Action 30 November 1942 Lunga Point War Damage Report 41* (March 20, 1944), 1-12 (Declassified) Retrieved from https://www.history.navy.mil/research/library/online-reading-room/title-list-alphabetically/w/war-damage-reports/uss-northampton-ca26-war-damage-report-no-41.html, accessed September 10, 2019

p.160 Map of Guadalcanal and Florida Islands, *World War II 75th Anniversary Commemorative Series Combat Narratives, Battle of Tassafaronga 30 November 1942 Japanese Evacuation of Guadalcanal 29 January-8 February 1943, Supra* At Face Page 1

P.164 Track Chart of Battle of Tassafaronga, Supra, at Face Page 2

p.166 Photo of USS *New Orleans*, bow blown off, *World War II 75th Anniversary Commemorative Series Combat Narratives, Battle of Tassafaronga 30 November 1942 Japanese Evacuation of Guadalcanal 29 January-8 February 1943.* Supra, at p. 9

p.167-168 Giberson, A. (1983, September 23) "Fighting Nora", *Gosport,* Vol. XLII No. 38, p. 11

Reduce size of footnote 11-See attached rewrite

p.167 fn. 11 *USS Dionne,* Retrieved from https://en.wikipedia.org/wiki/USS_Dionne, Accessed March 8, 2020

p.167-179 U.S. Navy Department Bureau of Ships, *USS Northampton (CA-26) Loss in Action 30 November 1942 Lunga Point War Damage Report 41* (March 20, 1944), 1-12 (Declassified) Retrieved from https://www.history.navy.mil/research/library/online-reading-room/title-list-alphabetically/w/war-damage-reports/uss-northampton-ca26-war-damage-report-no-41.html, accessed September 10, 2019

p.169 Diagram of torpedo damage USS Northampton (CA-26) Id at p.13

p.170 Giberson, A. (1983, September 23) "Fighting Nora" *Gosport*, Vol. XLII No. 38, page 11

p.173 fn.12 William S. McLaughlin Obituary (2006, June 15) *Dallas Post Star*, Retrieved from https://poststar.com/obituaries/william-s-mclaughlin/article_225c2b33--7e9f-52ae-acce2-1ddce711db91.html, Accessed September 15, 2019

p.173 fn.12 William S. McLaughlin, *The Hall of Valor: The Military Metals Database*, Retrieved from https://valor.militarytimes.com/hero/37698, Accessed September 16, 2019

p.176 fn.13 *Jason Robards*, Retrieved from https://en.wikipedia.org/wiki/Jason_Robards, Accessed October 6, 2019

p.177 Photo of PT-109, Naval History and Heritage Command, *Survivors of Tassafaronga # H-013-2*, Retrieved from https://www.history.navy.mil/about-us/leadership/director/directors-corner/h-grams/h-gram-013/h-013-2.html, Accessed on October 6, 2019

p.177 fn. 14 *Patrol torpedo boat PT-109*, Retrieved from https://en. Wikipedia.org/wiki/Patrol_torpedo_boat_PT-109

p.177-178 Droney, J. F. (1942, December 28). 21-Year-Old Local Sailor In Seven major Sea Battles. *The Lowell Sun*, p. 7

p.187 Photo of Lionel and Claire Turcotte's Wedding photo, (1942, December 28) *The Lowell Sun*, p.7 (Turcotte Family Collection)

p.186 *Christmas Island*, Retrieved from https://en.wikipedia.org/wiki/Christmas_Island, Accessed September 15, 2019

p.187 *Treasure Island, San Francisco*, Retrieved from https://en.wikipedia.org/wiki/Treasure_Island,_San_Francisco, accessed September 15, 2019

p.194 *Vought OS2U Kingfisher*, Retrieved from https://en.wikipedia.org/wiki/Vought_OS2U_Kingfisher, Accessed September 17, 2019

p.196 Photo of Bob and Lionel Turcotte in white navy uniforms (Turcotte Family Collection)

p.202 Declassified Report from Commanding Officer USS *Cincinnati* to Secnav, (June 9, 1943), *U.S. Navy Personnel File* 2-22986362171 Robert Turcotte, Aviation Chief Machinist, National Archives, National Personnel Records Center, (St. Louis)

p.203 Image of telegram to Helen Turcotte, U.S. Navy notification of Robert Turcotte missing in action (Turcotte Family Collection) p.209 Image of *Lowell Sun* Article, Robert Turcotte, Brother of Naval Hero Missing. (1943, June 30) *The Lowell Sun*, p.1

p.210-211 *Lockheed Corporation,* Retrieved from https://en.wikipedia.org/wiki/Lockheed_Corporation, Accessed September 27, 2019

p.211 *VP-131,* Retrieved from https://en.wikipedia.org/wiki/VP-131, Accessed September 27, 2019

p.212 Photo of Lockheed Ventura PV-1 Bomber, Evans,M. and Grossnick, R. Naval History and Heritage Command, *Collection of Articles on Naval Aviation in World War II, Vol. 1, Chapter 5, World War II 1940-1945* (2015), 172 Retrieved from https://www.history.navy.mil/content/dam/nhhc/research/publications/1910/5%20chapter5.pdf

p.214 *Naval Air Station Key West,* Retrieved from https://en.wikipedia.org/wiki/Naval_Air_Station_Key_West, Accessed September 19, 2019

p.217 Photo of Lionel Turcotte and Ventura PV-1 Bomber crew (Turcotte Family Collection)

p.218 Photo of Lionel Turcotte, Chief Aviation Machinist Mate (Turcotte Family Collection)

p. 221-222 *VP-131,* Retrieved from https://en.wikipedia.org/wiki/VP-131, Accessed September 27, 2019

p.221-222 *Zandery Field,* Retrieved from www.sixtant.net/2011/artigos.php?cat=u.s.-navy-bases-in-guyanas-and-trinidad&sub=the-guyanas-and-trinidad-airfields&tag=2)zandery-airfield, Accessed September 19, 2019

p.224 *Planes Lost in the South Atlantic WWII-1944,* Retrieved from https://sixtant.net/2011/artigos.php?cat=u-s-planes-lost-on-the-south-atlantic-ww-ii&sub=vp-navy-usn-usmc-usgc-nat&tag=3)us.acft-lost-in-south-atlantic-1943, Accessed September 19, 2019

p,225 Id.

p.226 Id.

p.229 *Plankowner,* Retrieved from https://en.wikipedia.org/wiki/Plankowner, Accessed September 15, 2019

p.230 Image of Lowell Sun article about Jim Turcotte, Droney, J. F. (1943, February 20). 21-Year-Old Local Sailor In Seven major Sea Battles. *The Lowell Sun*, p.1

p.231 Photo of USS *Iowa* (Naval History and Heritage Command #NH53264)

p.232 *USS Iowa (BB-61)*, Retrieved from https://en.wikipedia.org/wiki/USS_Iowa_(BB-61), Accessed September 17, 2019

p.233-234 Local Sailor Had Part In Tokio Attack. (1943, April 22) *The Lowell Sun*, p.1

p.234-236 *1943 Atlantic Hurricane Season*, Retrieved from https://en.wikipedia.org/wiki/1943_Atlantic_hurricane_season #Hurricane_Four, Accessed September 19, 201

p.233 Image of Lowell Sun article, Local Sailor Had Part In Tokio Attack. (1943, April 22) *The Lowell Sun*, p.1

p.233-23-235 Article about Doolitte's Raid Id.

p.239 Image of Jim Turcotte's Harvard admission photo (Turcotte Family Collection)

p.248-252 *U.S. Navy Personnel File* 2-22986362190 Lionel Turcotte, Aviation Chief Machinist Mate, National Archives, National Personnel Records Center (St. Louis)

p.248-252 *Planes Lost in the South Atlantic WWII-1944*, Retrieved from https://sixtant.net/2011/artigos.php?cat=u-s-planes-lost-on-the-south-atlantic-ww-ii&sub=vp-navy-usn-usmc-usgc-nat&tag=3)us.acft-lost-in-south-atlantic-1944, Accessed September 19, 2019

p.249 Telegram to Helen Turcotte, U.S. Navy notification of death of her son Lionel (Turcotte Family Collection)

p.250 Photo of Lionel Turcotte's burial in Dutch Guiana, February 1944 (Courtesy of Mary Turcotte O'Connell)

p.257 Image of Jim Turcotte's Harvard graduation yearbook, *Navy R.O.T.C. and V-12 Unit Harvard University* (Army and Navy Publishing Company of Louisiana,1945) (Turcotte Family Collection)

p.258 Photo of Walter "Bud" Turcotte as a young boy (Turcotte Family Collection)

p.259 Photo of Helen Turcotte during WWII with all her children except Jim (Turcotte Family Collection)

p.260 U.S. Navy Certificate of presumed death of Robert Turcotte (Turcotte Family Collection)

p.261 Photo of Walter "Bud" Turcotte and Mary Turcotte (Turcotte Family Collection) p.262 Walter Turcotte's application to the U.S. Navy (Turcotte Family Collection)

p.263 Parental permission allowing Walter Turcotte to join the U.S. Navy (Turcotte Family Collection)

p.264 Photo of fire suppression training at USNTS Sampson, Retrieved from www.rpadden.com/samp_training/training.htm (Published with permission of Dolores Dinsmore and Fred Bonn at the Sampson Museum), Accessed on November 21, 2019

p.268 Photo of Jim and Walter Turcotte 1945 (Turcotte Family Collection)

p.269-270 *Edith Nourse Rogers,* Retrieved from https://en.wikipedia.org/wiki/Edith_Nourse_Rogers, Accessed on September 19, 2019

p.272 Photo of Walter in white navy uniform (Turcotte Family Collection)

p.274 Jim Turcotte and Platoon 232 photo, Fort Schuyler 1945 (Turcotte Family Collection)

p.275 Jim's graduation photo from Midshipman's school

p.276 Images of Fort Schuyler's graduation exercise program and invitation (Turcotte Family Collection)

p.277 Image of cover of Ft. Schuyler graduation book (Turcotte Family Collection)

p.278 Photo of Jim Turcotte celebrating in NYC (Turcotte Family Collection)

p.279 Image of photo holder from Charlie Lowe's Forbidden City (Turcotte Family Collection)

p.280 Photo of Jim Turcotte, John Abdun-Nur and Joe Grilli at Charlie Lowe's Forbidden City (Turcotte Family Collection)

p.280 Image of John Abdun-Nur's scrap book (Courtesy of John Abdun-Nur Durrett)

p.281-291 History.com, *Battle of Okinawa,* (October 29,2009) Retrieved from https://www.history.com/topics/world-war-ii/battle-of-okinawa, Accessed September 18, 2019

p.281-291 Appleton, R. et. al *United States Army in World War II The War in the Pacific Okinawa: The Last Battle Chapter 16 Behind the Front (*1948) p. 411-417 Retrieved from https://history.army.mil/books/wwii/okinawa/chapter16.htm#b2, accessed September 20, 2019

p.303 Photo of Jim Turcotte as assistant navigator, USS *Missouri* (Turcotte Family Collection)

p. 303-304 *Port Hueneme, California,* Retrieved from https://en.wikipedia.org/wiki/Port_Hueneme,_California, Accessed September 27, 2019

p.304 *USS Missouri (BB-63),* Retrieved from https://en.wikipedia.org/wiki/USS_Missouri_(BB-63), Accessed September 29, 2019

p.306 Photo of dignitaries' card game aboard USS *Missouri*, 1946 (Naval History and Heritage Command #80-G365725)

p.316-318 *USS Missouri (BB-63) Mediterranean Cruise, April 1946*, Retrieved from https://ibiblio.org/hyperwar/OnlineLibrary/photos/sh-usn/usnsh-m/bb63-m1.htm, September 29, 2019

p.306-318 Hewitt, H. Kent and Cherpak, Evelyn M., *"HM 15: The Memoirs of Admiral H. Kent Hewitt"* (2004). Historical Monographs. 15. Retrieved from https://digital-commons.usnwc.edu/historical-monographs/15, p.235-244(2004) Accessed January 6, 2020

p.306-307 *Dardanelles,* Retrieved from https://en.wikipedia.org/wiki/Dardanelles, Accessed September 29, 2019

p.307 Photo of Jim Turcotte using sextant aboard USS *Missouri* (Turcotte Family Collection)

p.308 Photo of USS *Missouri* in Harbor at Istanbul (Naval History and Heritage Command #80-G-702557)

p. 308 *USS Providence (CL-82),* Retrieved from https://en.wikipedia.org/wiki/USS_Providence_(CL-82), Accessed September 29, 2019

p.309 Photo of USS *Missouri* saluting (Naval History and Heritage Command #80-G376893)

p. 309-310 U.S. Navy, Department of the Navy, (1952) *United States Navy Regulations* Chapter 12, Section 5 and Section 10

p.310 Photo of funeral procession of Turkish Ambassador to U.S., Istanbul, 1946 (Naval History and Heritage Command # 80-G-702555)

p.311 Photo of cover of commemorative Turkish cigarettes (Turcotte Family Collection)

p.311 *Dolmabahce Palace,* Retrieved from https://en.wikipedia.org/wiki/dolmabahce_palace, Accessed September 30, 2019 p.312 Photo of inside of commemorative Turkish cigarettes (Turcotte Family Collection)

p.312 Image of cover of commemorative book on Turkey (Turcotte Family Collection)

p.313 Lincoln R., *20 WWII Facts Every Jeep Owner Should Know*, August 15, 2016, Retrieved from https://www.warhistoryonline.com/military-vehicle-news/20-facts-world-war-ii-jeeps.html, Accessed September 30, 2019

p.314 Photo of Greek Archbishop aboard USS *Missouri* (Naval History and Heritage Command #80-G-702531)

p.315 Image of program to ball in honor of USS *Missouri* (Turcotte Family Collection)

p.316 Image of invitation to ball (Turcotte Family Collection)

p.317 Photo of Pope Pius XII with the crew of the USS *Missouri* (Turcotte Family Collection)

p.326 Photo of Walter Turcotte's knives (Courtesy of Patricia Cossette)

p.328 Image of postcard from Walter Turcotte to his sister Mary from Italy, 1947 (Turcotte Family Collection)

p.329 Image of postcard from Walter Turcotte to his parents (Genoa) (Turcotte Family Collection)

p.330 Image of postcard from Walter Turcotte to his parents (Naples) (Turcotte Family Collection)

p.331 Photo of Walter Turcotte in Navy P coat and hat (Courtesy of Patricia Cossette)

p.332 Photo of USS *Des Moines* (Naval History and Heritage Command # NH91829)

p.332-333 *USS Des Moines (CA-134)*, Retrieved from https://en.wikipedia.org/wiki/USS_Des_Moines_(CA-134), Accessed October 1, 2019

p.332-333 *USS Des Moines CA-134*, Retrieved from https://www.militaryfactory.com/ships/detail.asp?ship_id=USS-Des-Moines-CA134, Accessed October 1, 2019

p.333 Photo of officers of USS *Des Moines*, 1951 (Turcotte Family Collection)

p.334 Photo of silver plate given to Jim Turcotte by Des Moines Wardroom officers (Turcotte Family Collection) p.345 Image of Seventh Division, *Sixth Fleet Cruise Book USS Des Moines CA-134*, (Albert Love Enterprises, 1952) (Turcotte Family Collection)

p.336 Image of Ports of Call, Id., (Turcotte Family Collection)

p.337 *Robert Carney,* Retrieved from https://en.wikipedia.org/wiki/Robert_Carney, Accessed October 2, 2019

p.337 Photo of Gerald Creasy, Governor of Malta, aboard the USS *Des Moines*, Sixth Fleet Cruise Book USS *Des Moines* CA-134, (Albert Love Enterprises, 1952) (Turcotte Family Collection)

p.338 Retrieved from https://taskandpurpose.com/5-worst-navy-bases-stationed, Accessed October 2, 2019

p.340 Image of *Lowell Sun* article regarding return of Lionel's remains, Body of Local Hero Due Here Tomorrow. (1948, April 29) *The Lowell Sun,* p. 3

p.341 Image of article regarding burial of Lionel, Full Military Honors for L.O. Turcotte, (1948, May 4) *The Lowell Sun*, p. 3

p.342 Photo of the Turcotte family gravestone, Lionel, Carol Ann, Herman, and Helen Turcotte (Turcotte Family Collection)

p.343 Photo of Claire (Brennan) (Turcotte) Munro and Jack Munro in blue U.S. Navy uniforms (Courtesy of Ruth Gerke)

p.342 Wave Trainee. (1944, August 19), *The Lowell Sun*, p. 5, Retrieved from https://newspaper archive.com/lowell-sun-auf-19-44-p-29/, Accessed March 15, 2020

p.344 Photo of Claire and Jack Munro, circa 1990 (Courtesy of Ruth Gerke)

p.344 Image of Robert Turcotte's name on East Coast Memorial in Battery Park, NYC (Turcotte Family Collection)

p.345 Image of East Coast Memorial (Turcotte Family Collection)

p.348 Image of sign designating Turcotte Square, Lowell, MA (Turcotte Family Collection)

p.349 Photo of Helen Turcotte and Gold Star Mothers wearing white evening gowns (Turcotte Family Collection)

p.349 Photo of Helen Turcotte at Gold Star Mothers event (Turcotte Family Collection)

p.350 Photos of Helen and Herman Turcotte (Turcotte Family Collection)

Bibliography

Abdulhafedh, A. 2017. "The Panama Canal: A Man Made Engineering Marvel."
   Researchgate. March. Accessed October 29, 2019.
   https://www.researchgate.net/publication/337499463_The_Panama_Canal_A_M
   an-Made_Engineering_Marvel.

Appleman, Roy E., James M. Burns, Russell A Gugeler, and John Stevens. 1948. "Chapter
   1 Operation Iceberg." In *The United States Army in World War II, The War in the
   Pacific, Okinawa: The Last Battle,* by Roy E Appleman, James M Burns, Russell
   A Gugeler and John Stevens, 1-43. Washington DC: Center for Military History.

Appleman, Roy E., James M. Burns, Russell A Gugeler, and John Stevens. 1948. "Chapter
   16 Behind the Front." In *The United States Army in World War II, The War in the
   Pacific, Okinawa, The Last Battle,* by Roy E. Appleman, James M. Burns,
   Russell A. Gugeler and John Stevens, 403-419. Washington DC: Center for
   Military History.

Ashman, L.M. Cpl, Department of Defense, Department of the Navy, U.S. Marine Corp.
   n.d. *Photo of Bell Airacobra, General-Aircraft-black and White.* Accessed June
   16, 2019. https://catalog.archives.gov/id/74237205.

Bing Search Engine Editors. n.d. *Distance from New Caledonia to Espiritu Santo, Vanuatu.*
   Accessed June 7, 2020.
   https://www.bing.com/search?q=Distance%20from%20New%20caledonia%20to
   %20Espiritu%20Santo&qs=n&form=QBRE&sp=-
   1&pq=distance%20from%20new%20caledonia%20to%20espiritu%20santo&sc=
   2-45&sk=&cvid=120D2A681A1B42AD9371FC36095C4A75.

Children in History Editors. 2008. *World War II Pacific Island Territories: New Caledonia,
   Children in History.* May 22. Accessed October 28, 2019.
   https://www.histclo.com/essay/war/ww2/cou/island/pac/w2pi-nc.html.

Crookall, James. n.d. *Item: CVA 260-687[Bi-planes on deck of U.S. ship "Cincinnati"],
   City of Vancouver Archives.* Accessed June 25, 2019.
   https://searcharchives.vancouver.ca/biplanes-on-deck-of-u-s-ship-cincinnati.

Droney, John F. 1943. "21-Year-Old Local Sailor in Seven Major Sea Battles." *The Lowell
   Sun,* February 20: 1,6.

Editors, Hyperwars. n.d. *Halsey-Doolittle Raid: Bombing of Tokyo, Action Report: USS
   Hornet (CV-6).* Accessed November 6, 2019.
   https://www.ibiblio.org/hyperwar/USN/ships/logs/CV/cv8-Tokyo.html.

Encyclopedia Britannica Editors. 1998. *Aviation.* July 20. Accessed August 16, 2019.
   https://www.britannica.com/technology/aviation.

Evans, Mark L. and Grossnick, Roy A. 2017. *Chapter 5, World War II 1940-1945, United States Naval Aviation 1910-2010, Volume 1.* November 24. Accessed September 27, 2019. https://www.history.navy.mil/content/dam/nhhc/research/publications/1910/5%2 0Chapter5.pdf.

Frank, Richard B. 1992. *Guadalcanal, The Definitive Account of the Landmark Battle.* New York: Random House.

Giberson, Art. 1983. "The Fighting Nora." *Gosport*, September 23: 10-11.

Google Editors. 2005. *Japanese Occupation of Rabaul 1942-1944.* Accessed October 28, 2019. https://sites.google.com/site/simpsonhafen/home/japan-s-invasion.

Grosssnick, Roy A. 2014. *U.S. Navy Squadron Designations and Abbreviations, Appendix 4, The Dictionary of American Naval aviation Squadrons .* February 4. Accessed July 12, 2019. https://www.history.navy.mil/content/dam/nhhc/research/histories/naval-aviation/dictionary-of-american-naval-aviation-squadrons-volume-1/pdfs/Dict-of-Amer-Avia-Sq-v1.pdf.

Hewitt, H. Kent; Cherpak, Evelyn M. 2004. *US Naval War College Digital Commons, Historical Monographs, HM 15 The Memoirs of Admiral H. Kent Hewitt.* January 1. Accessed January 6, 2020. https://digital-commons.usnwc.edu/historical-monographs/15/.

Hickman, Kennedy. 2019. *World War II: Doolittle Raid.* July 3. Accessed October 3, 2019. https://www.thoughtco.com/world-war-ii-doolittle-raid-2360534.

History Editors. 2009. *History: Battle of Okinawa.* October 29. Accessed September 18, 2019. https://www.history.com/topics/world-war-ii/battle-of-okinawa.

History.com Editors. 2009. *Battle of Okinawa, History.* March 29. Accessed September 18, 2019. https://www.history.com/topics/world-war-ii/battle-of-okinawa.

Hornfischer, James D. 2011. *Neptune's Inferno, The US Navy at Guadalcanal.* New York: Bantam.

Hyperwar Editors. n.d. *Sixtant War II in the South Atlantic, Zandery Arirfield.* Accessed September 19, 2019. https://www.sixtant.net/2011/artigos.php?cat=u.s.-navy-bases-in-guyanas-and-trinidad&sub=the-guyanas-and-trinidad-airfields&tag=2)zandery-airfield.

—. 2011. *Sixtant War II in the South Atlantic, The Anneliesse Essberger.* Accessed September 28, 2019. https://sixtant.net/2011/artigos.php?cat=commander-south-atlantic-force&sub=usafsa-(38-pages--14-images)&tag=15)the-anneliese-essberger.

—. 2011. *Sixtant War II in the South Atlantic, The Neutrality Patrol, The Objective.* Accessed September 23, 2019. https://www.sixtant.net/2011/artigos.php?cat=the-neutrality-patrol&sub=neutrality-patrol-&tag=1)the-

objective#:~:text=THE%20NEUTRALITY%20PATROL%20-
%20NEUTRALITY%20PATROL%201%29THE%20OBJECTIVE,approaching
%20the%20US%20East%20coast%20or%20West%20Indies.

—. n.d. *Sixtant War II in the South Atlantic, U.S. Planes lost in the south Atlantic WWII-
1944, 17 Feb. 44,.* Accessed September 19, 2019.
https://www.sixtant.net/2011/artigos.php?cat=u-s-planes-lost-in-south-atlantic-
ww-ii&sub=vp-navy-usn-usmc-uscg-nats&tag=3)u.s.-acft-lost-in-south-atlantic-
1944#:~:text=3%29U.S.%20ACFT%20LOST%20IN%20SOUTH%20ATLANTI
C%201944%20109,the%20great%20effort%20of%2.

—. 2002. *USS Northampton (CA-26, originally CL-26),1930-1942.* January 3. Accessed
July 9, 2019. https://www.ibiblio.org/hyperwar/OnlineLibrary/photos/sh-
usn/usnsh-n/ca26.htm.

Polmar, Norman. 2007. *Historic Aircraft.* December. Accessed September 27, 2019.
https://www.usni.org/magazines/naval-history-magazine/2007/december/historic-
aircraft.

Potts, JR. 2017. *USS Des Moines CA-134, Heavey Cruiser Warship (1948), The Des
Moines-class was the last all-gun heavy cruiser.* August 16. Accessed October 1,
2019. https://www.militaryfactory.com/ships/detail.php?ship_id=USS-Des-
Moines-CA134.

Rickard, J. 2013. *USS Cincinatti CL-6.* January 2. Accessed June 25, 2019.
www.historyofwar.org/articles/weapons_USS_Cincinnati_CL6.html.

—. 2014. *USS New Orleans CA 32.* November 27. Accessed September 22, 2019.
https://www.historyofwar.org/articles/weapons_USS_New_Orleans_CA32.html.

Rickard, J. 2014. *USS Northampton CA 26.* March 10. Accessed July 19, 2019.
http://www.historyofwar.org/articles/weapons_USS_Northampton_CA26.html.

Riddle, Lincoln. 2016. *War History Online.* May 16. Accessed September 30, 2019.
https://www.warhistoryonline.com/military-vehicle-news/20-facts-world-war-ii-
jeeps.html.

Roy E. Appleman, James M. Burns, Russell A. Gugeler, and John Stevens. 1948. "Chapter
16 Behind the Fron." In *United States Army in WWII The War in the Pacific
Okinawa: The Last Battle,* by James E. Burns, Russell A. Gugeler, and John
Stevens Roy E. Appleman, 403-419. Washington, DC: Center of Military
History, United States Army.

Scharch, Stacy. 2018. *E.L. Scharch, USNR, AvCad V-5, Naval Aviator AV(N), WWII, NAS
Jacksonville, Florida.* Accessed August 16, 2019.
http://www.scharch.org/Ed_Scharch/08-nas-jax-oper.htm.

Snizek, Rick, Editor. 2016. *Lost at sea,WWII veteran finally comes home to R.I., Rhode
Island Catholic.* September 8. Accessed June 16, 2019.
https://thericatholic.com/stories/lost-at-sea-wwii-veteran-finally-comes-home-to-
ri,8380.

South Pacific WWII Museum Editors. n.d. *USS President Coolidge, The War in Pictures.* Accessed June 16, 2019. https://southpacificwwiimuseum.com/historical-gallery-uss-president-coolidge/.

Sterner, Douglas. n.d. *William McLaughlin, Hall of Valor: The Military Metals Database.* Accessed September 16, 2020. https://valor.militarytimes.com/hero/37698.

Sun Signs Editors. 2018. *Esther Williams, Sportswoman, Sun Signs.* January 15. Accessed October 5, 2019. https://www.sunsigns.org/famousbirthdays/d/profile/esther-williams/.

Taplett, Robert D. 2020. *HistoryNet, 'So This is War'-A Young Marine Officer's Account of the Days Before Pearl Harbor and the Stunning Start of Pacific Conflict.* August 3. Accessed December 15, 2020. https://www.historynet.com/so-this-is-war-a-young-marine-officers-account-of-pearl-harbor-and-the-pacific-conflict.htm.

Task & Purpose Editors. 2016. *The 5 Worst Navy Bases To Be Stationed, Task & Purpose.* March 10. Accessed October 2, 2019. https://taskandpurpose.com/joining-the-military/5-worst-navy-bases-stationed/.

Team Mighty. 2016. *Military.com The Meanings Behind 19 classic Sailor Tattoos.* July 15. Accessed September 24, 2019. https://www.military.com/undertheradar/2016/07/here-are-the-meanings-behind-19-classic-sailor-tattoos.

The Barrier Miner Editors. n.d. *06 Aug 1941-US Warships At Brisbane-Trove.* Accessed June 20, 2019. https://trove.nla.gov.au/newspaper/article/48393284#.

The Dallas Post Star Editors. 2006. *William S. McLaughlin, Sr., Obituaries.* June 15. Accessed September 16, 2020. https://www.legacy.com/us/obituaries/poststar/name/william-mclaughlin-obituary?pid=18118781.

The Government of Turkey. 1946. *Turkey.* Ankara: The Turkish Press Department.

The Lowell Sun Editors. 1948. "Body of Local Hero Due Here Tomorrow." *The Lowell Sun*, April 29: 3.

—. 1943. "Brother of Naval Hero Missing." *The Lowell Sun*, June 30: 1.

—. 1948. "Full Military Honors for L.O. Turcotte." *The Lowell Sun*, May 4: 3.

—. 1943. "Local Sailor Had Part in Tokio Attack." *The Lowell Sun*, April 22: 1,11.

—. 1942. "Turcotte-Brennan." *The Lowell Sun*, December 28: 7.

—. 1944. "Wave Trainee." *The Lowell Sun*, August 9: 5.

—. 1944. "Wave Tranee." *The Lowell sun*, August 19: 5.

The Royal Hawaiian Resort Waikiki Editors. n.d. *History of the Royal Hawaiian Hotel, History Overview, Glimpse into the Past of the Royal Hawaiian Hotel.* Accessed July 11, 2019. https://www.royal-hawaiian.com/history-overview/.

Thomas, Suzanne. 2006. *St-Jean-Baptiste celebrations.* February 7. Accessed June 10, 2019. https://www.thecanadianencyclopedia.ca/en/article/st-jean-baptiste-celebrations-emc.

United States Naval Reserve Midshipman's School. 1945. *Gangway.* Fort Schuyler, N.Y.: Ex Libris.

United States Navy. n.d. *1943 Intelligence Report Blockade Runner Summary, Research @Large.* Accessed September 27, 2019. http://researcheratlarge.com/Atlantic/BlockadeRunners/Summary/.

United States Navy. 1952. "Chapter 12 Flags, Pennants, Honors, Cermonies and Customs Section 10 Deaths and Funerals." In *United States Navy Regulations*, by United States Navy, 151-153. Washington DC: United States Navy.

United States Navy. 1952. "Chapter 12, Flags, Pennants,Honors, Ceremonies and Customs Section 5 Passing Honors." In *United States Navy Regulations*, by United States Navy, 131-132. Washington DC: United States Navy.

—. 1952. *USS Des Moines CA-134 Sixth Fleet Cruise.* Atlanta: Albert Love Enterprises.

United States Navy, Bureau of Ships. 2016. *USS Northampton (CA26) Loss in Action 30 November 1942 Battle of Lunga Point.* January 21. Accessed September 10, 2019. https://www.history.navy.mil/research/library/online-reading-room/title-list-alphabetically/w/war-damage-reports/uss-northampton-ca26-war-damage-report-no-41.html.

United States Navy, Naval Historical Center. 1999. *USS Missouri (BB-63) Mediterranean Cruise, April 1946.* January 22. Accessed September 29, 2019. https://www.ibiblio.org/hyperwar/OnlineLibrary/photos/sh-usn/usnsh-m/bb63-m1.htm.

United States Navy, Naval History and Heritage Command. 2017. *The Sullivan Brothers: U.S. Navy Policy Regarding Family Members Serving together At Sea.* November 7. Accessed July 25, 2019. https://www.history.navy.mil/browse-by-topic/disasters-and-phenomena/the-sullivan-brothers-and-the-assignment-of-family-members/sullivan-brothers-policy-family-members.html.

—. n.d. *Today in Naval History, November 21.* Accessed September 27, 2019. https://www.history.navy.mil/today-in-history/november-21.html.

United States Navy, Office of Naval Intelligence , Naval History and Heritage Command. 2019. *Naval History and Heritage Command: Doolittle Raid 18 April 1942.* May 10. Accessed September 20, 2019. https://www.history.navy.mil/browse-by-topic/wars-conflicts-and-operations/world-war-ii/1942/halsey-doolittle-raid.html.

United States Navy, Office of Naval Intelligence, Naval History and Heitage Command. 2020. *H-Gram 013: Night of the Long Lances, 2. Guadalcanal: Battle of Tassafaronga-Night of the Long Lances.* April 21. Accessed September 16, 2020. https://www.history.navy.mil/about-us/leadership/director/directors-corner/h-grams/h-gram-013.html.

United States Navy, Office of Naval Intelligence, Naval History and Heritage Command. 2016. *Naval History and Heritage Command, Coral Sea.* April 7. Accessed July 19, 2019. https://www.history.navy.mil/research/histories/ship-histories/danfs/c/coral-sea.html.

—. 2019. *Naval History and Heritage Command, Wasp (CV-7) 1940-1942.* March 14. Accessed July 25, 2019. https://www.history.navy.mil/browse-by-topic/ships/modern-ships/uss-wasp.html.

—. 2017. *World War II 75th Anniversary Commemorative Series Combat Narratives Early Raids in the Pacific Ocean: February 1 to March 10, 1942 Marshall and Gilbert islands, Rabaul, Wake and Marcus, Lae and Salamaua.* Washington DC: Naval History and Heritage Command.

—. 2017. *World War II 75th Anniversary Commemorative Series Combat Narratives, Battle of Midway June 3-6, 1942.* Washington DC: Naval History and Heritage Command.

—. 2017. *World War II 75th Anniversary Commemorative Series Combat Narratives, Battle of Tassaforanga 30 November 1942 Japanese Evacuation of Gudalcanal 29 January-8 February 1943.* Washington DC: Naval History and Heritage Command.

—. 2017. *World War II 75th Anniversary Commemorative Series Combat Narratives, Battles of Savo Island 9 August 1942 and the Eastern Solomons 23-25 August 1942.* Washington DC: Naval History and Heritage Command.

—. 2017. *World War II 75th Anniversary Commemorative Series Combat Narratives, Early Raid in the Pacific Ocean, February 1 to March 10, 1942 Marshall and Gilbert Islands, Rabaul, Wake and Marcus, Lae and Salamaua.* Washington: Naval History and Heritage Command.

United States Navy, USNTS Sampson. n.d. *USNTS Sampson, Training at Sampson, Fire Suppression Exercise 1944, Photo #21.* Accessed November 21, 2019. http://www.rpadden.com/samp_training/training.htm.

Unites States Navy. 1945. *Navy R.O.T.C. and V-12 Unit Harvard University.* Baton Rouge: Army and Navy Publishing company.

USS Elmore Project Editors. 2018. *USS Elmore (APA-42) The Admirals.* Accessed August 11, 2019. https://usselmore.com/war_effort/admirals/admirals.html.

Wanderlust Crew Editors. 2021. *How to visit the Molokai leper colony-Kalaupapa Hawaii.* February 10. Accessed March 15, 2021. https://wanderlustcrew.com/molokai-leper-colony-kalaupapa-hawaii/.

Wikipedia Conributors. 2007. *Aviation machinist's mate, Wikipedia, The Free Encyclopedia.* January 11. Accessed July 18, 2019. https://en.wikipedia.org/wiki/Aviation_machinist%27s_mate.

Wikipedia conributors. 2007. *Domain of the Golden Dragon, Wikipedia, The Free Encyclopedia.* December 22. Accessed September 24, 2019. https://en.wikipedia.org/wiki/Domain_of_the_Golden_Dragon.

Wikipedia contributors. 2005. *1943 Atlantic hurricane season, Wikipedia, The Free Encyclopedia.* January 13. Accessed September 19, 2019. https://en.wikipedia.org/wiki/1943_Atlantic_hurricane_season.

—. 2004. *American Volunteer Group, Wikipedia, The Free Encyclopedia.* March 26. Accessed June 14, 2019. https://en.wikipedia.org/wiki/American_Volunteer_Group.

—. 2009. *Byron McCandless, Wikipedia, The Free Encyclopedia.* August 30. Accessed July 5, 2019. https://en.wikipedia.org/wiki/Byron_McCandless.

—. 2001. *Christmas Island, Wikipedia, The Free Encyclopedia.* October 31. Accessed September 15, 2019. https://en.wikipedia.org/wiki/Christmas_Island.

—. 2006. *Clean sweep (naval), Wikipedia, The Free Encyclopedia.* October 30. Accessed June 10, 2019. https://en.wikipedia.org/wiki/Clean_sweep_(naval).

—. 2001. *Dardanelles, Wikipedia, The Free Encyclopedia.* April 30. Accessed September 29, 2019. https://en.wikipedia.org/wiki/Dardanelles.

—. 2004. *Degaussing, Wikipedia, The Free Encyclopedia.* October 26. Accessed July 22, 2019. https://en.wikipedia.org/wiki/Degaussing.

—. 2004. *Dolmabahce Palace, Wikipedia, The Free Encyclopedia.* March 29. Accessed September 30, 2019. https://en.wikipedia.org/wiki/Dolmabah%C3%A7e_Palace.

—. 2005. *Edith Nourse Rogers, Wikipedia, The Free Encyclopedia.* February 19. Accessed September 19, 2019. https://en.wikipedia.org/wiki/Edith_Nourse_Rogers.

—. 2003. *Espiritu Santo, Wikipedia, The Free Encyclopedia.* August 16. Accessed October 28, 2019. https://en.wikipedia.org/wiki/Espiritu_Santo.

—. 2004. *Esther Williams, Wikipedia, The Free Encyclopedia.* August 12. Accessed October 5, 2009. https://en.wikipedia.org/wiki/Esther_Williams.

—. 2003. *Flying Tigers, Wikipedia, The Free Encyclopedia.* July 7. Accessed June 14, 2019. https://en.wikipedia.org/wiki/Flying_Tigers.

—. 2004. *Gedunk Bar, Wikipedia, The Free Encyclopedia.* May 26. Accessed November 13, 2019. https://en.wikipedia.org/wiki/Gedunk_bar.

—. 2007. *History of Lowell Massachusetts, Wikipedia, The Free Encyclopedia.* February 27. Accessed June 9, 2019. https://en.wikipedia.org/wiki/History_of_Lowell,_Massachusetts.

—. 2003. *Jason Robards, Wikipedia, The Free Encyclopedia.* September 6. Accessed October 6, 2019. https://en.wikipedia.org/wiki/Jason_Robards.

—. 2004. *Line-crossing ceremony, Wikipedia, The Free Encyclopedia.* October 15. Accessed September 24, 2019. https://en.wikipedia.org/wiki/Line-crossing_ceremony.

—. 2004. *Link Trainer, Wikipedia, The Free Encyclopedia.* May 12. Accessed August 16, 2019. https://en.wikipedia.org/wiki/Link_Trainer.

—. 2004. *List of United States navy elisted rates, Wikipedia, The Free Encyclopedia.* March 24. Accessed July 6, 2019. https://en.wikipedia.org/wiki/List_of_United_States_Navy_enlisted_rates.

—. 2004. *List of United States Navy ratings, Wikipedia, The Free Encyclopedia.* June 16. Accessed July 6, 2019. https://en.wikipedia.org/wiki/List_of_United_States_Navy_ratings.

—. 2002. *Lockeed Corporation, Wikipedia, The free Encyclopedia.* April 22. Accessed September 27, 2019. https://en.wikipedia.org/wiki/Lockheed_Corporation.

—. 2003. *Molokai, Wikipedia, The Free Encyclopedia.* March 11. Accessed June 22, 2019. https://en.wikipedia.org/wiki/Molokai.

—. 2006. *Naval Air Station Key West, Wikipedia, The Free Encyclopedia.* December 10. Accessed September 19, 2019. https://en.wikipedia.org/wiki/Naval_Air_Station_Key_West.

—. 2005. *Naval Air Station Pensacola, Wikipedia, The Free Encyclopedia.* February 17. Accessed June 14, 2019. https://en.wikipedia.org/wiki/Naval_Air_Station_Pensacola.

—. 2008. *Naval Air Station Squantum, Wikipedia, The Free Encyclopedia.* January 4. Accessed June 30, 2019. https://en.wikipedia.org/wiki/Naval_Air_Station_Squantum.

—. 2003. *Naval Battle of Guadalcanal, Wikipedia, The Free Encyclopedia.* December 17. Accessed September 12, 2019. https://en.wikipedia.org/wiki/Naval_Battle_of_Guadalcanal.

—. 2004. *Neutrality Patrol, Wikipedia, The Free Encyclopedia.* March 8. Accessed September 23, 2019. https://en.wikipedia.org/wiki/Neutrality_Patrol.

—. 2003. *Patrol torpedo boat PT-109, Wikipedia, The Free Encyclopedia.* August 1. Accessed October 6, 2019. https://en.wikipedia.org/wiki/Patrol_torpedo_boat_PT-109.

—. 2004. *Petty officer third class, Wikipedia, The Free Encyclopedia.* March 26. Accessed July 18, 2019. https://en.wikipedia.org/wiki/Petty_officer_third_class.

381

—. 2004. *Petty Officer, Wikipedia, The Free Encyclopedia.* March 13. Accessed July 18, 2019. https://en.wikipedia.org/wiki/Petty_officer.

—. 2004. *Plankowner, Wikipedia, The Free Encyclopedia.* March 9. Accessed September 15, 2009. https://en.wikipedia.org/wiki/Plankowner.

—. 2002. *Port Hueneme, California, Wikipedia, The Free Encyclopedia.* October 18. Accessed September 27, 2019. https://en.wikipedia.org/wiki/Port_Hueneme,_California.

—. 2004. *Quonset hut, Wikipedia, The Free Encyclopedia.* December 4. Accessed June 30, 2019. https://en.wikipedia.org/wiki/Quonset_hut.

—. 2007. *Quonset Point Air National Guard Station, Wikipedia, The Free Encyclopedia.* June 11. Accessed June 30, 2019. https://en.wikipedia.org/wiki/Quonset_Point_Air_National_Guard_Station.

—. 2004. *Robert Carney, Wikipedia, The Free Encyclopedia.* October 6. Accessed October 2, 2019. https://en.wikipedia.org/wiki/Robert_Carney.

—. 2004. *Royal Hawaiian Hotel, Wikipedia, The Free Encyclopedia.* May 28. Accessed June 5, 2020. https://en.wikipedia.org/wiki/Royal_Hawaiian_Hotel.

—. 2002. *Saint Jean Baptiste Day, Wikipedia, The Free Encyclopedia.* August 21. Accessed June 9, 2019. https://en.wikipedia.org/wiki/Saint-Jean-Baptiste_Day.

—. 2006. *SS President Coolidge, Wikipedia, The Free Encyclopedia.* September 11. Accessed June 16, 2019. https://en.wikipedia.org/wiki/SS_President_Coolidge.

—. 2005. *Storekeeper, Wikipedia, The Free Encyclopedia.* December 12. Accessed July 18, 2019. https://en.wikipedia.org/wiki/Storekeeper.

—. 2003. *Treasure Island, San Francisco, Wikipedia, The Free Encyclopedia.* April 7. Accessed September 15, 2019. https://en.wikipedia.org/wiki/Treasure_Island,_San_Francisco.

—. 2004. *USS Cincinnati, Wikipedia, The Free Encyclopedia.* October 24. Accessed June 25, 2019. https://en.wikipedia.org/wiki/USS_Cincinnati_(CL-6).

—. 2003. *USS Constellation (1854), Wikipedia, The Free Encyclopedia.* September 19. Accessed September 2020, 2019. https://en.wikipedia.org/wiki/USS_Constellation_(1854).

—. 2004. *USS Des Moines, Wikipedia, The Free Encyclopedia.* March 29. Accessed October 1, 2019. https://en.wikipedia.org/wiki/USS_Des_Moines_(CA-134).

—. 2007. *USS Dionne, Wikipedia, The Free Encyclopedia.* July 28. Accessed March 8, 2020. https://en.wikipedia.org/wiki/USS_Dionne.

—. 2003. *USS Enterprise (CV-6), Wikipedia, The Free Encyclopedia.* March 11. Accessed June 29, 2019. https://en.wikipedia.org/wiki/USS_Enterprise_%28CV-6%29.

—. 2003. *USS Iowa (BB-61), Wikipedia, the Free Encyclopedia.* April 1. Accessed September 17, 2019. https://en.wikipedia.org/wiki/USS_Iowa_(BB-61).

—. 2005. *USS King (DD-242), Wikipedia, The Free Encyclopeida.* April 25. Accessed September 19, 2019. https://en.wikipedia.org/wiki/USS_King_(DD-242).

—. 2002. *USS Missouri (BB-63), Wikipedia, The Free Encyclopedia.* September 19. Accessed September 29, 2019. https://en.wikipedia.org/wiki/USS_Missouri_(BB-63).

—. 2003. *USS New Orleans, Wikipedia, The Free Encyclopedia.* March 21. Accessed September 22, 2019. https://en.wikipedia.org/wiki/USS_New_Orleans_(CA-32).

—. 2004. *USS Northampton (CA-26), Wikipedia, The Free Encyclopedia.* March 26. Accessed July 9, 2019. https://en.wikipedia.org/wiki/USS_Northampton_(CA-26).

—. 2005. *USS O'brien (DD-415), Wikipedia, The Free Encyclopedia.* December 18. Accessed July 25, 2019. https://en.wikipedia.org/wiki/USS_O%27Brien_(DD-415).

—. 2004. *USS Providence (CL-134), Wikipedia, The Free Encyclopedia.* March 30. Accessed September 29, 2019. https://en.wikipedia.org/wiki/USS_Providence_(CL-82).

—. 2003. *USS Wasp (CV-7), Wikipedia, The Free Encyclopedia.* April 12. Accessed July 25, 2019. https://en.wikipedia.org/wiki/USS_Wasp_(CV-7).

—. 2004. *Vought OS2U Kingfisher, Wikipedia, The Free Encyclopedia.* April 10. Accessed September 17, 2019. https://en.wikipedia.org/wiki/Vought_OS2U_Kingfisher.

—. 2016. *VP-131, Wikipedia, The Free Encyclopedia.* June 16. Accessed September 27, 2019. https://en.wikipedia.org/wiki/VP-131.

Wordpress Editors. 2011. *History of Frano Americans in Lowell Massachusetts.* November 1. Accessed June 9, 2019. https://francolowellma.wordpress.com/newspapers/.

Zimmerman, Dwight Jon. 2012. *Insulting the Fying Tigers, The Army Air Forces' blunder effectively dissolved the only fighter group that was winning against the Japanese.* March 30. Accessed June 14, 2019. https://www.defensemedianetwork.com/stories/insulting-the-flying-tigers/.

About the Author

James R. Turcotte was born in Wethersfield, Connecticut. Jim studied at Boston University earning a B.A., *cum laude,* in History, 1980. Jim attended Western New England University School of Law and graduated with a Juris Doctorate in 1984.

He worked for the Connecticut Division of Criminal Justice as a prosecuting attorney for over 34 years. Jim retired in April 2019. From 2006-2020, He also worked as an adjunct professor of law, first at UConn School of Law and then at Quinnipiac University School of Law.

Jim is the son of James H. Turcotte, one of the principal brothers in this book. Now that he is retired, Jim spends most of his time reading history, writing, researching his genealogy, fishing, and visiting friends and family.

Made in the USA
Middletown, DE
03 February 2022

60376400R00219